GULLY FARM

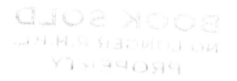

Barr colonist encampment, early 1900s. Frederick Steele. Photo LH-4911 courtesy of the Saskatoon Public Library Local History Room.

GULLY FARM

A Story of Homesteading
on the Canadian Prairies

Mary Hiemstra

FIFTH
HOUSE
PUBLISHERS

Front cover photograph, LH–4911, courtesy of the Saskatoon Public Library Local History Room
Hand colouring by Laurel Wolanski
Production by Jeremy Drought / Last Impression Publishing Service
Cover design by John Luckhurst / GDL
Series and logo design by Sandra Hastie / GDL

The publisher gratefully acknowledges the support of the Department of Canadian Heritage and the Canada Council for the Arts for our publishing program.

THE CANADA COUNCIL | LE CONSEIL DES ARTS
FOR THE ARTS | DU CANADA
SINCE 1957 | DEPUIS 1957

Printed in Canada
01 02 / 5 4

CANADIAN CATALOGUING IN PUBLICATION DATA

Hiemstra, Mary, 1897–
Gully farm
(Western Canadian classics)
Originally published: Toronto: McClelland Stewart, 1955.
ISBN 1–895618–96–7

1. Pinder family. 2. Pioneers – Lloydminster (Sask. and Alta.) – Biography.
3. Lloydminster (Sask. and Alta.) – History. 4. Barr Colony (Alta. and Sask.) – History.
5. Frontier and pioneer life – Lloydminster (Sask. and Alta.) I. Title. II. Series.

FC3549.L59Z48 1997   971.23'302'0922   C97–920078–4
F1074.5.L59H54 1997

FIFTH HOUSE LTD.

⮜·DEDICATION·⮞

To the memory of my Mother and Father

SARAH & WALTER PINDER

W HAT is it like to create the world? The settlement pioneers of western Canada came as close as any humans are likely to come to this experience. And while many were dazzled by the personal opportunities this afforded, only the more sensitive among them grasped the full significance of being part of a society starting afresh. For the perceptive and thoughtful, there was an awesome excitement in this new beginning. Yet, this enthusiasm was sometimes tempered by regret for what was being lost in their energetic acts of creation.

Mary Hiemstra (nee Pinder) was one of the more observant participants in the great rush of settlement that transformed the plains of western Canada in the early part of the twentieth century. In less than a generation, grasslands became bustling agrarian communities and thousands of settlers poured into the region. Hiemstra arrived in the spring of 1903, a child of six, whose father had brought his reluctant wife and three small children, as part of the Barr Colony expedition.

The "Barr Colony" was among the last and the largest group-settlement enterprises in Canadian history. Over 2,700 men, women, and children embarked from Britain to establish a British colony in what was still the North-West Territories. If Canadians had any talent for celebrating their history, these colonists would be the stuff of legend. They were responding to depressed economic conditions in Britain in the wake of the Boer War, to the sense of heady adventure as the British Empire bestrode the world, and to patriotic advertisements that urged increased immigration to "plant firm, Britannia's flag in Western Canada's fair domain."

These eager settlers crammed the decks of the *S.S. Manitoba* for a trans-Atlantic voyage every bit as pregnant with hope and trepidation as the crossing of the *Mayflower*. Few among them had any farm experience, and fewer still had any inkling of the harsh demands of pioneer life. This was due, in part, to their own naïve arrogance and also to the florid promises Isaac Barr had made in his soon-to-be-famous brochures. Barr had promised bracing, yet healthful, winters, lush growing seasons, and pleasant accommodations along the way. Some saw it all as a "grand tour," and as soon as problems emerged, they began to vent their indignation and then their fury on the beleaguered Isaac Barr.

Some colonists left along the way, as the journey stretched on, onerous day after onerous day. At Saskatoon, they faced a formidable overland trek by horse- or oxen-drawn wagons. When the tent-city rest stations along the way proved to be another of Barr's empty promises, the colonists had had enough. At a meeting in Battleford, they voted to reject Barr and turn leadership over to Reverend George Exton Lloyd, the accompanying Church of England chaplain. They even went so far as to vote unanimously to refer to themselves as "Britannia colonists" rather than "Barr colonists." There is today a Britannia municipality, where the bulk of the colonists settled, but otherwise, history has given Barr his revenge, and the term Barr colonists is now used exclusively.

The colonists went even further in rejecting Barr by naming the townsite after Reverend Lloyd, who insisted on the appendage of "minster" to draw attention to the role of the church that was immediately established in the little town, as being the "minster" or "mother church" to the surrounding communities. So it is that Lloydminster, now a city on the Alberta-Saskatchewan border, became the central town of the vast area of over 2,500 square miles (almost 4,000 sq. km) that Barr had persuaded the Canadian government to reserve for British homesteaders. That much of this area was settled by one wave of immigration in less than three years is another part of what could be celebrated as Canadian legend.

Hiemstra's account, though, is not the place to find the "political" history of this adventure. Indeed, she seems oddly unfamiliar with even the basic details of that settlement scheme. The major strength of her narrative is her ability with description. With subtlety and precision she captures the underlying nuances to evoke a sharing of emotions across the generations. Recounting her life in England in the months leading to the critical decision to emigrate to Canada, she describes the arrival of her baby brother in this way: "Life was very smooth and pleasant, and I thought it was always going to be that way. Then one damp day in October Dad strode into the little room. 'It's a lad,' he said, and his voice sounded like the organ at the start of Onward Christian Soldiers."

So it was that the die was cast and the compelling need to seek a better life for his son propelled Walter Pinder to join the Barr colonists. In so doing, the Pinders joined the millions from all over Europe, and later the world, who saw in Canada a chance to create a better world, if not for themselves, then for their children. But it was never easy, and six-year-old Mary Pinder speaks for all who have ever had to leave behind the familiar and open a new chapter in their lives, which only promised to be the key to later happiness. "Aunt Jane cried and held out her hands," Hiemstra writes, "but the door was closed and the train moving. She ran down the platform calling my name and crying. I stood at the window and called to her, and tried to blow a kiss, but the window was in the way and I was crying."

With similar skill in describing not only the external but also evoking the internal, Hiemstra recreates the voyage by sea, train, and finally by horse-drawn wagon over the last 180 miles to what would become the homestead of her youth. Along the way she brings to life the tensions and the mixed emotions of hope for the future and regret for the past left behind. The struggle is nicely counterpointed in the continual clash between her hopelessly optimistic father, Walter, and her ever-practical and determined mother, Sarah.

The homestead would become known as Gully Farm, later the title of Hiemstra's work. Along the way, the reader is immersed in the awe of encountering the virgin prairie, and the loneliness its immense dome of sky created in those from a smaller world. We experience the heart-stopping fear of battling a raging prairie fire, the numbing, day-after-day struggle to survive the brutal cold of the prairie winter, the comfort of new friendships, and the pride in misfortunes overcome. Brought to life again is the dangerous naïveté of the greenhorns and the grinding loneliness of the women tied to their draughty shacks by the needs of their children and the continuous daily labour of survival. Over all, there is a growing sense of the scale of the ultimate victory of the pioneers in establishing viable farmsteads and thriving communities in what was to some a "sub-arctic desert."

Not forgotten, though, is a sense of what was lost. Hiemstra writes: "Once many years later when we stood looking at a field of wheat Dad sighed and said: 'Do you remember how it used to be, Mary? All the trees! It's practically a desert now. It will never be the same again.' But [that first] night Dad showed me the sunset, western Canada was new."

There was a time, long ago now, when history was dominated by the accounts of the political, military, and economic elites. In recent years, especially, historians have turned their attention to rescuing the history of "ordinary people," the likes of whom are central to Hiemstra's work. *Gully Farm* serves as a valuable resource, allowing us a window into the lives of people who at one time did not surface on the pages of history.

Generations of Can. Lit. students have been exposed to Susanna Moodie's *Roughing It in the Bush* for its rare account of a woman's daily life in the backwoods of pioneer Upper Canada. *Gully Farm* deserves equal rank. It speaks strongly to western Canadians, and Hiemstra avoids the underlying outraged frustration that colours Moodie's recollection of what seemed to her a period of exile on a stump farm north of Belleville. Little Mary Pinder recognized the hardships of pioneer life, but she quickly accepted them as part of the sacrifice necessary to build the new and better life her parents and so many others sought.

So it is that *Gully Farm* joins the ranks of Western Canadian Classics. Remarkably consistent in maintaining a childhood perspective, deeply evocative, and tellingly written, *Gully Farm* rises above the cardboard reminiscences that so often characterize "pioneer writing." Those who lived her era are gone, with little left behind but unlabelled, tinted photographs of sober-faced people beside nondescript buildings, or rusted farm machinery in what is generously called a museum. Mary Hiemstra provides something far more valuable. Hers is one of the few accounts that allows us to feel what it was to be alive in that era. Through young Mary's account we sense the bond of common humanity that unites us over the ages. She tells the story of one pioneer family, but she tells it so well that it becomes the story of all pioneers.

Franklin Foster
Lloydminster, Alberta
1997

x

I

T was spring when we left England to go with the Barr Colony to Canada; 31st March 1903. Daffodils were in bloom in the gardens of the big house on Castle Hill, and there were tall buttercups and tiny yellow-centred daisies in the small hillside fields in front of our house. The leaves on the hawthorn hedges and the moss on the old stone walls were a fresh, tender green, and the ivy that covered our stone house right to the top of the chimney-pots was thrusting out new, inquisitive shoots. Near the pond creamy yellow cowslips were opening, and a nightingale was looking for a nesting-place in the big tree at the top of the lane.

There were five of us in the family then. Dad, short and thin, with thick dark brown curls, a proud aquiline nose, a wide forehead, and eyes that were a strange mixture of light and shadow. They were cloud grey edged with black, and undershot with that deep but living shade of ocean green that always holds a spark. Humour was there, and understanding, and a never-failing zest that lasted all his life.

Mother was a trim little woman even shorter than Dad. Her eyes were big and blue, and her pink-and-white face round and smiling. She had tiny hands and feet and a quick, energetic way of walking that gave her tiny figure a look of eager importance. She looked far too young to be the mother of three children: Lily, a serious little girl with big brown eyes and light brown curls, Jack, a baby of five months, and myself, a big girl just past six.

The decision to leave England hadn't been either sudden or easy. All our relatives and friends were there, and our ancestors, who now slept under the big oaks in the old churchyard, had walked on the narrow cobbled streets, and lived their lives in the stone houses that stood companionably side by side.

Dad, however, had never really liked the elbow-to-elbow way of living, and as soon as he could he moved to the farm on Castle Hill. There were five houses there, but they were surrounded by fields, and we had a feeling of space. The fields, of course, were small, and badly in need of fertilizer, but Dad seemed content with them until the summer before Jack was born.

There were long articles about Canada in the papers that spring, and Dad began reading them, casually at first, then with deeper and deeper interest.

'Seems to be a lot of people going to Canada these days,' he said one morning as he turned the pages of the *Manchester Guardian*. 'It must be quite a place.'

'Some people either haven't any sense, or their feet tickle.' Mother looked disapprovingly at the red-and-white roast of beef she was preparing for the oven. 'England's plenty good enough for me.' She put the meat into a shallow roasting-pan, crossed the hearth, and shoved the pan into the dark mouth of the oven. She closed the door with a snap, and began spooning flour for a Yorkshire pudding into a yellow bowl.

'Sounds like an interesting place,' Dad said after a while, and turned a page.

'What does?' Mother looked up from the pudding she was beating and smiled.

'Canada.' Dad tapped the paper with a thin finger. 'It says here that land there is free.'

'Papers don't seem to care what they print these days.' Mother dismissed them with a toss of her small, neat head. 'Put some coal on the fire, will you? And give the grate a shake. There seems to be a lot of cinders in the coal lately, and they charge plenty for it, too.'

'You can get wood for nothing in Canada,' Dad said as he laid his paper on the table.

Mother was busy beating the pudding and didn't reply. Dad picked up the coal-scuttle, stepped over the polished brass fender that curved around the hearth, and poured a shower of coals on the open fire; then he went out to see how the new calf was getting along, but he didn't entirely forget about Canada. Scraps about it littered his conversation, and created little ripples in the even current of our lives.

While this little breeze of words, that was no stronger than the wind that stirred the bluebells and carried the small white parachutes of the dandelions, eddied about us, life for me went on just as usual. I went to school, visited Grandmother and Aunt Jane in their little shop with the house attached, played hopscotch with Katie Daw, tossed stones into the Spen River, and helped make hay.

We had neither horse nor mowing-machine, and Dad said the field was so small hiring wasn't worth while, so he cut the hay with a scythe, raked it by hand, made it into hay-cocks, and left it in the field until he could hire a horse and wagon to haul it to the hayloft over the barn, or mistle as we in Yorkshire called it.

Everyone helped with the haymaking: Uncle Arthur, Dad's brother, and George Henry, a cousin who lived with us now and then. Even Mother worked for a while when she took lemonade to the sweating men. I was supposed to help, too, but I spent most of my time rolling in the sweet-smelling grass, looking for clover flowers, or sliding down the green hay-cocks when nobody was looking.

'If we had a bigger farm we could have a horse-drawn rake,' Dad said one afternoon when he paused to take a deep drink of lemonade and mop his hot face and damp curly hair. 'They say even the small fields in Canada are half a mile long.'

'You can't believe all you hear, and only half you see,' Mother said, and picked up a fork and began piling the lush hay. She wore a blue cotton dress and a big hat and looked like a morning glory.

'Some things must be true,' Dad insisted. 'They say the wheat grows as tall as a man.'

'There's drawbacks there just as there are anywhere else,' Mother said, and tried to look as if she thought Canada, and wheat as high as a man, were only fairy-tales, and not to be taken seriously; but when the man from Manitoba came she was quite worried.

He did not stay with us, he was visiting some friends in Littletown, but he spent a great deal of time at Castle Hill talking to Dad. Big and loose-jointed, he looked as if he had been out in a high wind and hot sun for a long time. His red hair was always rumpled, and his eyebrows, bleached to a pinkish shade, stood on end. Red freckles spattered his face and his big ears, and his eyes looked like the pond on a cold, windy day. The backs of his broad hands were also freckle-blotched, and hair the colour of his eyebrows grew between them. While Dad milked the solemn cows he leaned against the end of the stall and talked in a flat, monotonous voice that seemed to come partly from his nose.

I paid very little attention to the man from Manitoba. His voice was harsh to my ears, but Dad's eyes brightened and his face glowed as the words unwound steadily like string from a ball.

'It sounds like a good thing,' he said when the string of words paused, and he turned his head sideways and smiled while the thick white streams of milk gurgled into his bright pail.

When the milking was finished the man from Manitoba said good night and went whistling down the tree-lined lane, and Dad, his lean face still shining, went into the house. While he washed and scalded the milk pails and had his tea, he told Mother about Canada and the advantages to be had there.

'It must be fair wonderful,' he said as he sloshed scalding water into the bright pails. 'The grass touches the horses' bellies, and practically everything's free. There's all the meat you can eat: deer, elk, prairie chickens, rabbits, grouse. All you have to do is shoot them. And if you want to fish you just throw a line into a lake, and the fish stun one another trying to grab your bait. You can build your own house and barn, too. It won't cost you a thing.'

'There must be a catch in it somewhere,' Mother said, and poured boiling water into the blue teapot. 'What about the gamekeepers?'

Dad said there weren't any, and no need of them. The land wasn't owned by a few as it was in England. There was a lot of vacant land, and anybody could have a piece free. 'Just think on it,' he said as he drew his chair to the table, his face shining, 'a hundred and sixty acres, a quarter section, free. Pretty nearly twenty times more land than we have here, and not even any rent. You'd be driving your own carriage in no time, Sally.'

'I don't want a carriage; horses frighten me.' Mother cooled my tea by pouring it from my white mug with the brown dog on the side to the green mug with the cat on it. 'I can walk to my father's, and that's as far as I want to go.'

'And Mary could have a horse to ride.' Dad stirred his tea, and stared at the roses on the wall-paper, but he wasn't really looking at the big pink flowers, he was looking at a wide sweep of wheat on the other side of the ocean.

Mother took a slice of bread from the plate in the middle of the table and ate it slowly. 'What are you going to do after tea?' she asked, not looking at Dad. 'Spread manure?'

'Eh!' Dad blinked and looked confused for a moment, then he shook his head as if to clear it of a dream. 'What's that?' he asked.

'That manure. I thought you were going to spread it to-night.'

'Oh, ay,' Dad said, and moved his feet uneasily. 'I spread most of it this afternoon. I think I'll go to the club for a bit to-night. That fellow from Manitoba might come around.'

'Him!' Mother pressed her lips together. 'Isn't it about time he went back to where he came from?'

'He'll be gone soon.' Dad got up and took his coat and cap from the hook behind the door. 'I'll be back in a bit,' he said, and went out. Mother tossed her neat head and got up and began clearing the table.

I went out into the pale evening sunshine, hoping that Ernest Ives, the little boy who lived two doors away, might be able to come out and play. I had pushed him into a mud puddle in the afternoon, and his mother had put him to bed and told me to go home and stay there. Three hours, however, were half a lifetime by my reckoning, and I'd almost forgotten about the mud puddle. I trotted down the walk and knocked on the Ives' green door. Mrs Ives stuck out a frizzed head and frowned. 'Can Ernest come out?' I asked.

'No.' The green door banged.

I hopped down the stone steps and wandered into the Ginnel. It was a narrow lane that tilted sharply downhill. There was a stone wall, old and crumbling, on one side, and a high hedge on the other. The path was rough and rock-strewn, and in places there were uneven steps. The Ginnel ended in a fence with a stile. A dark rider on a black horse haunted it, and George Henry wouldn't come up it unless someone stood at the top and shouted down to him.

The Ginnel was a short cut to Littletown, and I started down it pretending I was going to Aunt Jane's. At the stile, however, I stopped and looked at Listing Lane for a while, then I turned and began the steep climb back.

The sun was low and the air warm and mellow. Moss smells rose from the old wall, and leaf smells came from the hedge. I climbed slowly, kicking at the stones, and pausing often to pull myself up and peep over the wall. When I was almost at the top I looked up, and there was a black horse and rider coming towards me.

I moved to one side to let them pass, expecting the horse to move over a little too, but it didn't. It came on just as if I wasn't there, and its big hoofs almost stepped on me. I was irked by its rudeness and threw a stone after it, then I dawdled the rest of the way home. 'You know what?' I said as I took off my bonnet. 'A horse in the Ginnel nearly stepped on me.'

'Hush,' Mother said. 'It was only a shadow.'

'No, it wasn't,' I insisted. 'It was a horse with big black feet. I threw a stone at it.'

Mother looked startled, but before she had time to say anything there was a tap on the open door, and Uncle Sam came in.

Mother and Uncle Sam thought a lot of each other, and no wonder. He was only fourteen months older than she was, which made them almost twins. They looked a lot alike, too, except for the sparkle. When Mother laughed her blue eyes danced, and when she walked she bounced, but Uncle Sam's feet always seemed to drag a little, and his pale eyes were always anxious even when he smiled. His straw-coloured hair was already getting thin, and his narrow shoulders looked tired.

Uncle Sam was a cabinet-maker and worked in Grandfather Gomersall's shop, but adventure had once beckoned, and he had tried to follow its enticing hand.

When he was about eighteen he had dreamed of being a soldier and going to India. He had tried again and again to enlist, but he was too thin, and although he ate a fantastic amount he couldn't gain an ounce. The army being out of the question he started to learn a trade that held out some prospects of travel, at least in England, but something happened; either the man died or the firm went out of business, and Uncle Sam came home and learned cabinet-making. He was a good workman, but the yeast had gone out of him.

Mother forgot all about the dark horse and rider when she saw Uncle Sam. She poked up the fire and put the kettle on for tea, and told me to go and play with my dolls for a while, which was quite all right with me. I'd expected to be put to bed.

While they waited for the kettle to boil Mother and Uncle Sam talked. They spoke of the weather and Aunt Lily's cold, then Uncle Sam lowered his voice and said: 'Sarah, I hear Walter's thinking seriously about going to Canada.'

'Where did you hear that nonsense?' Mother asked.

'A fellow that goes to the club a lot told me. He said Walter talks of nothing else.'

Mother laughed a little. 'It won't amount to anything,' she said confidently. 'As soon as that man from Manitoba goes he'll forget all about Canada.'

'I wish he'd go then.' Uncle Sam wrinkled his pale, high forehead.

'Don't let it bother you.' Mother poured boiling water into the teapot. Uncle Sam, however, continued to worry. He said the situation was much worse than Mother thought, and he wouldn't be a bit surprised if Dad really went. Mother told him he was quite wrong, but after a while her voice lost some of its confidence, and a pleat appeared in her white forehead.

When they were on their third cup of tea Uncle Sam leaned across the table and said in an intense voice that made my ears perk: 'Even if he goes, Sarah, you don't have to go with him.'

'He won't go without me,' Mother said, and there was happy pride in her voice, and confident grace in her shoulders.

'You never know.' Uncle Sam stirred his tea. 'He seems quite smitten with Canada. Be firm if he tries to persuade you, but remember, I'll help you with the bairns if he insists on going.'

Mother smiled and said there was nothing to worry about, but when Uncle Sam left the smile fell from her lips, and when I asked for a bedtime story she said there wasn't time.

CHAPTER TWO

O<small>UR</small> little stone-floored house, with the roses growing in the wall-paper and the geraniums blooming in the window, wasn't very cheerful after Uncle Sam's visit. Dad and Mother didn't argue, but they didn't smile much, either. The air somehow felt stretched, and Mother's blue eyes were worried.

Some of the tightness went away after a while, but there was always a little of it around even after Dad said: 'Well, if this next isn't a lad I'll forget about Canada.'

This promise, however, pleased Uncle Sam, but when Mother said she'd like a boy anyway he looked unhappy all over again.

Dad looked a little depressed, but nothing more was said about Canada for a long time. I was allowed to spend more and more time with Grandmother and Aunt Jane, which pleased me very much. Their house was much closer to school than the house on Castle Hill, there was a constant supply of candy, and several children just around the corner to play with. Life was very smooth and pleasant, and I thought it was always going to be that way. Then one damp day in October Dad strode into the little room. 'It's a lad,' he said, and his voice sounded like the organ at the start of 'Onward, Christian soldiers.'

Grandmother and Aunt Jane both talked at once, and even Grandfather Pinder, ill with a heart ailment, looked pleased.

When the excitement had simmered down a little Dad told me to put on my coat and bonnet, he was going to take me to look at my new brother. I wanted to know how big he was, but Dad told me to wait and see, and together we walked up Listing Lane to Castle Hill.

Mother was in bed, and that frightened me a little. I'd never seen her in bed in the day-time before, but she smiled and said she was all right, so I ventured into her room and asked where the boy was.

Mrs Hall, a kind-faced woman with grey hair, lifted Jack out of his cradle.

I was terribly disappointed. I'd expected a boy as big as Ernest Ives, who was five, but this little creature wasn't even as big as my big doll, and more than half of him was long white robe. Tears came to my eyes. Mrs Hall asked if I wanted to hold him, but I shook my head.

Disappointing as the baby was, however, I still thought he ought to have the nicest name in the world, which in my opinion was Ernest. I talked about it constantly, and he was finally named John for Mother's father, and Ernest to keep me quiet. I called him Ernest for a long time, and Mother called him John, but Dad's name, Jack, finally won.

Jack's christening party was quite an event for me. Mother took the protecting stockings off the mahogany legs of the table. Grandfather had made it and given it to her for a wedding present, and the legs were always kept covered to protect them from my restless feet. I had never seen them before, and spent a lot of time under the table admiring them. I even made Lily look at them, though she wasn't much interested.

Jack wore his best robe for the party. The front was almost solid embroidery, and when Mother held him on her lap the hem touched the floor. Everybody admired him, and said how much like Dad he looked, though I couldn't see any likeness. Dad, however, was very pleased, and his thin face was one big smile all afternoon.

Everybody, of course, wanted to know what Jack had been named, and what we were going to call him for short. 'Ernest,' I said quickly before anyone else had a chance to reply. Mother laughed and said we'd see, but all afternoon I stood beside Mother's chair pushing my name. I missed most of the refreshments, but when the last guests were leaving I climbed on the table, captured a dish of strawberry jam, dived under the table, and had a feast.

Soon after the christening party the peace of our house was again disturbed by talk about Canada. It was like a restless wind that refused to die down or go away.

Dad sent for pamphlets, and when they came he read them aloud to Mother. According to the leaflets everything in Canada was free: land, schools, meat, fish, fruit, which grew wild, and vegetables, which grew practically by themselves the land was so rich.

Mother agreed that Canada sounded all right. 'But that's just the bright side,' she insisted. 'There must be some drawbacks.'

Dad said there weren't, at least nothing serious. Mother, however, wasn't convinced, and thought it would be foolish to give up the farm on Castle Hill just when the fertilizer was beginning to show results.

They would have to start all over again in Canada., and someone else would get the good of all the work Dad had done in the last three years.

Dad said they wouldn't be losing anything. The land in Canada was so good it didn't need fertilizer. Wheat grew three feet or more all by itself. 'And it's hard wheat, too,' Dad added. 'We can take it to the mill and have it made into flour. Just think of how much that will save. Our own meat, eggs, vegetables, and bread. Living won't cost us a thing. We shall be well off in no time.'

'There must be something wrong somewhere,' Mother insisted. 'Nobody gives good land away.'

Dad said there wasn't a thing wrong, and the land was wonderful, but there was a lot of it, and the Government wanted it settled and improved. 'Imagine,' he said, looking out of the window and far across the fields, 'no taxes, no rent, and a hundred and sixty acres for nothing. It's the chance of a lifetime.'

'It might be if there was just the two of us,' Mother said. 'But money doesn't grow on trees even in Canada, and with three bairns to provide for we ought to be careful.'

Dad said the bairns were the big reason for going to Canada. What was there for them in England? Nothing. The lasses would go into the mills and get married, and Jack might get a small farm if he happened to be lucky. But where would he be in ten years? Nowhere. And if he went into the mills or the coal-mines it would be the same: work from daylight to dark, and soot and grease year in and year out until he was old. He might get to be a foreman, but he'd always be working for somebody else, and somebody would always be telling him what to do and when to do it. 'I want summat better than that for my lad,' Dad finished.

'Priestly was a doffer once,' Mother said, 'and now the mill belongs to him.'

'And look at him,' Dad said. 'Old before his time. You don't want Jack to look like old Priestly, do you?'

Mother looked at Jack's round pink face and admitted she didn't, but Canada was a long way from home and they didn't know a soul there, except the man from Manitoba, and she didn't think much of him. The argument swayed back and forth like a tree in the wind, and after a while Christmas came, and Canada slipped into the background for a month or two.

Except for the children's stockings that Santa Claus filled with apples, oranges, nuts, candies, and a toy, there was no giving at Christmas in those days. Instead there were hearty handshakes, cheery good wishes, and much visiting between family and friends. We spent an afternoon in the little house by the Spen eating rich, dark cake and sipping purple port. A day or so later we went to Grandfather Gomersall's and had roast beef and Yorkshire pudding. Later in the evening, and because it was Christmas and the shadow of Canada lurked in the background, Grandfather prepared tall glasses of something hot that had Irish whisky as a base.

Uncle Sam and Elizabeth, the girl he was going to marry, and Aunt Lily and the man she was engaged to came to our house one afternoon and had tea and cake. There was red-and-green holly on our mantel, and snow on the field in front of our house, and ice on the pond that year.

Coopers, who lived next door, had a party to which we all went after a day of skating and sliding. And one evening when the lamp was lit the carol singers came. They carried a lantern and stood outside in the snow and sang 'Here we come a-wassailing' and 'O come, all ye faithful,' then Mother opened the door and asked them to come in, and gave them tea and cake, and some money. They warmed their hands at the glowing coals, rubbed their red noses, stamped their feet, and left little pools of water on the clean stone floor.

Early on Christmas morning the church bells rang clear and gay in the crisp air. They played 'Hark, the herald angels sing' and 'Nowell.'

Lily and I, with help from Dad and Mother, had hung our stockings from the mantel the night before. Lily's stocking was too small, so she hung one of Mother's long hand-knitted woollen stockings. That gave me an idea, and I hung one of Dad's stockings, also knee length and hand knitted. Then we shouted our wants up the chimney and went to bed.

The first peal of the church bells brought us tumbling downstairs. There above the cold grate hung our stockings, and from each a big, fair-haired doll smiled. They were the biggest dolls we had ever had, and, marvel of marvels, they could close their big blue eyes.

Mrs Cooper, who came in a little later in the day, said the dolls looked a bit too big for us. Mother agreed with her, then she sighed and said she had decided to give us big dolls while she could, next Christmas we might not get anything if Dad had his way. Canada, an uneasy shadow, still hovered over us.

When Christmas, and my sixth birthday, 1st January, had passed, Dad began to be really serious about Canada. He wrote for more pamphlets about the Barr Colony, and talked constantly of what an opportunity it was, and of how little the trip would cost.

'Don't go with him,' Uncle Sam urged when he came to Castle Hill to see Mother. 'If he really has Canada fever let him go alone.'

Aunt Jane, Dad's only sister, opposed our going even more fiercely than Uncle Sam. She was nine years older than Dad, and she had given up one thing after another all her life.

Grandfather Pinder had lost his health when Aunt Jane was still young, and she had felt it her duty to refuse one suitor after another and help Grandmother, who had a sore ankle, to bring up the three boys. Later, when the boys were grown and gone, her suitors were gone also. She never complained about the sacrifices she had made, a girl gave up her life for her family almost as a duty in those days, but the constant giving had robbed her. She was gentle and kind, and full of patience, but the sparkle had gone out of her eyes. Like Uncle Sam, she looked a little tired.

Even though her brothers were gone, Aunt Jane still had Grandfather and Grandmother to think about, and she worked hard to provide a living for them. Her little shop was opposite Priestly's mills, and every day at noon she brewed a huge boiler of tea and sold it to the mill-workers at a penny a mug. She also sold candy, pies, cakes, bread, and a delicious meat loaf she made herself. She got up early and went to bed late, and except for church on Sunday and a week at Blackpool once a year she seldom went anywhere.

Except for her beautiful long brown hair that would have curled softly if she had let it, Aunt Jane, I suppose, was a plain woman. Her skin was clear, but sallow from lack of sun, and her eyes, cloud grey and touched with green like Dad's, lacked sparkle, but to me her rather long, thin face was perfect, and at night when she combed her hair I thought she was beautiful.

Aunt Jane slept in a small white room not much bigger than a cell, and when I stayed at the house by the Spen I slept with her. Together we went up the stone stairs, Aunt Jane holding the candle in its round iron candlestick. First I was tucked into the white bed, then Aunt Jane took off her tight dark bodice and long skirt and put on her night-gown. It was made of heavy white cotton, and was long and full with wide sleeves gathered at the wrists, and there was a ruffle around the high neck. When the night-gown was buttoned Aunt Jane took out her hairpins and shook loose her lovely curls. Dark and shining, they tumbled over her shoulders to well below her waist. All Aunt Jane's lost sparkle seemed to have gone into them, and they gleamed and glowed in the candlelight. When the curls stopped falling, Aunt Jane tipped her head backward and lifted her arms and ran her fingers through her gorgeous hair. The simple action transformed her completely. Her wide white sleeves became half-extended wings, and the soft candlelight on her gentle face became a halo. 'You're so pretty, Aunt Jane,' I told her.

'No, lassie, I'm not. I'm an old maid and plain,' and she sighed. I did not contradict her, but to me she was far more beautiful than the angel that lived in the church window.

The other aunts and uncles said they couldn't understand why Aunt Jane spoiled me the way she did, but there was nothing unusual about her love for me. I had her eyes, her hair, and her name, and I had been born at my grandmother's house, as Blanche, her first niece, had been.

Aunt Jane had worshipped Blanche. Aunt Miriam, Blanche's mother, hadn't been well for some time after Blanche arrived, and the little girl spent most of her short life at Grandmother's. When she died Aunt Jane was heart-broken.

I never quite took Blanche's place. Aunt Jane's voice always stumbled when she spoke of her, but I had a place of my own in Aunt Jane's heart. She never refused me anything, and no matter what I did she never scolded me. I, of course, took advantage of her kindness. I never went to bed until she did, often I insisted on being read to when she was tired. I ate only what I pleased, and every day at noon I demanded and got a mug of the strong tea she brewed for the mill-workers.

Once when I stamped my feet and screamed Grandmother said: 'Jane, you ought not to let her behave like that. A little slap won't hurt her.'

'She'll get enough slaps in her life without me giving her any,' Aunt Jane said. 'Besides, it isn't her fault she's upset. She's tired.' And picking me up she carried me upstairs, tucked me into bed, and sat beside me until I went to sleep. Sometimes, of course, I patted her thin cheek and told her how much I loved her, and somehow that seemed to make up for my tantrums.

When she went to Blackpool for her short yearly rest Aunt Jane always took me with her. Hand in hand we walked on the wide yellow sands listening to the minstrels, or watching Punch choke Judy. Sometimes we sat on the sand and built castles with turrets and towers. I always hoped to find the castles again in the morning, but I never did. The tide came in during the night and washed them away.

Sometimes we stood on the sand and watched the tide come in. The little waves ran towards us, then turned and hurried back to the ocean as if afraid, but after a moment they ran forward again, coming a little closer than they had before. Each spray-tipped wave was bolder than the last, and after a while the sand and the sand castles were covered by blue-green water.

'My castle's gone,' I cried. 'The sea melted it.'

'Nothing lasts, Mary,' Aunt Jane said gently, 'not even this, though I hope it won't go soon.' Then she took my hand and we went home. The tide of time, however, was bringing changes that neither she nor I could stop.

Aunt Jane did her best. 'What is there in Canada that you haven't got here?' she asked when Dad talked of leaving England. 'You're better off than you've ever been. The farm's doing well. You're saving money. You have a nice home. Why do you want to throw it all away and go to a wilderness half-way across the world?'

'There's more opportunity there,' Dad said unhappily. 'Especially for a lad.'

Aunt Jane didn't think so. She also told him how much Grandfather and Grandmother would miss him, and reminded him of how lonely Uncle Albert had been in both South Africa and Philadelphia. 'If you don't like Canada you'll be worse off than ever when you come back,' she warned. 'The farm will be gone, and you'll have to start all over again.'

Dad's unhappy eyes glanced around the little room. He looked at the old plates on the wall, at Grandfather breathing heavily in his chair, and at Grandmother's crutch leaning against the sofa. 'I'll think it over,' he promised, but there was longing in his eyes.

The more he thought, however, the more he wanted to go, and at last Aunt Jane asked Grandmother to talk to him. 'He'll stay if you ask him to,' she said. 'All you have to do is say a word or two and all this nonsense will be over and done with.'

'I know.' Grandmother's voice was gentle. 'Walter was always one to listen to me. But it isn't for me to interfere, or you either, Jane. If he really wants to go to Canada it's the Lord's will, and right for him to go.'

'I've no patience with the Lord's will,' Aunt Jane said. 'I want him to stay, and Mary Jane too.'

'Don't talk like that, Jane.' Grandmother's thin face was pinched, and her fine grey eyes sad. 'I know how hard it is for thee,' she said, 'but have patience.'

Grandfather Gomersall, Mother's father, also refused to interfere. He was a stout old gentleman with white hair, smiling blue eyes, and a fringe of white whiskers that went around his chin from ear to ear. Life hadn't been any too kind to him. He had buried two wives and three children, and one of his daughters, Aunt Louisa, had already gone to Australia, but he refused to influence Mother one way or the other.

He had not always been a cabinet-maker. Music had been his first and early love. He had, however, decided that the father of nine children ought to do more than play the piano, so he had become a cabinet-maker on week-days and a musician on Sunday. When other men lounged in the Sunday sunshine smoking and talking, Grandfather Gomersall played the piano. And instead of going to the corner for a glass of beer, he put on his frock-coat and tall silk hat and went to church. He and his third wife, who always wore an impressive long black dolman and neat bonnet, were a dignified pair.

It was as a cabinet-maker, however, that I liked Grandfather Gomersall best. With his sleeves rolled up and a white apron tight over his stomach he looked like Santa Claus getting ready for Christmas. He also had a Santa Claus knack with dolls, and whenever a doll lost an arm or leg I took the sufferer to him, and she was soon cured.

Even when my dolls were in good repair I found his shop interesting. He had once operated a big store as well as a workshop, but there was no longer much demand for his fine, hand-carved chests and sideboards, so the store had gone, and only the shop remained. It was a delightful place in which to play. There was clean, sweet-smelling sawdust to walk in, and hammers, saws, and gimlets to work with. Sometimes when Grandfather sawed a board the saw cried as if in pain, sometimes it purred like a happy cat. The chisels Uncle Sam used to scoop out leaves and flowers often grumbled and complained as if weary of the work they did, and longing to escape from the sweet smell of glue, the crisp smell of varnish, and the spicy fragrance of the shavings that curled from Grandfather's plane.

The plane sliced the shavings off the boards, and they fell in long golden curls to the floor, and lay there in fluffy yellow piles. I loved to turn them over and over, sniffing their clean wood smell and looking for extra-long curls. When I had thoroughly sorted the pile I stood and watched Grandfather make more curls. 'Be careful,' I urged as his plane skimmed along the edge of the board and the shaving curled from it. 'Don't let it break. Don't let it break.' But somehow the shavings always broke sooner or later and I was disappointed.

'Things seldom go just the way you want them to,' Grandfather said when one shaving after another broke. 'But don't let it bother you, lass. We can always try again.' And he smiled at me, squinted along the edge of the board, and knocked off another curl or two.

'If you'd only talk to Sarah and Walter,' Uncle Sam said one day when I was turning over a pile of yellow curls, 'you might get him out of his notion of going to Canada, and hers of going with him.'

Grandfather ran his finger slowly along a groove, and his blue eyes, so like Mother's, looked troubled. 'It's for them to decide,' he said at last.

'But that wilderness is no place for a woman,' Uncle Sam said. 'She ought to let Walter go alone, and she would if you'd ask her to. She thinks a lot of your opinion. You ought to talk to her.'

'Sarah knows I'll help her all I can if she stays,' Grandfather said slowly. 'But if a woman wants to go with her husband that's where she belongs.'

'We'll never see her again if she goes to that god-forsaken place.' Uncle Sam's voice was bitter, and his thin face unhappy.

Grandfather Gomersall didn't reply, but his round body seemed to shrink a little, and the smile left his face. Suddenly he looked quite old and tired.

'You hate to see her go as much as I do,' Uncle Sam said.

'That may be.' Grandfather bent over his plane. 'But it isn't for me to try to separate them, or for you either.'

Uncle Sam didn't argue any more, but he didn't give up. He asked Aunt Polly, Mother's half-sister, and her husband, Uncle Elstub, to talk to Mother. They came to see us when Dad was at the club, and talked for a long time. Their visit caused so much turmoil that I was sent to the house by the Spen until it was over.

The house by the Spen wasn't any too peaceful, either. Aunt Jane was unhappy, and every time Dad came, which was almost every day, she told him how foolish he was to even think of going to Canada. 'What is there in Canada that you haven't got here?' she asked. 'You're making a good living. What more do you want?'

'I want more than a bare living.' Dad put down the bright can in which he had brought milk, and looked at Grandmother and the crutch beside her. 'And I want more than a living for Jack, too.'

'He'll do just as well here as he will there,' Aunt Jane said, stirring the little fire in the open fire-place. 'Besides, he can always go to Canada when he grows up if he wants to.'

'The good land will be gone by then,' Dad said. 'And it'll be better for him to grow up where he's going to live. If we go now I'll have made a start for him. Got things going.'

'You're thinking more of yourself than you are of him.' Aunt Jane's voice was sharp with misery. 'You'd go even if he was a lass.'

'There's no future here,' Dad said. 'Nothing to look for'ard to. The ruts are near too deep to get out of, and everything's that crowded. These narrow streets, and the houses cheek by jowl, and them bits of fields! They shut a man in, and there's no elbow-room. And look at the folk! Them that don't see beyond the end of their noses, what do they do if a man tries to get on? They laugh at him. Tell him it's no use, and he's making a fool of himself, trying to be something he isn't. After a bit, if things go wrong, he believes them, and starts doing as they do. He goes to the pub Saturday night, saves a shilling now and then for a decent funeral, and that's all. I want summat better'n that.'

'How do you know you'll get summat better in Canada?' Aunt Jane asked. 'You might do a lot worse.'

'I'll have tried to do better, anyway,' Dad said.

'At the expense of your old mother's loneliness.'

'No, Jane! You mustn't say such things,' Grandmother protested.

'But it's true,' Aunt Jane said.

Dad looked miserable but determined, then a bright idea hit him. 'I don't see what you have to fret about,' he said, brightening. 'As soon as I get going out there what's to stop you coming as well? I'll build a house for you right next to ours, it won't cost a penny, and we can be near one another again.'

'If you go to Canada it will be the last we'll ever see of you,' Aunt Jane said.

'No, it won't. Even if you don't come out you'll see us in a year, or two at the most. I don't intend to stay in Canada for ever,' Dad said.

Aunt Jane started to reply, but Grandmother interrupted. 'Let's have a drink of tea,' she said gently. 'Canada's a long way off, but it isn't another world.'

The tea ended that argument, but there were many more. To get away from them I often went to Katie Daw's home.

Katie was a thin child, and when the discussions about Canada were going against him Dad always held her up as an example of what might happen to me if we stayed in England.

Her brown eyes were about three sizes too big for her thin, sallow face, and her ankles, above her wood-soled, iron-shod clogs, looked like matchsticks. She lived with her grandmother in a tiny house just around the corner from Aunt Jane's, and although only just past ten years old she was a half-timer in a mill, and worked about thirty hours a week, for which she was paid about four shillings. She also went to school half-days, and helped with the housework. At night she was usually tired, but I liked to visit her.

Mrs Daw, Katie's grandmother, was considered a character, and some people said she smoked a long clay pipe, and took a drop now and then. Actually she was a hard-working old lady, and looked a lot like a steamed pudding.

While Katie dozed in her chair by the fire Mrs Daw sat and talked to me. Somebody had brought her an Indian doll from Canada, and she brought it out and let me look at it. Its dress was fringed leather, and around its head was a beaded band with a tiny feather stuck through it at the back.

I thought it a queer hat and said so. Mrs Daw said all Indians wore headbands around their hair, unless they had been scalped, and had no hair. She described the scalping process, and said it often happened to people in Canada. One pull and all your hair was gone. She seemed to think it a rather grim business, but the prospect of losing my hair to a scalping-knife didn't worry me at all. In fact I rather looked forward to the operation. My curls were always full of snarls, and combing hurt. What would be nicer than getting rid of the whole business by means of one quick jerk?

Aunt Jane, however, didn't think much of the treatment, and said I'd better not go to the Daws' again for a while. Katie had to get her sleep, and the night air wasn't good for me. So I stayed at the little house behind the shop, or at Castle Hill, and listened to the planning that was going on around me.

In spite of all the arguments against it Dad had decided to go to Canada with the Barr Colony, and Mother was going with him.

Uncle Sam, however, hadn't given up. He came often to Castle Hill and tried to persuade Mother to change her mind. They sat in the rosy firelight, close to the bright brass fender, and talked in low voices.

'If you were going to a town I wouldn't care so much,' Uncle Sam said, his thin face pale in spite of the fire glow. 'But a wilderness with three children! It's madness.'

'I know, but Walter has set his heart on going.' Mother's voice was low, but not miserable like Uncle Sam's.

'What will you do if the children get typhoid?'

'I don't know.' Mother sighed.

'Then why don't you stay here? You could get a cottage. Jane will help, and so will I. I'll put off getting married. Walter will be back in six months if you don't go.'

Mother looked thoughtfully at the fire and frowned. 'No,' she said at last, and shook her little head. 'They're Walter Pinder's children, and it's up to him to take care of them. If he goes we all go.'

'If you'd married Edmond Bastow this wouldn't have happened,' Uncle Sam said bitterly.

'Him!' Mother's chin tilted disdainfully. 'He was too old for me.' She didn't sound sorry.

'There was only five years' difference. That's nothing.'

'It was more than I wanted.' Mother smiled.

'It wasn't until you met Walter Pinder. Sometimes I doubt if you care a ha'p'orth for anybody but him. You know he wouldn't go across the street if you put your foot down, but you won't. Sometimes I think you want to go as much as he does.'

'No, I don't.' Mother picked up the poker and stirred the coals, making them flame red and yellow. 'But if he doesn't go he'll never be satisfied, and I'm not going to be left.'

Aunt Jane also tried to persuade Mother not to go. She offered to take care of me and help with Lily and Jack. The shop was doing well, and she could manage it.

Mother looked tempted for a moment, then she shook her head. 'No, Jane,' she said, 'it's good of you, but you have enough to look after. Don't fash yourself too much about this. Albert didn't stay long in either Philadelphia or South Africa. Walter may not stay long in Canada. But if he doesn't go and see for himself what it's like he'll never be content. A good big dose of Canada is the only thing that will cure him. That man from Manitoba told me a few things. There aren't any penny-trees even on the prairie.'

This view cheered Aunt Jane a little, but she was still worried. Uncle Albert had crossed the sea while he was single; if he'd had a wife and three children with him for company he might have stayed. Still, it was a thread to cling to, and to strengthen it a little Aunt Jane put out a thread of her own. Why not leave me with her until they were sure about what they wanted to do? I could always go out later if they decided to stay.

Dad and Mother and all the aunts and uncles discussed this idea for some time. They all thought the family ought to stay together and said so, but Dad and Mother hesitated for a long time. Dad hated to hurt Aunt Jane's feelings, and Mother didn't want to leave me behind, though she admitted I might be better off in England where I could go to school. She also thought I might be the tie that would bring them back.

'What do you want to do, Mary?' Aunt Jane asked one Sunday afternoon when we were sitting by the fire in the little house.

I hesitated. Dad had told me a lot about Canada: of the pony I could ride, the flowers I could pick, the streams I could wade in, the fields of grass, and the wagon and horses that would be ours.

'Jane, she's too little to know what's best,' Grandmother said gently.

'She ought to have something to say about where she's going,' Aunt Jane said. Her thin face above her high, dark collar was very pale and tired.

'I could come and see you,' I said.

Tears came into Aunt Jane's eyes. 'No, you couldn't. It's too far.'

'Farther than Cleckheaton?'

'A lot farther. It's even farther than Leeds.'

'Then I think I'll stay here.' I hated to see Aunt Jane unhappy.

She was delighted with my decision, and told Dad I didn't want to go to Canada. Dad didn't say anything, but when everything else had been settled—who was to have the farm, and when, and what price the cows ought to bring—Dad and Mother said they thought I ought to go with them.

Aunt Jane was heart-broken. She stood in the middle of the little room, a lonely and forlorn figure, and twisted her thin, worn hands. 'What have I done that everything I love is taken from me?' she asked bitterly. 'First Blanche, now Mary.'

Dad looked at the floor, and Mother looked at the row of candy jars in the window, and there was silence in the little room until Grandmother said gently: 'Jane, why don't you go with them?'

'To Canada?' Aunt Jane's face, that had been so unhappy a moment before, was suddenly bright and alive.

'Yes,' Grandmother said. 'Why not?'

'It would be grand!' Aunt Jane's thin face, curly dark hair, and even her plain dark dress seemed to glow. She lifted her head, and her eyes, wider and brighter than I had ever seen them, stared far beyond the little room, as if she were seeing the life she had missed, but still might find in a new and wider world. 'I could be ready,' she said eagerly, then she turned and caught sight of Grandmother's crutch leaning against the end of the sofa.

Aunt Jane stiffened and stared at the crutch, and all the light went out of her. Her shoulders sagged, her crisp hair seemed to wilt, her mouth shrivelled, and age like a cloak settled over her. 'I can't leave you,' she said hoarsely, staring at the crutch. 'What would you do?'

'There'll be someway done,' Grandmother said. 'It isn't right that you give up everything. You've a right to a bit of life. Katie Daw will come in and help. It will be easier for her than the mill. And there's Emma.'

'No.' Aunt Jane shook her head. 'Emma has her own home, and one of these days Katie will be married. My place is here.' And walking stiffly, as if she were made of wood, Aunt Jane turned and went slowly across the little room and upstairs.

There was a long, sad silence after she had gone. Grandmother, her pale hands folded, looked at the fire. Dad looked at his feet, and Mother smoothed Jack's soft hair. 'I think we had better be going,' Dad said at last. He helped Lily into her coat and bonnet, and Mother wrapped Jack in his big shawl, then they went quietly away.

CHAPTER THREE

GETTING ready to leave England took quite a long time, and most of the preparations were sad. Dad said there was no need to make a fuss, we were not going to Canada for ever. In a year, two at the most, we would be back. Grandmother said 'Yes, of course' and smiled with her lips, but her grey eyes were bleak, and she looked at Dad's cheerful face as if trying to fix it in her memory for ever.

The other relatives said: 'Oh, you'll be back, Canada won't be all clover.' But their voices sounded hollow, and the aunts wiped their eyes and the uncles coughed.

Two of our relatives, however, Gladstone and Walter Walker Pinder, Dad's nephews, thoroughly enjoyed saying good-bye.

They were about ten and eight years old, and they seemed to enjoy the prospect of never seeing me again. They also did their best to frighten me half to death.

They had never been on a ship, or even seen one, but they knew all about ships, and the dark holes that went right through them to the water. The sides of the holes were also quite slippery, which made them easy to fall into, and impossible to get out of. Swarms of monsters were always waiting at the bottom of each hole—waiting to eat little girls, a finger at a time. But these monsters were nothing compared to the whales and sharks that followed the ship. These creatures not only lurked in the water, they even jumped on deck and bit chunks out of children's legs. 'Don't ever go near the edge of the deck,' the boys warned. 'And never go on deck at night. If you do you'll be pulled overboard, and the sharks and whales will nibble at you for days.'

According to them Canada was also full of peril. There were buffaloes in every field waiting to chase anyone who went near, and toss them high in the air. The forests were full of big black and brown bears, all hungry. Wolves, of course, were as thick as flies, but the bears were by far the worst. They often broke into the houses at night and pulled little children my size right out of bed, and carried them to their dens and ate them a little at a time. Much to the boys' disgust I enjoyed their stories, and urged them to tell me more, but a bear on my bed was my favourite nightmare for a long time.

When the cousins' visit was over I went to stay in the little house by the Spen, and life, except for the sadness on Aunt Jane's face, was much as it always had been. The mill-workers crowded in every noon for their mugs of strong tea, children clutching a penny came to buy candy, women with shawls over their heads came and bought potted meat, cake, and thread. The bushes by the Spen put out tiny green shoots, and in the gardens that surrounded some of the big houses daffodils bloomed. I skipped in the space behind the shop, and when Katie Daw had a minute to spare we played jacks on her doorstep. Canada seemed a long way off, and almost forgotten. Then one day Dad came and told me to put on my bonnet, we were going to Castle Hill.

I went eagerly, for a trip of any sort with Dad was fun. He was always cheerful, everything interested him, and he shared his interest with me. He called my attention to the clouds, and told me why he thought it was going to rain, showed me birds' nests with eggs in them, helped me gather acorn cups under the oaks, and violets among the new leaves. Often he had a supply of hazel-nuts in his pocket, and amused me by cracking them between his fingers. He showed me how to do the trick, but the hard shells always defeated me, and I thought Dad had some special kind of magic in his fingers.

That afternoon, however, Dad's pockets were empty, there was no sparkle in his dark, green-flecked eyes, and his thin face looked tired.

We walked up Listing Lane without pausing once to look for either hedgehogs or frogs, and when I stopped to gather acorns Dad didn't seem to notice.

As we walked up the narrow, tree-shaded path that went from the lane to the top of Castle Hill Dad paused once or twice and looked at the little fields edged with stone walls and greening hawthorn, and his thin lips were pressed tight together. I found a pretty stone and showed it to him, but he didn't seem to see it though he said it was fine.

We walked past the big house with the high stone wall around it. The iron gates were open, and we could see the daffodils and primroses growing in the garden. I longed to step through the gates and smell the flowers, but I didn't dare. Once a gardener had shouted at me when I stopped to admire some pansies. We turned the corner and there was our little house at the end of the lane.

Ivy, thick and green, covered it right to the chimney-pots. There was a little space in front where grass grew, and until that day the front window had been full of geraniums. Now, however, the window was empty, and it looked unhappy and lonely, as if it missed the flowers Mother had loved. I missed them, too, and the bare window gave me a strange, hollow feeling.

Dad turned the iron key in the lock and opened the green door. He stepped inside, but I paused with my foot on the threshold. This was no longer our house. It was empty, cold, and strange.

The rugs Mother had brodded in the long winter evenings were gone, and the stone floor was bare. There was no bright brass fender around the hearth, no fire in the fire-place, no happy kettle, no hissing pans. The whole hearth was dull and dead. The table with its leg protections had also gone, and so had the chairs and their crocheted antimacassars. Even the roses in the wall-paper looked lonely and unhappy.

I knew that people often moved from one house to another. Aunt Emma had moved after Wilfred was born. But we had always lived in this house. I had played on the floor, and Bob, our dog, had slept before the fire. Now all our things were gone, and the house seemed strange. I rubbed my eyes, and my fist was wet.

Dad seemed to have forgotten all about me. He walked slowly around the room looking at the marks the chairs had made, and the places where the pictures had hung. He touched the mantel, and looked for a long while at the spot where the cradle had stood, then he went upstairs. He was gone a long time.

When he came down he walked around the room again, and looked at the lonely roses in the wall-paper, and at the empty window where the geraniums had bloomed. He seemed to want to impress every bit of the house on his memory, and no wonder. It was the first home he and Mother had ever had. There they had been young, and there Lily and Jack had been born.

After a while Dad came over to where I stood close to the door. 'Take a good look,' he said, and there was strain in his voice. 'You might never see it again.'

I did as he told me. I looked at the place by the hearth where my little rocking-chair had stood, and at the step where I had so often sat and played with my dolls, but there was a cold mist in my eyes, and I was glad when Dad took my hand, led me outside, and closed the green door behind us.

We walked down the little lane to the top of the Ginnel, and there Dad paused again. Before and below us was the Spen Valley, Littletown where Dad and Mother, and generations before them, had been born, the mills where they had worked, the fields where as children they had gone to gather daisies and buttercups, the streets down which they had walked. There also was the church where Lily, Jack, and I had been baptized, and the churchyard where so many of our ancestors, now long forgotten, were buried. Their tombstones, leaning, weather-beaten, and moss-covered, were there under the ancient oaks. The names and the dates of birth and death were still upon them, but all else was gone.

We stood for a long time and looked at the house-tops, the church spire, and the chimneys from which slow smoke rolled, then Dad reached for my hand, and together we walked down the Ginnel and along Listing Lane to Grandmother's house in Littletown.

Years later I returned to Castle Hill. The ivy had gone from the little house, and its stone walls looked bare and old. The green door had faded, and the paint was peeling. I looked at the door for a long time, but I did not open it. Dad was no longer with me.

CHAPTER FOUR

A day or so after Dad and I said good-bye to Castle Hill we left England. I had known for a long time that we were going, everybody had talked about it for months, but to me the actual leaving was sudden and unexpected.

The day before we left had been like any other day. I had watched the mill-workers stream out of the mill entrance when the whistle blew, thrown stones into the Spen River, played hopscotch, and gone to bed just as usual, but next morning my world was all out of joint.

Aunt Jane, her eyes red and her thin face tired, woke me when it was still night. She stood beside my bed holding the iron candlestick, and told me it was time to get up. I tried to turn over and go back to sleep, but Aunt Jane began to pull on my stockings. Then she dressed me, carefully, and combed my hair with gentle hands.

When we went downstairs coals glowed in the open fire-place, and the gas was lit, but the little room was full of sorrow. Grandfather Pinder, who spent most of his days in an arm-chair by the fire because of a heart condition, wore his best suit even though it wasn't Sunday, and tears rolled slowly down his swollen cheeks.

Grandmother also wore her best black dress, and a little shawl to keep the draught from her shoulders. Her white hair was parted in the middle, combed smoothly, and knotted at the back of her head. Though unhappy, her pale, fine face was as dignified and composed as the face on a coin. Beside her, propped against the horse-hair sofa, was her crutch.

Grandmother Pinder had never indulged me as Aunt Jane had, but she had never scolded me either. She never needed to. I had obeyed her quiet voice without question, for there was a goodness and a strength about her that made me want to please her more than I wanted to please myself. I never saw her upset about anything. No matter what happened her quiet courage was equal to it. Even when the cab came to take us to the station, and it was time to say the last good-bye, she did not falter.

Grandfather Pinder shook hands with Dad and Mother, and put his swollen hands on Lily's head, then on mine, but he could not trust himself to either stand or speak. He simply sat and looked at us, his blue eyes full of tears.

Grandmother, however, stood straight and firm in spite of her crutch. She kissed us and said a word or two, and her voice was steady even when she told me to be a good girl. She did not cling to any of us, though Dad was her youngest and she might never see him again. Her thin, kind face was peaceful, and her fine lips did not quiver. Dad was doing what he thought he ought to do, and she made it as easy as possible for him. Only her eyes, so like Dad's, showed the depth of her feeling. They looked like bleak pools into which snow had fallen.

When the farewells were said Dad picked up Lily and went towards the door, and Mother, carrying Jack, followed him. I went a step or two, then I turned and looked once more at the little room. I looked at the small fire on the hearth, at the tiny arm-chair that had been mine, and at the old mugs and platters that Grandmother prized. And at last I looked at my grandmother's gentle face.

She did not smile or speak, and yet I felt her love warm and friendly around me.

'Come, Mary,' Mother called from the doorway. 'We must be going.'

I knew I had to go, but I could not turn away from the kind face I loved. Instead of turning I backed slowly towards the door.

Seeing my difficulty, Grandmother, with the help of her crutch, came towards me, but she did not take me in her arms or even touch me. There was a vase of daffodils on the table, and she took the bright flowers out of the water and handed them to me. 'Here, darling,' she said gently, 'take them with you.'

I had admired the flowers extravagantly the day before, and had longed to hold them, but now I could not look at them. I clutched them tightly, and backed slowly out of the door, still looking at my grandmother's kind face. Having the flowers to hold, however, did comfort me a little, especially when Aunt Jane finally had to let me go.

Aunt Jane went with us to Liversedge station. She would have liked to go to Liverpool with us, but she did not want to leave Grandmother for a whole day. I sat on her lap in the cab, and at the station she clung to my hand while we waited for the train.

The drive to the station was dull in spite of the excitement of riding in a cab. Rain was falling, and the streets were wet and dark, and all the huddled little houses looked cold and half asleep.

The little knot of people huddled on the platform waiting for us looked cold also, and rain and tears mingled on their cheeks.

Grandfather Gomersall smiled with his lips, but his blue eyes looked full of rain. Aunt Lily and Aunt Polly, Mother's sisters, were crying. Uncle Sam looked pale and a little withered. Uncle Elstub, Aunt Polly's husband, looked bored. He was going to Liverpool with us so that Uncle Sam, who was also going, wouldn't have to go home alone. Uncle Arthur, who was taking over our farm, looked depressed, and Aunt Emma, his wife, kept dabbing at her eyes. They stood there in the chill wind and talked in strained, unhappy voices, waiting for the train, yet hoping it wouldn't come.

Suddenly there was a clatter on the cobble-stones, and Katie Daw, clutching a shawl under her thin chin, came running through the rain. Her big brown eyes were full of tears, and some of them spilled over and mixed with the rain. 'I came to say good-bye,' she said, looking at me.

I stared miserably at her familiar face. Always before I'd had so much to say to her that my tongue wagged at both ends, but that morning I was without words. I simply stood and looked at her plain but friendly face.

'Say good-bye to Katie,' Mother said gently.

I refused to say a word. Somehow I hoped that if I didn't say good-bye she wouldn't go away, and this strange morning, so unlike every other morning I had ever known, would melt away: go back into the dream world where it had come from, and leave me in peace. If Katie stayed I felt sure I would wake up, and it would be time to go to school, and this unhappiness would be over.

'I have to go to work,' Katie said at last. 'Good-bye, Mrs Pinder.' She shook hands with Mother, then she turned to me. 'Good-bye, Mary.' She kissed me quickly and ran away into the rain.

The train came soon after Katie left, and the little group on the platform began saying the last words they might ever say to each other. I knew everybody well, but at that moment they were mostly a forest of long skirts and trousered legs. All except Aunt Jane. She stayed a little apart and put her arms around me.

People got off the train and others got on, and the doors slammed. The guard walked by and blew his whistle.

Dad, carrying Lily, and Mother, carrying Jack, got into a compartment, and Uncle Sam and Uncle Elstub followed them. Aunt Jane's arms tightened around me, and for a moment time seemed to wait.

I stood on the platform, a damp, miserable little girl clinging to Aunt Jane and the daffodils. I didn't want to leave Aunt Jane and all the love and protection she represented, but I didn't want to be left behind either. I wanted my world to remain unchanged, and I was hurt and resentful because it wouldn't respect my wishes. Why did grown people have to upset things so, when they didn't really want to go away either?

'Come, Mary,' Mother said, but I didn't move. Mother glanced at Dad, but he hated to hurt Aunt Jane so he said nothing. It was one of the few times I ever saw tears in Dad's eyes.

At last the guard came to our compartment and put his hand on the door handle. He glanced from one group to the other and hesitated a moment, then the train began to move. Everyone seemed to have stopped breathing. I wanted to cry to the train to stop, but I couldn't. Another second and the door would have been closed and I would have been left behind, but Aunt Polly grabbed my arm, pulled me away from Aunt Jane, and shoved me through the almost closed door in what seemed to be just one movement. 'She belongs with the others,' she said.

'Oh, no!' Aunt Jane cried and held out her hands, but the door was closed and the train moving. She ran down the platform calling my name and crying. I stood at the window and called to her, and tried to blow her a kiss, but the window was in the way and I was crying.

CHAPTER FIVE

THE sky was still grey when we arrived in Liverpool, and a thin drizzle of rain fell like hopeless tears on the gloomy city. Uncle Sam called a cab and took us to a restaurant, but the good food he ordered wouldn't go past the tightness in our throats, and we ate very little. It was a relief to us all when another cab came and took us to the dock where the ship, *Lake Manitoba*, waited.

I did not realize at first that the long dark bulk with the white railings and superstructure, the smoking chimneys, almost as big as the mill chimneys, and the queer funnels was a ship. It was far bigger than anything the cousins had described. The misty rain hid the far end of it, and I was quite sure that anything so big must go all the way across the ocean like a bridge. Going to Canada wasn't going to be much of a problem after all. It was just a walk up the gang-plank, along the ship, then down the gang-plank at the other end. Obviously the cousins had been all wrong about the ship. Such a big structure couldn't possibly float. As for the holes, I didn't see any, and no fish could possibly climb those steep sides. For the first time I began to wonder if Gladstone and Walter Walker really knew everything. One thing I was sure of, and it comforted me very much: Canada wasn't as far away as Aunt Jane thought. To visit us all she had to do was take a train to Liverpool, then walk across the ship. I tried to explain this to Uncle Sam, but he only said 'Yes, Mary' without any understanding at all.

We had to wait for a while on the dock while Dad went to see about the baggage, and check the tickets, and make sure this was the right ship.

The dock was as grey as the town had been, and the wind was raw and cold. The rain, though little more than a thick mist, dampened everything. It clung in tiny drops to the fur over Mother's shoulders, wet my hair and my dark blue coat and bonnet, and moistened Jack's round pink cheeks. It made Lily's hand, that I held part of the time, feel cold, and it came up through my shoes and made my feet feel wet. It hid the sea beyond the ship, and dulled the outline of the town.

Although grey and dismal the dock was busy. Porters hurried about carrying baggage and pushing clanking carts. Men on the dock and on the deck shouted. Gulls, wet and grey, swooped out of the mist, hovered, mewed, and flew away, only to swoop back and mew again. And there were people everywhere: unhappy little groups that seemed to have already lost contact with England. They stood there in the drizzle, their dark coats damp, their hats tilted by the cold wind, their faces bleak: a group of unhappy adventurers teetering on the edge of the unknown.

I held my daffodils in one hand and Lily's coat in the other, and listened to the conversations going on about me. Uncle Sam was still urging Mother to change her mind. His voice was low and unhappy, and I lost interest in the tiresome discussion and turned my attention to another little group close beside me.

They were no happier than we were. Rain moistened their faces and clung to their clothes just as it did to ours, and their eyes looked lonely and their lips trembled. They tried to smile, but their lips either bent stiffly or sagged out of control, and they hid them behind their handkerchiefs.

They tried hard to encourage one another. 'We aren't going to Canada for ever,' the young woman told her mother. 'In a year we shall be back with plenty of money. Take good care of my kitten, won't you?'

'I surely will,' the older woman said, and her tired mouth bent a little, but her eyes searched her daughter's face as if she were trying to fix its every curve and plane in her memory for ever. 'You'll write often, won't you?' she asked. 'And don't forget the flannel on your chest when it's cold.'

'Of course, Mother.' The young woman looked at the ship. 'I wonder where Herb is?' she said impatiently.

After a while the unhappy little groups began to divide. They kissed and shook hands, then the younger ones went slowly up the gangplank, pausing often to look back and wave a limp handkerchief. Those remaining on the dock waved also, and bit their lips, and wiped their eyes.

There were a few older people among the colonists, but most of them were young. Couples like Dad and Mother with small children, newly-weds going to a new country to start their new lives, and many single men eager for adventure, and hoping to acquire a quick fortune.

Few of them, however, had any idea of what the new country would be like.

They knew they were going to a place called the North-West Territory where everything was free, but most of them had never been outside a city, or away from such conveniences as roads, water in a faucet at the sink, trams, gaslights, roofs that didn't leak, real floors, and, most important of all, relatives at the end of the street and friends next door. They had been told that life in Canada might be rough at first, but they did not realize how vast the prairies were, how savage the storm, how bitter the cold. They had never seen a mosquito or heard of a sand-fly.

Standing damp and cold on the dock, or leaning wearily against the rail of the ship, the Barr colonists didn't look anything like the stuff pioneers are supposed to be made of. They were neither big nor raw-boned, and there was no cock-sure swagger in either their shoulders or their feet. They were simply a group of unhappy people leaving home and friends for what they hoped would be a better life. Some of them were home-sick already, and the women at least said they wished they'd never heard of Canada. A few, however, were looking forward with hope in their eyes, and Dad was one of these.

He came towards us through the misty rain: a short, thin man in a brown coat and cap. Not a pioneer as far as looks went, but there was a pleased smile on his lean face, and excitement in his step. 'Everything's settled,' he said cheerfully. 'You're going to Canada, lass.' He gave my bonnet a pat. 'Let's get on board.' He picked up Lily and started towards the gang-plank.

'You don't have to be so pleased, do you?' Mother asked as she followed him.

The rail of the gang-plank was wet, and I scooped drops of cold water into my hand. At the top there was a little delay, and a small argument, then Uncle Sam gave someone some money and we went on board.

The deck was cleaner than the dock, and there were interesting doorways, and glimpses of narrow stairs, but nobody paid any attention to them. Everybody seemed to be crying.

I sniffed at the daffodils Grandmother had given me, and wondered why everyone was so miserable. If they didn't want to go to Canada why were they going? They were mostly grown up, and could do as they pleased. They didn't have to do as they were told as I did. No one would push them into a train.

While I was pondering the odd ways of the old a band began to play. Mr Barr had arranged for the music, hoping it would cheer the colonists a little. Mother, however, said it was the last straw as far as she was concerned: especially the last number, 'Dolly Gray.' The first line of it was 'Good-bye, Dolly, I must leave you,' and before the band got half-way through it everyone but Dad was in tears, and two or three women were having hysterics.

At last, when everybody was thoroughly cold, damp, and miserable, a long, deep-throated hoot came from somewhere in the middle of the ship. It was the signal for those not going to Canada to go ashore.

Handshaking broke out all over again, and there were more tears and more promises to return. I stood beside Mother more confused than ever by the goings-on of grown people. They were doing what they wanted to do, but what a fuss they were making! Finally even Lily began to whimper, and Dad put her down and told me to look after her. I took her little hand and told her to shut up, but she paid no attention to me.

Uncle Sam hugged and kissed us all, then he turned to shake hands with Dad, but Dad had disappeared. Uncle Sam blinked and looked again, but Dad just wasn't there. 'He must be somewhere about,' Uncle Elstub said, and he and Uncle Sam hurried about looking behind piles of bags and boxes, and into the faces of men about Dad's height, five foot four, but they couldn't find him.

People began to stream down the gang-plank, and a steward near us looked uneasy. 'Come with us, Sarah,' Uncle Sam urged, and picked Lily up. 'He's gone, maybe ashore. You're free now.' He started towards the gang-plank.

'No!' Mother's voice was thin but determined, and she grabbed the back of Lily's coat. 'They're his children, and they're going with him. He'll be here in a minute. He hates to say good-bye, that's all. Don't you worry about us.' She smiled confidently.

Uncle Sam hesitated. Mother's sudden smile puzzled him. He put Lily down, and backed away a little as if bewildered.

'Sir,' the steward said, 'if you aren't going to Canada you'd better go ashore. They'll be raising the gang-plank in a minute.'

Uncle Sam looked wildly around the ship. 'Sarah!' he said, and pulled at Mother's arm.

'That'll do, Sam.' Uncle Elstub, large and friendly, stepped forward. 'Sarah and Walter will be all right. They belong together. Let's be going.' He took Uncle Sam's arm and pulled him towards the gang-plank.

The minute the uncles were gone and the gang-plank up Dad appeared. He waved to the uncles, now on the dock, then he turned and smiled sheepishly at Mother. 'I thought you'd like to say good-bye to Sam by yourself,' he said.

'That isn't it at all,' Mother said sharply, though she looked relieved. 'You wanted to get out of the last good-bye, and you know it. Where were you? We looked everywhere. I very nearly went back with Sam, and it would have served you right if I had.'

Dad smiled, and insisted he'd slipped behind some bales so that she could have a last moment with her brother, but Mother refused to believe him. She said he had lost his nerve at the last minute, but wouldn't admit it.

Dad said no such thing, he never lost his nerve, and his eyes twinkled, and he smiled so convincingly that Mother was more irked than ever. She tossed her pretty head, and said in that case he ought to be ashamed of himself, worrying her that way, and she sometimes wondered why she had ever married such a thoughtless man. Edmond Bastow would have been a far better choice, and wouldn't have dragged her off to Canada, either.

'Oh, him! You wouldn't even go to the bob-dolly show with him,' Dad said, smiling.

'Yes, I would,' Mother replied, but her voice wasn't convincing.

'I think we're moving.' Dad turned and went towards the rail. Mother followed. There was a wide gap between the dock and the ship, and people were waving frantically. Mother and Dad waved, too, but rather carelessly I thought.

Several women began to sob, and one of them fainted, but Mother was quite calm. The little argument Dad had provoked had eased the tension of leaving, and they stood side by side and watched as the city of Liverpool and the shores of England slipped slowly backward until they finally disappeared in the wet mist.

CHAPTER SIX

THE *Lake Manitoba* wasn't a regular passenger ship. It had been chartered especially for the Barr Colony. There was nothing fancy about it: no bar, no lounge or amusement deck. It had been arranged to carry a large number of people with reasonable comfort, but no frills. There may have been special cabins reserved for special passengers such as Mr Barr, the man who organized the colony, and Mr Lloyd, the minister who went with us, but most of the colonists were housed just as we were: in little cubby-holes that surrounded and opened into a big room with tables and benches in the middle.

Our cubby-hole had four bunks and a port-hole. Nothing more. Somehow, however, Dad managed to get the little folding chair that Mother had insisted on bringing out of our baggage, and with it set up we felt more at home.

Most of the crowd, however, were very gloomy that night. The big room wasn't any too warm, everybody had red eyes and short tempers, and supper when it came was cold and tasteless. Lily and I were too tired to eat, and as soon as the meal was over Mother put us to bed. I had tucked my daffodils into my bunk before supper, and when I got into bed I put my arm around them. There was still a lot of comfort in their bright heads and green stems, and I was soon asleep.

Lily was still asleep when I woke up next morning, but Dad and Mother and Jack had left the little cabin. I wriggled into my clothes and went out into the big room. A cold green light came through the skylight, and the people, most of them leaning on the tables and holding their heads in their hands, were also green. Mother sat in her little chair looking pale and miserable. Dad sat on the end of a bench holding Jack, who, unlike everybody else, was smiling.

I asked Mother what ailed her, but she shook her head and didn't answer, only pointed to the table where the stewards were serving breakfast.

Nobody seemed to be eating, or to care what I ate, so I had some strong tea with lots of sugar in it and some toast smothered with jam, then I put on my coat and bonnet and went up the narrow stairs at the end of the room and found myself on deck.

The first thing I saw was the water: miles of it stretching away right to the sky. I had seen the ocean at Blackpool, but there it had always seemed friendly, and the security of the land was under my feet and at my back. There was no land anywhere that morning. Nothing but blue-green water heaving and tossing in the bright sunshine. The waves undulated towards me, deep green and mysterious in the troughs, blue and emerald near the foam-crested tops. The distant waves out near the horizon looked small and happy as they dimpled in the sun, but the near waves were big and dangerous. They reared up, high green hills with foaming tops that curled over and broke off and slid down the green slopes. The waves seemed higher than the deck, and I fully expected them to roll right over us, but they never did. At the right moment the ship rose and the waves slipped under us. Only the spray, caught and tossed by the boisterous wind, came on board. It was damp and tasted of salt, but its cold sting was pleasant.

When I realized that the ship knew how to stay afloat I ventured out on deck for a better look at the ocean. The wind flipped my petticoats and pushed me as no land wind had ever done. It also smelled queer. There was no smoke or soot in it, only salt and seaweed. I took a deep breath, then I looked at the passengers and lost interest in the wind and the sea.

The passengers were a dismal sight, far worse than the night before. They were red-eyed, haggard, and green, and most of them couldn't even stand. They leaned against the rail, slumped on the benches, lolled against the skylight, and even sprawled on the deck. My bonnet started to blow away, but nobody noticed it. I doubt if anyone would have noticed if I had blown away, so immersed were they in their own misery. I asked one red-headed woman what she was crying for, but she didn't answer. 'Oh, Lord, let this ship go down,' she prayed, and went right on crying.

I wondered what we would do and where we would go if the ship went down in all that water, but nobody cared where we went as long as we got off the ship. Some said they wished they'd never heard of Canada, others wished they'd had sense enough to stay at home, but most wished the damned ship would sink. A few hoped Mr Barr was as sick as they were. I wandered around the windy deck for a while and watched first one sick passenger, then another. They all told me to go away and stay away, so I went downstairs to the big room, sure that Dad at least would be well.

Dad, however, was as ill as anyone. He sat still on the bench, his thin face pale and drawn, and his usually happy lips pressed tight together. I had never seen Dad ill before and it frightened me. Mother had been in bed when Jack was born, Lily and I had had measles, Grandfather and Grandmother had been ill now and then, but never Dad. He did not hold with illness, at least for himself, and the sight of him sitting haggard and miserable was too much for me. The waves had been frightening, but this was far worse. The security I had always felt sure of was slipping. I began to cry. Nobody, however, paid any attention, so I slipped into bed and stayed there until most of the passengers got what Curly, a steward, called their sea legs.

Somehow, while I was hiding from illness, my daffodils disappeared. They had been wilted when I left them to go on deck, but not enough to put away, I thought. When I found Dad ill I had forgotten about them for a while, and when I finally reached for them they were not there. I looked under the mattress, and under the bunk, but every leaf and stem had vanished. Mother, who had intended to press them the moment I was ready to give them up, said the stewardess who made up the bunks that first morning must have thrown them away. She was sad because they were gone, but I never really lost them. Daffodils, because of my grandmother, still mean courage to me.

Most of the trip to Canada was uneventful, and some said it was dull, but I enjoyed it. Mother had Lily and Jack to take care of, so there was little time for me, but I managed very well.

I soon discovered that if I sat half a table length away from Mother I could eat anything I wanted, mostly jam. The minute the bell rang for a meal I rushed to the table and found a seat near a bowl of jam. I helped myself generously before anyone else had a chance at it. After a while, however, the supply of jam must have got low. The bowls were not nearly as full as they had been, and I had to be quick if I wanted a large helping. I usually managed to grab a bowl, but one day a fat woman told me I was greedy and tried to take it from me.

Though little and thin I didn't give up easily. I snatched at the dish and screamed. The jam spilled, and the disturbance brought Mother. She told the fat woman she ought to be ashamed of herself, taking food from a child, then she took me to her end of the table and told me to sit by Lily.

I was supposed to watch Lily when Mother was busy with Jack. She was a good little girl, plump and cuddly as a kitten. Her hair, like soft light brown silk waves, curled tenderly around her serious little face, and her big brown eyes, fringed with dark lashes, were solemn and thoughtful as the eyes of a fawn. 'How sweet she is!' women exclaimed. 'Just like a doll. Come, let me hold you.'

'No,' Lily said firmly, and refused to be petted.

Curly, our favourite steward, spent a lot of time trying to coax Lily to smile, but he was never successful. Life to her was a serious business, and she regarded Curly's antics with sober pity.

Although she never cried, and ate what Mother gave her, Lily had a mind of her own, especially about dolls, the way she wore her bonnet, and the ship biscuits.

For some reason Lily seemed to resent all dolls. She had taken one look at her Christmas doll and promptly bashed its head on the stone floor. Mine would have suffered the same fate, but I guarded it carefully. One morning, however, Lily got up before I did, and my doll, sitting at the foot of my bunk, caught her eye. She grabbed it and banged its head on the floor before Mother could stop her.

I was heart-broken, and wept bitter tears. The worst of it was that Lily didn't seem a bit sorry for what she had done. I thought Mother ought to spank her, and said so. Mother, however, said Lily hadn't intended to break the doll, banging its head was her way of playing with it. Besides, Lily was little and I was big, and big girls didn't cry about every little thing.

'Then I'm not going to be a big girl any more,' I said, and went to breakfast, leaving Lily to struggle with her own shoe buttons.

I soon discovered, however, that I couldn't help being a big girl, at least when compared to Lily. I wasn't really big, of course. I was only six and small for my age, but I was the oldest. I was also rather plain. My dark hair was coarse and frizzy, and my face was narrow and pale.

All my bones seemed to end in points, and I wasn't the least bit cuddly. Lily was small, round, and helpless-looking, and everyone thought I ought to take care of her, and see to it that she wore her bonnet right.

Like her coat the bonnet was a soft shade of blue, and Lily's round little face would have looked adorable in it if she had worn it the way it was supposed to be worn, but she had ideas of her own about how to wear a bonnet, and nothing could change them. She wore her bonnet front to back, and even Mother couldn't do a thing about it.

When she dressed Lily to go on deck Mother put the bonnet on properly, but Lily immediately untied the blue satin strings and turned the bonnet around. She couldn't retie the ribbons, but that didn't bother her. She went on deck with them untied.

'Why don't you take better care of your little sister?' women passengers said, frowning disapprovingly at me. 'You're big enough to put her bonnet on right, and tie the string, too.'

'She likes her bonnet that way,' I explained, but it was clear they didn't believe me. So I turned the bonnet and tied the strings until I was tired, but it was time wasted. If Lily had yelled when I turned her bonnet it might have helped, but she didn't. She stood perfectly still and let me turn it, then without even looking disturbed she turned it back again.

After two sessions of turning and tying I gave up and allowed Lily to have her way. The bonnet looked queer, the binding that ought to have been at the back of her neck was just above her big brown eyes, and the *ruche* that ought to have been in front was around her neck. Everyone said it looked odd, and frowned at me for my carelessness. It was my first brush with public opinion.

Lily was as firm about the ship biscuits as she was about her bonnet. She couldn't eat them, nobody could. They were as hard as rocks and wouldn't even crumble, but Lily would never settle for half a biscuit. It was either a whole one or nothing.

Why whoever bought the food wasted money on the biscuits was a mystery. Some said they were bought because they would float, and if the ship went down we could gather them off the water and use them for food. Others said they hadn't been bought at all. They had been on the ship for ever, and Mr Barr was making a nice little profit out of them. He'd been paid to dispose of them.

The biscuits certainly looked delicious. They were about three inches across, half an inch thick, and they had all been baked to a delicate, tempting brown. Although we couldn't possibly eat them, they wouldn't even soften in tea, we always took as many biscuits as the stewards would give us. They were fine for rolling. 'Give me another. Give me just one more,' we begged when the steward opened a barrel.

'You have enough. Get!' The steward frowned at us and we backed away, all except Lily.

'Me,' Lily said, and held out her fat little hand.

He offered her half a biscuit. 'It's more than you'll eat,' he told her.

'No.' Lily stood there solemn and determined.

Every steward except Curly argued with her, but it was waste of breath. Lily always got her way. Her accusing stare was too much for even the toughest steward.

When the stewards discovered we used the biscuits for rolling they refused to give us any more. They said we were too much underfoot as it was, and we ought to go on deck to play.

Our mothers, however, thought the deck unsafe unless they were with us, so the ten or twelve children living in the cubby-holes around our big white room amused themselves as best they could. We raced around the tables and benches shouting 'Gangway.' We played ring-around-the-rosy, and sang as loud as we could. Our table-hopping, jumping from one table to another, almost drove the stewards wild. They said at least one of us would break a leg, be scalded to death, or be killed by falling plates before the voyage was over. The only casualties, however, were a few broken dishes, and a lot of frayed nerves among the stewards. They said they had never crossed with a colony before, and so help them they never would again.

I did not spend all my time pestering the stewards. One Sunday morning I went to church.

Mr Lloyd, the minister who accompanied us, preached the sermon and led the singing, but it was not a cheerful service. Fog hid the ocean and the sky, and made even the rail and the funnels seem dim and far away. It swirled about us as we sat on deck huddled in our coats. Mr Lloyd's words were muffled by it, and the familiar hymns sounded thin and strange, as if they were surprised and a little frightened at finding themselves so far from home. They did not swell and billow around us as they had in the church at Littletown, giving us courage for the coming week, and a feeling of security. Instead, they hurried into the fog and left us, and we returned to the cold white room with the stiff benches and tables feeling chilled and deserted, and a little afraid. Were we so lost that even the Almighty could not find us? 'We shall go down,' a woman said, and started to cry. Then the fog-horn began to blow, and somehow its hoarse voice brought comfort and encouragement. We were not completely lost after all. Somewhere in the grey and eerie vastness were other ships, and even a shore.

Everybody, of course, knew there was a shore somewhere, but after ten days at sea many were beginning to wonder if we were ever going to find it. The ship was rather crowded, the food, especially the jam, was getting low, and tempers were getting short.

The women with young children were fairly busy, but the men, and the women without children, had nothing at all to do. Quarrels broke out, especially among the newly-weds, and the men began spending most of their time on deck talking to each other. This so irked one young woman, married only a week before we sailed, that she had hysterics, and threatened to go home the minute we landed.

Dad also spent most of his time on deck. He said the big room was stuffy and gave him a headache. Sometimes he took me upstairs with him, but the deck was always cold and windy, and I preferred the games in the big room.

I was playing hopscotch downstairs the day we sighted the iceberg. Dad came down walking fast, and told me to put on my coat and come and take a look at it. Mother said I was too little to know about such things, but Dad said I might never see another iceberg and hurried me upstairs.

The iceberg was huge, about the size of the ship, I thought. It floated majestically in the blue water, and Dad and I leaned on the rail and watched it for a long time. I recalled some of the stories my cousins had told me, and was sure I could see monsters clinging to the ice.

Dad said there wasn't a thing on it, then he told me where icebergs came from, and where they went, and why the wind was so much colder than it had been. He also told me about flying-fish, and how deep the ocean was. I asked a number of questions and was surprised to find that Dad knew practically everything.

The day after we saw the iceberg Dad took me on a tour of the ship. We went down narrow stairs to a place where huge wheels turned and big rods went back and forth. Dad said the wheels drove the ship through the water, but I couldn't understand how they did it when there wasn't any land for them to turn on. Dad explained, but I still couldn't understand. 'Isn't she a bit small?' a man with dark grease on his hands and face asked. 'No, I'm a big girl,' I told him proudly, and climbed up the narrow ladder all by myself. But for a long time I was sure that the wheels of the ship ran on the bottom of the ocean.

CHAPTER SEVEN

WE arrived at the port of St John, Canada, on 14th April 1903. Everybody was thrilled and excited, but the town was a disappointment to me. I had expected Indian wigwams, and Indians with feathers in their hair. St John was only a lot of houses, and ordinary people. The houses, however, were a little different from the houses in England. Instead of being either brick or stone they were made of wood, and most of them seemed to be white. The streets also were different from the streets in England. They were not paved with cobble-stones, and some of them were quite dusty.

The train that was supposed to be waiting for us wasn't ready, and we had to stay in St John overnight. Dad had a hard time finding a room for us, the town was so crowded, and for a while we thought we might have to sleep outside. Finally, however, someone took us in, and next day we boarded the train that was to take us to Saskatoon, practically the end of the journey, we thought.

'You'll wish you were back on this ship many a time before you get where you are going,' Curly warned when Mother was happily packing to go ashore. 'You think this trip has been bad, but it's nothing to what you're going to get.'

'You wouldn't be trying to throw a drop of cold water on us, would you?' Mother asked, smiling. 'At least the train will be a change.'

'You'll see.' Curly gave Lily one of the biscuits reserved for special passengers. 'Them trains is awful narrow.'

We soon found that Curly had been completely right. Five of us were crowded into an upper and lower berth. Dad slept in the upper, and the rest of us crowded into the lower. On the ship there had been plenty of room in which to play, but on the train there was none at all. The aisles were narrow and people were always going up and down them, so we children had to stay in our seats most of the time.

Nobody had told us there wouldn't be any food on the train. Dad and everybody else had understood that our food would be provided until we reached Saskatoon. But it wasn't, and there was no diner. We all went to bed supperless that first night, and there wasn't anything for breakfast, either. Finally the train stopped at a station, and Dad and all the other men hurried to buy provisions.

There were no cooking facilities on the train. A small stove at one end of each coach supplied us with heat and hot water for tea, and that was all. The porter was supposed to keep the fire going and the kettle boiling, but sometimes the fire went out, and the overworked kettle was cold.

Even when the fire was burning merrily there was a long wait for hot water. The stove was small, and the kettle didn't hold enough for everybody. The early risers didn't have much advantage, either. They had to wait until the kettle boiled. Late-comers often found the fire low, and those who tried to strike a medium found several others with the same idea in line ahead of them.

Dad was our line stander. He was usually up first, and while Mother dressed Lily and Jack he took the blue teapot and hurried down the aisle. We always tried to wait until he came back before we started eating the crackers, cheese, and jam Mother set out, but often Lily and I had eaten our fill before he returned.

Sometimes, when Mother was lucky enough to find the fire going and no one waiting, she managed to cook us some rolled oats, but such treats were rare. Crackers, cheese, and jam were our mainstays. Dad tried to buy bread at every station, but there were no bakeries in the little towns.

Everybody, of course, complained a great deal, and wondered where Mr Barr was, and how they could get hold of him. Fortunately for him he wasn't on our section of the train.

How Mother managed to keep herself and three children, one a small baby, neat and clean on that long trip I don't know, but somehow she did. Her long, lovely hair was never unkept and frowzy. She always combed it first thing in the morning and twisted it into a neat, thick roll on top of her small head. Her dress was as tidy as her hair. There was never a gap between her trim skirt and bodice, and she never walked about with her shoes unlaced as some of the women did.

Our clothes were never pinned together, either. Somehow Mother kept our buttons and strings sewed on, and our stockings washed and mended. She kept our hands and faces clean, too, but it was a continual struggle. The train was terribly dirty.

We had to open the windows for air, and smoke and cinders blew in constantly. The seat cushions were soon grimy, and there was cinder grit everywhere: on the window-ledge, on the table the porter put up for us, in our hair, on the floor crunching under our feet, in bed at night, on our crackers, and we could even feel it, smoky-tasting and rough, between our teeth. Mother said we were beginning to look and smell like smoked herring, but her skin was always a clear pink-and-white, and her eyes, though sometimes worried, were as blue as the early morning sky.

I suppose our train wasn't any slower than most trains in those days, but the colonists insisted that it was. They said we stopped for every freight and cattle train, and sometimes for nothing at all. Some of the men were quite angry about it, but there was nothing anyone could do. Mr Barr was out of reach, and our money had been paid. The stops in the towns were not bad. While Dad went to buy cheese and crackers the rest of us swarmed out on to the platform for a breath of fresh air, and a look at the strange, new country. Often the stores were a long way from the sidings where the train stopped, and Dad and the other men had to run for it when the whistle blew. I was always afraid Dad would be left behind, and instead of enjoying the little outing I spent the time watching for Dad and listening for the train whistle.

Most of the stops, especially those in the day-time, were fairly short, but the one in the middle of nowhere lasted all afternoon.

There was no town at all at that stop, only prairie on both sides of the track. It was grey with last year's grass, and there seemed to be no end to it. There were neither trees nor willows, only grass that went on and on until it finally met the sky at the edge of the world.

After we had been stopped for some time the porter opened the door and told us we could get out and stretch our legs if we wanted to, we might be stalled for quite a while. The sun was warm and the grass, though dead, looked inviting, but the embankment was high, and there was quite a jump at the end of the train steps. Most of the women decided to stay where they were, but the men swarmed out and raced off across the prairie after the gophers that were everywhere.

The gophers were the first wild creatures most of the men had ever seen outside a zoo, and when they found it was quite all right to catch them if they could the men began running in every direction. Nobody had a gun, or even a trap, but the gophers looked so stupid that everybody thought that catching them would be very simple, and some of the women were quite sorry for the little creatures.

The gophers, however, were not as dull as they seemed. When they were chased they ran, but only for a short distance. The moment the men got a little too close they popped down a convenient hole, flicking their tails derisively.

Thwarted, the men paused and looked slightly foolish, but a moment later they caught sight of other gophers sitting on their haunches, their forepaws hanging meekly, their little rodent faces looking completely helpless, and more than a little stupid. Whooping loudly the men dashed at the foolish-looking creatures. The gophers sat there, flicking their tails as if they didn't know what to do, but the moment the men got almost within striking distance the gophers popped down a handy hole.

Some of the men pulled out their pocket knives and tried to dig the gophers out. Others stretched out on the dry grass near a hole, and with knives poised waited for the gophers to come out. The gophers came out all right, but from holes a short distance away. They looked around carefully, their eyes bright and inquisitive, then scuttled to the top of a little mound of earth near the entrance to their holes and sat upon their haunches, flicking their expressive tails, and looking at the reclining men as if to say: 'Well, well, are you still there?'

The hunt went on for hours without any casualties whatsoever, and at last the engine coughed and the whistle blew. The men jumped up, put away their knives, scrambled up the embankment, and got on the train. 'Did you get any?' they asked as they hurried down the narrow aisle brushing brown earth and dry grass off their trousers.

'Not I' the man who stumbled over my feet replied. 'But did you notice the way the little beggars flicked their confounded tails?'

'I did that,' another man replied. 'Looked as if they were laughing at us, didn't they?'

'And no wonder,' Mother muttered as she wiped cinders off Jack's face. 'Anybody silly enough to come to this country deserves to be laughed at.'

The gopher hunt, however, even though unsuccessful, was a pleasant break in the journey, for the men, at least.

I don't know how long we were on the train, but I think it was close to two weeks. We got used to the rumbling and jolting, and even acquired a taste for cinders, but the cramped space got on everybody's nerves. The porter did his best, but the coach got terribly dirty, and as a result tempers got shorter and shorter. There were arguments over hot water, complaints about the noise the children made, and the couple across the aisle had a long-drawn-out private battle.

Mother said if we didn't get something to eat besides crackers and cheese soon we would all be ill, and a lot Mr Barr would care. She even began to doubt that there was a place called Saskatoon, except in Mr Barr's imagination. 'This is nothing but a wild-goose chase,' she said, looking at the wide sweep of the prairie on every side. 'Why would anybody build a town in this wilderness?'

'It's there, all right,' Dad said confidently. 'Canada's a big place.'

'It's far too big for me.' Mother frowned at the bare prairie on the other side of the train window. 'There isn't a hedge or a wall anywhere, nothing but grass and sky, and a few bushes now and then. If it wasn't for the railroad I'd think we were lost, and I sometimes doubt if the train knows where it's going.'

'We'll get there all right,' Dad said cheerfully, and went into the next coach for a game of whist.

⌁ ·CHAPTER EIGHT· ⌁

I T was late in April when we finally arrived in Saskatoon. It was not the end of the journey, only the end of the railroad: the place where we expected to rest before we went looking for the free land we had been promised. All of us had been looking forward to Saskatoon ever since we left Liverpool. It was the promised land. There, we had been told, would be shelter, real bread, a real bed that didn't sway and jerk, and not so very far away there was the hundred and sixty acres of land we had come so far to find. 'When we get to Saskatoon!' The words had been on everybody's lips. All our troubles would be over, all our problems solved once we arrived at that magic town.

'It can't be that perfect,' Mother said when Dad told her not to worry, all we needed would be in Saskatoon waiting for us, but like everybody else she looked forward to leaving the dirty train. She also looked forward to doing a big washing, baking real bread, and giving us a bath in a tub. She even went so far as to hope for a roast of beef, and some good Yorkshire pudding.

Dad hoped to find good land close to the town, a team of strong horses, a cow, and a wagon at the reasonable prices the pamphlets had promised. I looked forward to space in which to play, and somebody to play with, stores with jars of candy in the windows, and houses with backyards. But we had all been looking forward for so long we were almost stunned when the porter suddenly called: 'Saskatoon. Saskatoon. We're almost there.'

'Well, this is it, Sally,' Dad said, and jumped up, his eyes shining.

'I don't see any town,' Mother said doubtfully.

The train, however, finally jerked to a stop and everybody scrambled to get off. The porter said there was no hurry, this was the end of the line, and the train wasn't going anywhere else that night, but nobody paid any attention to him. Everybody gathered up bags, baskets, and children and trooped out on to the platform.

We had all expected a real town something like the towns in England, with paved streets, plenty of real shops, and houses in long rows side by side. There wasn't even a real station, only a small house and a long platform. A short distance ahead a few houses huddled on one side of the track, and a group of white tents, round and small, crouched on the other side, and that was all.

Mr Barr had promised us lodgings in Saskatoon, and we all expected someone to meet us and tell us where we were to go. We stood on the platform and waited, but nobody appeared. The men milled around on the platform and asked the train conductor what we were supposed to do. He didn't know. It was his job to get us here. He knew nothing about lodgings.

After a while, when it was plain that nobody had any interest in us, Dad and some other men started to walk to the little town. Mother sat down on the food box and took Jack on her lap, and Lily and I stood beside her feeling a little frightened. Canada was so awfully big. The town and the tents were mere dots almost lost on the vast prairie, and the grey, hostile sky was even bigger than the land. It seemed to go on and on for ever: a huge lid that had somehow closed over us.

Mother looked at the grey, inhospitable prairie, and her eyes became troubled and her mouth thin. 'So this is Canada,' she said at last. 'I wish I'd never heard of it.'

We sat on the platform for a long time. Darkness crept up from the horizon and stole across the empty prairie. A cold wind nipped at our knees and fingers, and went snuffing about like a hungry animal. The train backed away.

'If I could only get my hands on old Barr,' an angry woman said.

After a long time lights began to bob in the darkness. 'Here they come,' a woman said happily. 'I hope they've found something.'

Most of the men hadn't found anything, but Dad had been lucky. A young couple named Bell had offered to share their tent with us, and Mr Bell had come to help with our baggage. I'm not quite sure where the rest of the colony spent the night. I think they persuaded the conductor to let them go back to the train.

The tent the Bells so kindly shared with us was very small. It was round, and a pole in the middle held it up. Two mattresses filled it completely, one on each side of the tent-pole. In the day-time the mattresses were rolled up, but the tent was still quite crowded, and we spent most of the time outside. We spent two or three nights with Mr and Mrs Bell. Tents were scarce in Saskatoon, and Dad had a hard time finding one. When he finally got one we felt we had all the room in the world to live in.

Although our tent was small, putting it up was difficult. Dad put up the pole with the tent canvas over it, then Mother held the pole while Dad drove the tent-pegs into the ground, adjusted the tent-ropes, and tightened them. The ropes had to be just right; if they were not the tent leaned, and looked as if it would topple in the first wind.

Even when the ropes were adjusted we couldn't forget them. Rain, or any moisture, tightened both the ropes and the tent canvas, and the ropes had to be adjusted all over again or the tent-pole would go through the top and the whole thing fall on us. Rain in the day-time was bad enough, but a storm at night was a real hazard. Often Dad had to run out into the rain, wind, and darkness without taking time to put on his coat, and struggle with the wet ropes. As soon as the sun came out and dried the ropes and canvas the ropes had to be tightened again, or the tent leaned and was in danger of blowing over.

Another danger to the tent was people passing at night. The tents had been pitched in fairly straight rows, but in the darkness people sometimes lost their bearings and fell over the tent-ropes. Even with all these drawbacks, however, the tent was reasonably comfortable. We had our big flock mattress to sleep on, a box for a table, Mother's little folding chair to sit on, and a stove.

The stove was a real luxury; after we got it we had crisp bacon and hot oatmeal for breakfast every morning. Mother heated water on it for washing and for baths, and in the small oven she baked the first bread we had eaten since we left the ship.

The first batch of bread was terrible. Mother didn't know how to use the hard round cakes of yeast, and the dough didn't rise at all. We did our best to eat it, but the leathery slices were too much for us.

One of the settlers, however, knew how to use the new yeast. She came to our tent and showed Mother how to set the sponge, and the next batch of bread was wonderful: big brown loaves that smelled so sweet we couldn't wait until they cooled. What a feast we had that day! All the fresh, hot bread we could eat with jam on it.

Even having my hair washed was an exciting experience. Mother did the job outside, and all the other children looked on, so I couldn't make a fuss when the soap got in my eyes. It was the first time my hair had been washed since we left England.

Why there wasn't an outbreak of typhoid fever among the colonists I don't know. Our water came from a slough, and some people didn't even boil it before they drank it, but there was almost no sickness among us: not even measles.

While Mother made bread and washed us, Dad inquired about land. The people at the land office, and everybody else, said all the good land around Saskatoon had been homestead, and if he wanted anything really worth while he ought to go farther west. There was still some fair land near Battleford, but he would have to hurry to get any. It was going fast.

To go to Battleford we had to have a team and wagon, so one day Dad and I went shopping for them. We walked from the tent town on one side of the railroad tracks to the real town on the other. The road was only a wagon track, and it was muddy in places. The unpaved streets of the town were also muddy, and there were pools of water in the low spots. Some of the stores had wooden sidewalks in front of them, others had only two or three steps between the ungraded street and the door. The buildings were not even close together; some had wide spaces of grass between them. It was not the least bit like Littletown. 'When are we going to get there?' I asked as we walked down the sticky street.

'We're there now,' Dad said, and went up three steps into a harness shop.

It was an interesting place. Harness of all sorts hung on the walls, there were yellow saddles, and bright bits, horse-collars, and hames with shiny knobs on them, bright red and green saddle-blankets, and brown horse-blankets in piles on the floor. The whole place was full of the sweet, spicy smell of new leather and fresh lumber, but the thing that really fascinated me was the horse in the window.

He was a dapple-grey with a long silver mane and tail, and on his wooden head was a yellow bridle, and on his back a lovely light brown saddle and a bright green saddle-blanket. I fell in love with him immediately, and urged Dad to buy him at once.

Dad, however, said the grey wouldn't be any use to us, and after asking the price of some harness he took me to look at some real horses.

They were in a big, muddy pole corral, and after the trim dapple-grey in the window they looked extremely dull and uninteresting. Most of them were either dark brown or black, and their manes and tails were short and dingy, and wisps of hay clung to them.

Dad and I climbed part way up the side of the corral and leaned over to get a better look at the miserable creatures. 'How do you like that one?' Dad asked, pointing to a big dark animal.

I didn't like it at all. After the dapple-grey's dainty feet its big hoofs looked clumsy, and its gentle eyes seemed dull. 'It's an ugly old thing,' I said.

Some other men were also looking at the horses, and Dad began to talk to them. They discussed fetlocks, shoulders, and spavins, and after a while one of the men jumped into the corral, opened the mouth of one of the horses, and looked at its teeth.

They were the biggest teeth I had ever seen: long and yellow and sharp. 'Dad, come back,' I screamed when Dad went to look at the teeth.

'Come and take a look, it won't hurt you,' Dad said, but I refused to leave my perch on the edge of the corral. The men could be eaten if they hadn't any more sense than to get near those teeth, but I preferred to be safe.

The horse, however, didn't seem to mind having its teeth looked at. When the man let go of its mouth it yawned, showing its big white tongue, then it shook its head and blew through its nose.

After we had looked at the horses for a while we went to look at wagons. They were all alike: oblong green boxes on red wheels. Some of the wagons were topped by big white canvas covers supported by wooden bows. These were the most expensive, and by far the best looking, almost like tents on wheels. Dad, however, thought they looked top-heavy, and said they would tip over easily.

We did not buy anything that day. Dad wanted to talk to Mother first. I wanted to talk to her, too. I thought she might be able to persuade Dad to buy the dapple-grey.

Mother, however, was even less interested in the dapple-grey than Dad was. An argument in a tent a short distance from ours had upset her, and she listened only perfunctorily when Dad told her of the brown horses and the canvas-topped wagons.

'I never heard such a row,' Mother said as she put the kettle on for tea. 'The way he shouted at her, and she so far from home.'

Dad told her not to worry, it was just another upset and would soon blow over, and after Mother had had two cups of tea she agreed that it no doubt would, but she still looked a little uneasy.

Rows, however, were not unusual among the tents. The tiresome train trip and the inconvenience of the tents had got on people's nerves and they argued about trifles. Home-sickness was also a problem, especially among the women. Everything in this bare country was so different from anything they had ever known: they missed their fire-places and their sinks, the trams and the shops, but most of all they missed their parents, and their brothers and sisters.

The men were no doubt as lonely as the women, but they had more exciting things to do. They went to town and bargained for horses, tents, and supplies, and talked to other men about the adventures ahead. The women had none of this excitement. They stayed near the tents, caring for their children, washing in brown water, cooking over smoky stoves, and worrying about what lay ahead, or dreaming about what they had left behind. 'It's the nights that bother me,' one woman said to Mother. 'In the day-time it's lonely enough, but at night it's awful.'

Most of the men came back to the tents in the late afternoon and spent the evenings with their wives and families, but a few went back to town after supper and spent the evening there. When they came home, long after we had gone to bed, they often lost their way, stumbled over the tent-ropes, and talked in loud, thick voices.

The big man who had quarrelled with his wife that afternoon was one of those who came home late almost every night. Even in the day-time he had a loud voice, and a habit of waving his arms, but at night his voice was like thunder. He and two or three other men usually returned from town together. I used to lie awake listening to their hoarse voices, and worrying a little about the tent. I was afraid they would stumble over the ropes and pull it down.

The big man's wife was a quiet woman with a thin, pale face and lonely eyes. She spent most of her time taking care of her two small children, and didn't visit much at the other tents. 'She spends too much time by herself,' Mother said on the night of the row. 'He ought to stay at home more instead of running around with those single men.'

Dad agreed with her, then he smiled and his cloud-grey eyes, that were shot with ocean green, twinkled. 'But it isn't every woman that has a man like me,' he said.

Mother sniffed and tossed her small head. 'Some people think a lot of themselves,' she said, then she began to ask questions about the team and the wagon, and the row in the tent a short distance from ours was forgotten, as Dad and Mother got more and more interested in where we were going next.

Mother wanted to stay as close to Saskatoon as possible. We were much too far from England as it was. If we stayed where we were, going back when the time came would be simple. All we had to do was get on the train, and then the ship, but if we went farther west there would be all that back-tracking to do.

Dad, however, said there was no good land left here, so why stay? After all, we had come a long way, a few more miles wouldn't matter, and anyway the railroad would soon stretch clear across the country, and we could get on a train there just as well as here.

Mother was doubtful about the railroad, but Dad got out a map someone had drawn for him and showed her the dots on it that some day would be towns. 'Well, all right,' Mother said at last, 'but it still looks as if there's nothing there.' Dad said there would be plenty in a year or two; towns, shops, and everything.

'You'll never be satisfied till you see how bad it really is, will you?' Mother asked, but her voice wasn't sharp, it was patient and a little tender, the same voice she used when she told Uncle Sam she wasn't going to be left.

'I'd like to take a look at it, anyway,' Dad said as he lit the lantern and hung it on a nail driven into the tent-pole.

'Come, Mary, time to go to bed,' Mother said. 'Wash your hands and face.'

'It isn't even dark outside,' I protested, but the stars were coming out, bright pin-heads in the sky, and the moon was a silver boat with its own star lantern to guide it. Dad unrolled the mattress, and Mother arranged the blankets. I got into my place in the big bed. It was on the far side, nearest the low tent wall. I was a big girl now, old enough to sleep on the outside edge of the bed. Lily, being little, slept on the inside.

Sleeping near the tent wall had one advantage: I could lift up the canvas and look out. Sometimes I saw Dad and Mother talking to Mrs Bell, sometimes I saw Beth talking to her young man, and often people passed. But there was one big disadvantage that I didn't like; I could hear the big man when he came back from town shouting and swearing in the dark, and I could feel the tent-ropes jerk when he fell over them.

It was quite dark, and I seemed to have been asleep for a long time when the big man fell over the tent-ropes that night. As usual he shouted, and said something that sounded terrible, even though I couldn't hear it very well, partly because I had pulled the blankets over my frightened head, and partly because his mouth seemed full. He had a harder time than usual getting up, even though his friends tried to help him, and our tent quivered and shook until I was sure it would fall.

'Walter, hadn't you better go and help him?' Mother whispered.

'No.' Dad sounded disgusted. 'Let the darned fool help himself. If he bangs himself up a bit it might knock some sense into him.'

'And his poor wife so lonely,' Mother said. 'He ought to be ashamed of himself.'

Dad muttered something I couldn't hear, and after a while the big man got himself untangled and went away swearing and shouting. I put my fingers in my ears, his voice frightened me so, but I couldn't go back to sleep for a long time. I hadn't seen the big man, but somehow I knew that his long arms were waving, his face was white and spongy like dough, and his mouth was wide and slack like a purse with a broken string.

The tent above my head was pale yellow in the early sunlight when I opened my eyes next morning. I stretched sleepily, thankful that the darkness and the big man had gone, but my satisfaction didn't last. Even before I got out of bed I knew that something was terribly wrong.

All the cheerful morning noises of our tent town were absent, or so low they seemed buried under a blanket. No voices came from the tent next door, no frying-pans clattered, no kettles spluttered as they boiled over on to the hot fire, and, worst of all, Mother wasn't anywhere about.

I slipped out of bed and went to the door of the tent. Dad sat by the stove holding Jack. 'Where's Mother?' I asked, my voice loud in the stillness.

'She'll be back in a bit.' Dad's voice was low, and his thin face looked pinched and pale. 'Get dressed.' He began stirring the oatmeal with a slow spoon.

I went back into the tent, but I didn't get dressed. Dad's voice, low and queer like crunching sand, and his face all pulled together, frightened me. Even when we said good-bye to Grandmother his face hadn't been so knotted. I crept quietly into bed and kept very still, hoping that whatever troubled Dad would soon go away.

From where I lay I could see the tent door and Dad's thin shoulders. I tried to close my eyes and go back to sleep, but my eyelids refused to stay shut, and my ears, not wanting to hear, were extra keen. I heard soft-treading feet go past the tent, and a long skirt move furtively across the grass. In the tent next door somebody seemed to be crying, and even a team of horses tied not far away seemed to be extra quiet, as if they also feared the horror that had come in the night.

I lifted the tent wall a little and looked out. Everything was hushed and still. Not far away a man sat alone on the tongue of his wagon. He looked at the ground between his feet, but he didn't seem to see it. The morning wasn't cold, but his hands were shaking.

After a while the man got up and came over to our tent. 'What do you make of it?' he asked in a whisper.

Dad shook his head. 'The fellow was a fool to leave her alone so much,' he said, and gave the oatmeal a sharp stir.

'Then you don't think...?' The man twisted a button on his coat.

'I don't know,' Dad said.

'I'm glad I wasn't with him last night.' The button came off.

Dad's eyelids half closed, and his mouth tightened, but he didn't speak. After a little while the man went away.

I got up and went to the tent door, and sat down on a box close to Dad. Neither of us spoke, but near him I felt less afraid, and after a little while some of the hardness left his thin face.

We were still sitting there when Mother came back. We didn't hear her coming, she simply seemed to appear at the tent door. I was glad to see her, but her face frightened me all over again. She was pale, and her blue eyes were full of water and rimmed with red. Her nose looked as if it had been squeezed, and her mouth, though tight, looked as if it might fall apart if she tried to speak. Her chin was puckered, and so was her forehead. She didn't speak to either Dad or me, she simply walked past us into the tent as if she didn't see us.

I got up to go after her, but Dad popped Jack into my arms and I had to sit down again. I turned around as soon as I could, but Dad had closed the tent flap. Mother's voice, however, came through the canvas. 'Poor thing!' she said over and over, 'poor thing!'

'You shouldn't have gone,' Dad said at last. 'That's an old woman's job.'

'I had to do what I could,' Mother said. 'She had so very little, not even a decent sheet, and him drinking. It's no wonder she…' Mother's voice choked, and I didn't hear any more. I rocked Jack back and forth, and when he was quiet I leaned forward and put some wood on the fire, and after a while Dad came out of the tent and made some tea.

Mother drank several cups of the strong brown brew, then she gave Lily and me some oatmeal. 'The bairns have to eat even if we can't,' she said, and wiped her eyes, though she was not really crying. Tears simply rolled down her cheeks, and she couldn't stop them.

I ate my oatmeal quickly, then I put on my own clothes and helped Lily with her shoes. Sometimes if I hurried Dad took me with him when he went into the town. Dad, however, showed no signs of going anywhere that morning. He seemed tired, and all the spark and energy had left him; even his dark curls were not as crisp as usual.

I went to the tent door and looked out. The sun was still low, and the shadows lay long on the grass. A team and wagon came slowly along the trail that went to town. They went past our tent, but when they came to the tent of the big man they stopped. The man on the wagon jumped down, and the little crowd of men near the closed tent door stood aside and made a way for him, then they all took off their caps and held them in their hands. I was about to go over to the big man's tent and see what was going on when Mother called me and asked me to play with Jack. As far as I could see Jack was quite all right, but Mother told me to watch him, so I sat down beside him. While I dangled one of Jack's shoes I told Mother about the wagon and the crowd, and asked what they were doing. 'Nothing,' Mother said, 'nothing at all.' But her voice shook a little, and although she turned away and began combing her hair as if this was just another morning, I knew that the tears were still rolling down her cheeks.

I didn't ask any more questions, so I never knew what really happened to the wife of the big man. I never knew what became of the big man, either, but one thing I was glad of, he never again fell over our tent-ropes.

CHAPTER NINE

W ELL, what do you say, Sarah?' Dad asked a day or two later. 'Shall we go on or not?'

Mother's face was still pale, and her blue eyes had a little fog in them. She looked at the shabby little town at the other side of the track, then she glanced over her shoulder at the tents, white in the sun. 'You'll never be satisfied if you don't go and see what's out there.' She nodded in the direction of the trail that twisted over a distant rise. 'So if we're going let's be gone. I don't care for it much here.'

'Then I'll go and buy that team if it's still there.' Dad got up and put on his cap.

'And take Mary with you,' Mother said. 'She's better off away from here.'

I skipped along beside Dad, and tried once more to persuade him to buy the dapple-grey. Dad, however, said it was only a wooden horse, and couldn't even walk, much less pull a plough.

I was sure he was mistaken. If the dapple-grey got out of the window he would be able to walk as well as any other horse. It was just being stuck there that made him seem so stiff. 'Well, all right,' Dad said, 'we'll take another look at him.' So we went to the harness shop again, and I had to admit that Dad was right. But I still loved the dapple-grey, and was disappointed when we had to go away and leave him.

The two big dark-brown horses were still in the corral, and Dad bought them and the harness that went with them. Then we bought a green-and-red wagon, and a wagon seat with springs, a white canvas wagon cover, and two bows. Dad said four were dangerous.

The man from whom we bought the wagon helped Dad hitch the team to it, then we got into the wagon, sat down on the high seat, put our feet on the little shelf at the front of the wagon box, and drove home.

I clutched the sides of the wagon seat with both hands at first, for the horses seemed quite wild. They swished their tails, shook their big heads, and rattled their bits in the most alarming manner. Dad, however, said they were as tame as cows and wouldn't hurt a fly, then he asked if I would like to try driving them.

I was so surprised I nearly choked, but if Dad thought I could drive those big things…I nodded and reached for the reins.

Dad looked surprised, but he gave them to me. 'Get up,' I said, and shook the reins the way Dad had done. The horses went right on walking just as they had before I took over.

Dad showed me how to pull on the reins when I wanted the team to turn, and much to my surprise the horses responded. They were really so gentle and well trained they hardly needed any driving at all, but I thought I was doing something terribly dangerous, and I was being very brave. I sat upright on the green seat, my small feet braced against the rim of the wagon box, and shook the reins, and felt as proud as a cock sparrow.

Dad said since I could drive the horses so well I could also name them. This was another responsibility I hadn't expected, and I hadn't any idea what sort of names the horses would like. Dad said they wouldn't care what we called them, and suggested several names. I tried them out loud so that the horses could hear, and finally settled on Darkie and Nelly. They were short, and I was sure the horses pricked up their ears when they heard them.

When we got near the tents Dad wanted to take the reins, but I was sure I could manage. Besides, I wanted my friend Annie Jefferies to see how big I was.

Annie wasn't anywhere about, but a lot of people I didn't know stared as we went past. When we got to our tent I shouted 'Whoa' and the team obediently stopped. 'Mother,' I called, 'come and look. I can drive.'

Mother came out of the tent, a scared look on her round face. 'What in the world are you thinking of?' she asked, glaring at Dad. 'Letting her drive them big things! First thing you know she'll be killed.'

Dad looked a little guilty, but his eyes twinkled. 'To tell the fair truth I couldn't stop her,' he said. 'She's going to make a rare farmer.'

Mother said she didn't know about that, but one thing she was sure of: Canada seemed to be changing everybody, and not for the better. Then she told me to come down from the wagon seat, and to leave the driving to Dad.

I climbed over the big red wheel, and swaggered into the tent not at all deflated. We had a team, and I could drive. I was sorry that Gladstone and Walter Walker couldn't see me.

Next day Dad went to look for implements and tools. I wanted to go with him, but Mother said she couldn't trust Dad, he might let me drive again, so I stayed at home.

Dad brought back an interesting assortment. There was a plough to turn the sod, and a disk to cultivate it; a big cross-cut saw with teeth an inch long for felling trees, an axe for splitting wood, a spade and an adze for digging a well, and a stout logging chain that could be used for pulling us out of mud if we got stuck, and for dragging logs out of the brush. At the back of the wagon was the most interesting item of all: a red-and-white cow.

Mother didn't think much of the plough and the disk, she said they would take up an awful lot of space in the wagon box, and where would the rest of our things go? But she was very pleased with the cow. Her pleasure, however, was short-lived. The cow wasn't the least bit like the cows we had had in England, even though she looked about the same.

She was a rather small cow with a white star on her forehead, and a huge white curl at the end of her tail. Her colour was an ordinary red with a great deal of white sprinkled through it, but she was no ordinary cow. She was definitely an individual with a mind of her own.

One of her horns curved downward between her right eye and her ear, and the other, small, sharp, and thin, curved forward. Her big brown eyes were crossed, and not the least bit gentle. They had a gleam in them, and when she was excited they became quite wild.

Dad said she was a ranch cow and not used to people, but she would soon get over her wildness and be as gentle as a new kitten. Mother said she hoped he was right, but she'd never seen a cow with a squint before.

We decided to name the cow Star because of the mark on her forehead, but somehow the name didn't fit. One glare from her wild eyes and we forgot all about stars. Daisy suited no better, and after a while we stopped trying to find names and simply called her the Old Cow.

We tried to pet her and make friends, but she wasn't friendly. She tried to jab us with her horns, and her legs always had to be tied before she could be milked. The rope didn't have to be tight, but it had to be there. If it wasn't she sent the pail flying. Kicking if her legs weren't tied seemed to be a matter of principle with her. She would lash out suddenly and go right on chewing her cud. Mother said wildness was all you could expect of a Canadian cow, anyway. Anything tame wouldn't last long in this rough country.

We were now ready to leave Saskatoon and go looking for our farm. Mother baked a big batch of bread, and Dad loaded the wagon. He put the plough and the disk and the big packing-boxes in the night before, then next morning, as soon as we had eaten our oatmeal, he put out the fire and lifted the stove into the back of the wagon close to the end gate. The tent went in next, then the mattress.

Mother said she was sure the wagon wouldn't hold everything, but somehow it did, and up front, under the two bows that supported the wagon cover, there was room for the wagon seat, and behind it on the mattress a place for Lily and me to sit.

When the team was harnessed there was a lot of handshaking and good wishes, then Mother climbed over the red wheel and sat down on the seat, and Dad handed Jack up to her. He then climbed up himself, sat down, and shook the reins. 'Well, here we go, Sally,' he said happily. 'When we come this way again we'll be riding in a carriage, and our pockets will be overflowing with money.'

'Full of holes, more likely,' Mother said. 'Money doesn't grown on trees even on the prairie.'

'No, but a lot of other things grow.' Dad clucked to the team and the wheels began to turn, and so we started on the long trip that always afterwards was spoken of as 'coming up the trail.'

ᘰ·CHAPTER TEN·ᘱ

ETTLERS going west left Saskatoon every day, and our wagon
was just one in the straggling line that bumped across the grey
prairie.

Some of the wagons had full sets of bows, and these were called
prairie schooners. Others, like ours, had two bows in front, and some
had no bows at all, or even covers. A few wagons were drawn by four
horses harnessed tandem, others were drawn by oxen, but most were
drawn by a team of horses like ours. Most of them were overloaded,
and a few had a crate of chickens tied on at the back. Ours was the
only wagon with a cow behind it.

The trail, just two wagon tracks, wound casually across the prairie,
skirting sloughs that were full of brown water, avoiding hills not yet
green, and slipping around clumps of dark, stiff-looking trees. It went
over badger holes and stones, and the little mounds the gophers made.
The steel-rimmed wheels of the springless wagons made the most of
every little hill and hollow, and the wagons creaked and swayed as
they jolted over the ruts. When the riders were tired of the everlasting
bumping they got down and walked for a change.

We did not all travel at the same pace, or even try to. The four-
horse tandems trotted smartly past the plodding teams, and the teams
went slowly around the placid oxen. Often we seemed quite alone in
the wide wilderness, but at night when the sun had gone below the
distant hills, and darkness was rising like a mist from the prairie, we
could see camp fires yellow in the distance.

Sometimes there was only one team tethered near a slough, and
one tent pitched near a fire, but usually there was a little group of
tents, and several small fires huddled in a hollow near the trail. 'How's
this?' Dad would ask, smiling at Mother. 'Think we've gone far enough
for to-day?'

Mother was always glad to get down off the bumping wagon.
Having Jack to hold she couldn't get down and walk when she was
tired of the jolting. Dad folded a coat for her to sit on, but when she
got down she always said she felt paralysed. Lily and I were also tired,
and it was pleasant to walk about and stretch our legs until the tent

was pitched, the fire burning, and the smell of bacon and bannock was sweet on the crisp air.

Sometimes two or three families used the same fire, and there was always a lot of visiting, but we never really became friends with anyone on the trail. Some of the colonists hurried ahead, and some lagged behind, and every night there were different faces around the fires.

Occasionally, if we were lucky, we camped in one of the big tents that had been pitched along the trail for our use. They had wood floors, and stoves for cooking, and when we stayed in them Dad and Mother were saved the work of unloading and pitching the tent at night, and taking it down in the morning. The stoves were also much easier to cook on than the camp fires. But there was no privacy in the big tents. We simply spread our mattresses on the floor a foot or so apart and went to bed.

Even though we had a good team we didn't cover much ground in a day. The cow had to be milked and taken to a slough to drink. The horses had to be fed and watered, and when we used the tent it had to be taken down. This was quite a job because all the tent-pegs had to be pulled out of the ground, and the tent folded and loaded. Then we had to have breakfast, usually tea, bread while it lasted, bacon when we had any, jam, and all the milk we could drink. In the middle of the day the team and the cow needed rest and food, and at night we had to stop in time to do the milking, watering, and feeding, and the tent-pitching all over again.

After we had been on the trail a few days the bread Mother had baked in Saskatoon gave out. We hadn't time to stop and bake more, and we would have had to go back to the cracker diet if an old-timer hadn't come along and showed Mother how to bake bannock. Actually it was baking-powder bread. Flour, baking-powder, and a little bacon grease, if we had it, were mixed together and made into a dough with either milk or water. The dough was shaped into a round cake and baked in a skillet. When Mother baked the bannock on a camp fire she baked the underside, then turned it over. Sometimes it was burned, and sometimes underdone, but when it was fresh and warm, and eaten with either bacon or jam and hot tea, it wasn't bad at all, even though the middle was a little sticky.

Our water for both drinking and washing came from the sloughs, and an occasional stream. It was pale brown, and tasted and smelled of dry grass. Mosquito larvae, and dozens of other queer wrigglers, some round and red, others long and yellow with rows of fins, inhabited it. We strained the water through a cloth to get the wrigglers out, then boiled it well before we made tea. Mother said the tea tasted horrible because of the dry grass flavour, but after a while we got used to it, and tea made from tasteless water seemed flat. Having milk for our tea was a great help. Sometimes we even drank the milk plain and didn't bother to make tea at all.

A great many of the colonists had come from London and other big cities, and had never ridden in a wagon until they got to Saskatoon. They didn't know a horse-collar from a clevis, and when they bought their teams and wagons they had quite a time learning how to put the harness on. This ignorance amused the old-timers, and they had many laughs at our expense, and dubbed us greenhorns.

Most of us had never even seen a full-sized axe, and although we knew that saws were used for sawing, we had never sawed anything. But we learned. A few men chopped their feet instead of the wood, and the old-timers laughed and suggested that the greenhorns ought to stand in tubs when they cut wood, but in a short time we knew dry wood from green, and we could swing an axe with anybody.

Naturally there was an accident now and then. Horses shied, and teams ran away, but nobody was seriously hurt, though Mother said it was a wonder the people dumped into the little river were not at least maimed for life.

We were a few days from Saskatoon when this accident happened. The snow had gone and the prairie trail was fairly dry, but there was still plenty of brown water in the stream beds, and in some it was quite swift and deep.

Dad always approached the streams carefully, and if they were extra wide we stopped if we were alone and waited for another settler to come up and help us across. With the help of the logging chain we doubled up—hitched one team in front of the other—and hauled the wagons across one at a time.

One afternoon we arrived at a stream that was both swift and wide, and the earth was so churned on either side that Dad decided it must have a soft bottom. He got down off the high seat and walked a short distance along the bank. When he came back he looked uncertain. 'It seems to be a bit muddy,' he said, 'but I hate to waste time. What do you say we chance it?'

'We shall waste a lot more time if we get stuck,' Mother said. 'Somebody will come by soon.'

Dad decided that perhaps Mother was right. He pulled over to the side of the trail so that the horses and the cow could eat the short, dry grass, then we all climbed off the wagon to rest our legs.

We didn't have long to wait. In a short time an outfit came over the far hill and hurried towards us. When the outfit got close we saw that it was a proud, four-horse tandem: bays with slender bodies, thin legs, and narrow, nervous faces—not the least bit like our big, thick-bodied team.

The driver of the tandem, a lean man with a pale face and pointed nose, was as proud as his horses. He didn't even nod to us, though he must have seen us. He looked straight ahead as if wagons with only two bows and two horses were beneath his notice, and he meant to pass them as quickly as possible. When he was abreast of us he flicked the rear horses with the tip of his store-bought whip, as if to make quite sure they did not hesitate.

'Well, I'll be damned!' Dad said as the big, white-topped prairie schooner sailed past.

The tandem didn't even slow down as it approached the stream. Evidently the driver had as little time for upstart streams as he had for two-bow wagons.

The stream, however, resented the driver's attitude. It was only a temporary thing created by the melting snow and the spring rains, and it hadn't any real bed, only a depression that crossed the wide prairie. In a short time all the brown water would be gone, and the place where it had been would be covered with millions of tiny golden buttercups and silvery-white strawberry flowers. Prairie chickens would nest among the willows that edged it, gophers would run where it had been and flip their impudent tails, and butterflies would hover

over it, their red-and-yellow wings bright in the sun. At that moment, however, the low banks of the little watercourse were full to the brim with racing amber water. It was a tributary of the mighty Saskatchewan, and some respect was due it or there would be trouble.

The tandem, however, advanced as if the stream wasn't even there.

Annoyed, the little stream gurgled deep in its brown throat, then it whipped up a handful of foam and tossed it into the faces of the oncoming bays. They shied and plunged sharply to the left, pulling the following team after them, and the wagon, high white top and all, rolled over into the stream.

There were screams and shouts. Horses and people floundered in the water, and boxes and pans and a bright copper kettle floated out of the overturned wagon and went bobbing off downstream. Dad and a new arrival ran and caught the frightened horses, then they helped the dripping man and woman out of the water, and rescued as many of the pans and boxes as they could.

As soon as she could get a fire started Mother made tea for the shivering couple. The men righted the wagon and pitched a tent. Then they spread the wet blankets out to dry, tethered the still trembling tandem, and turned their attention to getting their own wagons across the stream.

Using the logging chain they hitched the new arrival's team in front of ours, then we scrambled back on to our wagon. The other man got on the back of one of his horses, Dad climbed to the wagon seat, and slowly and carefully, and with many soothing words of encouragement, we approached the stream.

The horses lowered their heads and sniffed at it, then they put out a cautious foot, snorted, and hesitated. The men urged them gently, and after a moment the horses waded into the stream, and it was plain they didn't like the swirl of water that touched their bellies.

The stream was deeper than Dad had thought, and the bottom both rough and muddy. The wagon swayed dangerously. One moment we thought we were going to tip over, the next we thought we were stuck. Mother shut her eyes and clung to Jack. Lily and I, huddled in our little nest behind the wagon seat, clung to each other. Finally, after one last lurch and scramble, we were on dry land once more.

We were safe and dry, but the horses had to face the stream again. This time they were a little more sure of themselves, and the other wagon was hauled across without any difficulty. The driver of the tandem decided not to cross the stream that night. He said they might go back to Saskatoon. The prairie was more dangerous than they had thought. Mother said they had the right idea, but Dad said one little stream wasn't anything, and we hurried on.

We camped that night near a family that had lived not far from us in the tents at Saskatoon. They were older than Dad and Mother, and they had several children, including Beth, the girl I had often watched in Saskatoon.

Unmarried women were as rare as apple blossoms in August in those days, but single men were as plentiful as mice in a wheat field. The many young men in the Barr Colony were not yet aware of this situation. Girls had been over-plentiful in England, there had been six or eight on every street, so it wasn't necessary to grab the first that came along. There was plenty of time to look the field over and make a careful selection, so none of them paid much attention to Beth. Besides, most of them were already engaged, or so wrapped up in their dream of a quick fortune that they had no eyes for practically the only marriageable girl in the whole Barr Colony.

But the young Canadian who farmed near Saskatoon was well aware of the woman shortage, and the moment he saw Beth he started to court her. He was a tall, quiet man, well browned by the sun and wind, and good looking in a severe way. Every evening he had come to the tents, well washed and shaved, and wearing a tie. He sat outside on the wagon tongue, talking to Beth's father, and stealing a word with Beth when he could.

She was, as they would say in Yorkshire, a likely lass. She had heft in the places where heft ought to be, and there was sunshine in her hair, a dab of colour in her cheeks, and a bit of violet in her eye. According to Mother anybody would be lucky to get her.

Although she was seventeen Beth's parents thought she was still a little girl, and when the tall young man asked if he could marry her they were shocked stiff, then spluttering mad. They told him to go away and never come near their tent again if he valued his health.

The young man said he was sorry if he'd upset them and went off, his feet dragging and his head low. Next night, however, he visited at the tent next door, and Beth, just by chance, was sitting outside wearing a sprigged blue cotton that was very becoming, though it covered from her ears to the toes of her high-laced shoes. She smiled at the tall young man when she thought no one was looking, then she blushed and looked demurely at her feet.

The tall young man looked as if he hadn't noticed the smile, but the next night there he was again, and again Beth smiled.

Beth's father, however, saw that second smile, and being a cautious man he packed up at once and started up the trail.

The tall young man was stricken when he saw the bare spot where their tent had been, but he wasn't completely discouraged. Instead of going home and getting on with his ploughing he hitched his team to his buggy and followed Beth.

Her parents tried to outdistance him, but his team was faster than theirs. They couldn't keep him from camping near them, either. He had as much right to camp on the prairie as they had. At last they told Beth she had to stop encouraging him, and tell him to go away and leave her alone. To their horror she said she wanted to marry him.

Beth's mother cried when she came to our tent to buy some milk and tell her sad story. 'We can't do a thing with her,' she said, wiping her eyes. 'She says she's going with him, and him a complete stranger. I don't know what's come over her. She never used to be stubborn.'

'It's this awful country,' Mother said, and shook her neat little head. 'In England a man would have sense enough to stay away when he knew he wasn't wanted. Where are they going to be married? There isn't even a minister here.' She looked around at the wide, empty prairie.

'She's going back to Saskatoon with him first thing in the morning,' Beth's mother said. 'I tell her she's taking an awful risk going off like that, unmarried and all, but she won't listen. She says they'll be married by night, but how do I know?'

'He looks like a fairly honest man,' Mother comforted.

Beth's mother agreed, but added that looks sometimes lied, then she went home still wiping her eyes.

The sun was a red ball on the rim of the prairie and the long shadows still looked sleepy when we got up next morning, but Beth was already up and dressed, and saying good-bye to her family.

For a girl who was getting her own way Beth looked very unhappy. Her cheeks were puffy and her eyes red. Tears rolled down her cheeks when she kissed her father and her brother and sisters, but when she hugged her mother she sobbed outright. 'Now, now, you'll be all right in a bit,' her mother said gently, and patted her shoulder.

'I hate to leave you,' Beth sobbed. But in a few minutes she wiped her eyes and went over to the buggy where the tall young man, the cause of all the trouble, waited.

'Poor thing,' Mother said as the buggy drove away, its shadow running behind it.

'What was she crying about?' I asked.

'She didn't want to leave her folks.' Mother started mixing bannock.

'Then why did she? Nobody made her get married.'

'You don't understand.' Mother turned the bannock dough into the skillet, patted it into a flat cake, and put it over the fire to bake.

I certainly didn't understand. Grown people in my opinion did the queerest things. On the dock they had cried because they were leaving England, but nobody had made them leave. They hadn't been pushed into a railway carriage. They were leaving of their own accord, so what had they to cry about? As for Beth, nobody was making her get married, and yet she had made an awful fuss. It didn't make sense to me at all.

Another thing I didn't understand was the taste for tragedy that some grown people seemed to have.

Everybody along the trail, including me, knew about the Topot baby. It hadn't arrived yet, but it was expected any time, and when we camped Mother always asked the other women if they had heard how Mrs Topot was. I never heard the answer to the question. The women always lowered their voices at that point, but I wasn't much interested in Mrs Topot. It was the baby's problem that bothered me. Babies, I had been told, came in the doctor's bag. I hadn't seen a doctor since we left England, so how had the baby managed the trip? And even supposing it got across the ocean to Saskatoon hidden on the boat and the train, how would it ever manage to find Mrs Topot when she moved every day?

The worst of it was that nobody seemed a bit concerned about the baby. They said the Topots were foolish to start on such a trip when she was in that condition, and even more foolish to leave Saskatoon when she was so far along. They all hoped everything would be all right, and that Mrs Topot got as far as Battleford before anything happened, but there was never a word about the poor baby, probably somewhere on the prairie lost and cold.

I worried a lot about that baby, but he managed very well. He arrived one night when the tent was pitched beside the trail. There was neither doctor nor nurse, and no light except that given by a smoky barn-yard lantern. The woman in a nearby tent got up and did what she could with what she had, and that was all.

The Topots couldn't go on for a day or two, and we overtook them the following evening. As soon as our fire was started the woman who had helped Dickie Topot into the world came over to our tent, ostensibly to buy milk for the new mother, but mostly to tell Mother about the birth.

Dad was milking the cow, and Mother was sitting on the little folding chair she had brought from England mixing bannock for supper. When the visitor came Mother got up and offered her the chair.

The woman sat down and said how nice it was to sit in a real chair again, then she sighed and said she had a lot to be thankful for even though she hadn't a chair. Her two children, thank goodness, had been born where things were a bit more civilized.

'Weren't you frightened all alone like that?' Mother asked, and poured a little melted bacon grease into the bannock.

'I was that,' the woman said. 'And that poor thing! I don't know how she stood it.'

'Did she have a bad time?' Mother stopped stirring.

'Bad!' The visitor glanced over her shoulder, pulled her chair closer to Mother, and began talking quickly in a low, excited voice.

I didn't hear what she said. Jack was tired and restless and I was trying to amuse him with some twigs, but I knew from the 'Oh' and

'Ah' and the widening of Mother's eyes and the puckering of her lips that the visitor's story was interesting, even a little horrifying.

'It's a good thing everything came out all right,' Mother said at last.

'Yes, but you never know.' The visitor pursed her lips. 'She isn't out of the wood yet. I've known many a one to come down with third-day fever.'

'Let's hope she won't,' Mother said.

'Yes.' The visitor looked at the distant horizon, now faded to a misty blue. 'But you never can tell,' she said dismally. 'There's plenty that could happen even yet.' She did not smile or even look pleased, and yet there seemed to be a touch of hope in her face, and in her low voice. She sounded almost as if she had enjoyed Mrs Topot's illness, and would be disappointed if nothing more happened.

Dad came out of the blue dusk with the milk pail and put an end to the conversation, which disappointed me a little. He filled the visitor's pail with fresh milk, and told her to come and get more in the morning. The visitor offered to pay for the milk, but both Dad and Mother refused the money. 'It's little enough to do for her,' Mother said. 'I hope it gives her strength.'

The visitor said she hoped so, too, but she sounded as if the prospect was very poor.

'Is Mrs Topot going to die?' I asked when we were eating our bannock.

'Goodness, no!' Mother said. 'Whatever gave you that idea?'

'That woman seemed to think she would.'

Mother smiled. 'That was just her way of talking,' she said. 'Mrs Topot is fine. Hurry and finish your milk. It's time you were in bed.'

I did as I was told, but long after I was tucked in on the far side of the mattress against the tent wall I wondered why the woman had sounded excited about Mrs Topot's illness, and rather disappointed because no complications had set in. Grown people were certainly queer, I decided at last. They cried when they got what they wanted, and when things went well they seemed sorry even though they pretended not to be.

⌣·CHAPTER ELEVEN·⌣

Our objective when we left Saskatoon was Battleford, a town on the north branch of the Saskatchewan River. There was supposed to be plenty of good land still available there, and shops where we could buy supplies. But long before we got anywhere near Battleford our flour and bacon, sugar and tea, were almost gone. We travelled much slower than Dad had expected, and the prairie was far wider than he had thought.

Dad asked an old-timer we met how much farther we had to go, and when the man told him Dad knew our food wouldn't last. There was only one thing to do: go back to Saskatoon for more food. But not with the heavily loaded wagon, that would take too long.

Dad didn't want to leave us alone on the empty prairie, but the old-timer, a lank man with bristles on his chin and a shapeless felt hat on his head, said it was the only thing to do.

"'Tain't pleasant,' he said, sitting on a log and whittling a stick, 'but it's safe. And if you don't get a move on all the good land will be gone. You can travel twice as fast with an empty wagon as you can with a loaded one.'

Dad asked about the Indians. The ones we had seen seemed harmless, but we had heard a lot of wild stories. The Indian men didn't wear feathers in their hair, but it was often long and braided, and their buckskin coats, brightly beaded, gave them a savage look, at least to us. Even the squaws, wrapped in their gay blankets, didn't look any too dependable.

The old-timer, however, said the Indians had been quiet for a long time, and anyway, the Mounted Police had everything well in hand.

'But it wasn't always that way.' The old-timer grinned, showing long yellow teeth. 'You should have been here during the Riel rebellion. They were on the war-path then, all right. The fighting at Duck Lake was something. We all made for the forts as fast as we could to save our scalps. I was that scared, if any Indian had scalped me he'd have had a scrubbing-brush, my hair was that stiff.'

'Maybe they'll go on the war-path again,' Mother said, and looked over her shoulder at the wide emptiness behind her rapidly filling with night.

'We-e-ell,' the old-timer drawled, 'anything can happen, but they've been quiet for a good spell now.' He sent a stream of brown tobacco juice into the fire.

'Where did all them bones come from?' Dad pointed to some bleached bones scattered not far from the tent. 'They're all over the prairie.'

'Buffalo.' The old-timer threw his whittlings on to the fire. 'The prairie used to be covered with them, but they're all gone now. Killed for hides mostly. Canada ain't what it used to be, and it's getting worse. All this'—he waved his long arm at the miles of emptiness on every side——'will be ploughed in a year or so.'

'Now you are having us on,' Mother said, smiling. 'Where would anybody find enough ploughs to turn all this land over?'

'They'll find them. All the good land's gone now, even though there doesn't seem to be anybody about, and what's left is going fast. This time next spring there'll be shacks all over, and the prairie ripped to hell-and-gone. Me, I think I'll go north. Frost stays a mite too long for farming there. I'll give you a hand with that unloading if you like,' he added, turning to Dad.

Dad said he thought he would wait until morning to unload, it might rain in the night, but when the old-timer had gone to his wagon and we were in bed, Dad told Mother he was a little worried about him. 'He's a stranger, and you never know,' he said. 'Not that he doesn't look honest.'

'Maybe he'll be gone by morning,' Mother said.

The old-timer, however, was still there when we got up just at sunrise. He had a fire going, coffee boiling, and batter for flapjacks mixed. He called to us and offered us coffee, then he began to cook his flapjacks.

I stood wide-eyed and watched him. First he rubbed his skillet with a little bacon, then he poured in a little batter, tipping the skillet from side to side so that the batter spread evenly, forming a thin cake. He let the cake cook for a minute, then he shook the skillet and gave it a toss. The flapjack flew high in the air, and I gasped, sure it was going to fall in the fire. The old-timer, however, slipped his skillet under it at the right moment and caught it raw side down, then he grinned at me and went on with his cooking. When the flapjack was done he flipped it on to a tin plate and went through the fascinating process all over again.

'Ever eat these?' he asked when he had cooked three nicely browned cakes. I shook my head and inched nearer the fire.

The old-timer poured syrup over the cakes, found a fork, and handed the plate to me. 'Try some,' he invited.

I hesitated a moment. I was a little frightened by his bristles, his queer hat, and the big knife he used to whittle wood and slice bacon, but the smell of the flapjacks overcame my fear. I put out a timid hand and took the plate. It was the best meal I ever ate.

The old-timer cooked flapjacks for the rest of us, then, while Lily licked her plate, and I wished I wasn't a big girl and could lick mine, he told Mother how to make them. Mother thanked him and gave him all the fresh milk he could drink, which he seemed to enjoy even more than his flapjacks.

With the old-timer's help, unloading our wagon and covering the plough and the packing-boxes with the wagon cover didn't take long, and in a very short time Dad was ready to start back down the trail.

The old-timer went quickly, but Dad hesitated. He adjusted a bridle and checked a trace. He and Mother had never been apart for more than a night now and then ever since they were married, and leaving her alone with three small children in what she called the middle of nowhere wasn't easy.

'Keep the gun handy at night,' Dad said. 'But be careful, it's loaded. And don't forget about the axe. Take it in with you when you go to bed.'

'We'll be all right,' Mother said firmly. 'See that you take care of yourself.'

'Don't bother about me.' Dad's lips bent, and his deep grey eyes flecked with dark ocean green sparkled like water in the sun, but they were not happy. He went towards the wagon, walking sideways and still looking at us. At the wheel he hesitated, and for a moment I thought he was coming back, then he got in quickly and the team started.

'Good-bye, good-bye,' we called, and Lily and I waved both hands.

Dad turned and waved to us until the wagon went over a little hill and disappeared.

The prairie had seemed empty before, but without Dad it was desolate: a vast, empty space that cared nothing at all about us. Wherever we looked there was nothing but grey grass and pale sky that had been there since time began, and would still be there long after we had gone. The trail, of course, was still there not far from the tent, but it wasn't any comfort. Wagon wheels and the feet of oxen and horses had made it, but the oxen and the horses had gone, and the trail was now a part of the great emptiness. I began to feel frightened, and my throat ached.

Mother looked as if her throat ached, too, and her eyes, half closed from watching the trail, looked wet, but she didn't cry. 'Well, he's gone,' she said briskly, 'and standing here won't bring him back any sooner. I'm going to bake some bread, do some washing, and give you all a bath while I have the chance.' She hurried into the tent, brought out a shawl, spread it on the grass, and put Jack in the middle of it. 'You mind him, Mary, while I get some water,' she said. Then she put a little shawl on her neat head, knotted it under her chin, picked up two pails, and walked quickly towards the slough, her long skirts whispering as she crossed the dry grass.

Lily, Jack, and I huddled together on the green shawl. Jack waved his fat little hands, gurgled, and tried to crawl, but I pulled him back and made him sit still. The space around the shawl didn't seem safe for some reason.

After a while Lily and I tried to talk, but we soon stopped. Our voices sounded queer in the emptiness, and the words seemed to wander away and get lost. Lily edged closer to me and I edged over to her, then we looked over our shoulders at the space behind us. It seemed bigger than ever, and we both turned our backs on it and watched Mother.

The slough wasn't far from our tent, but it was in a little hollow, and willows grew around it. Mother went into the hollow, and quick as a wink the willows swallowed her. I leaned forward trying to catch a glimpse of her, but she was gone. Lily, Jack, and I were completely alone. I was almost afraid to breathe, the emptiness seemed so close. A little wind came from nowhere and pulled at my coat, and a cloud floated over the face of the sun and cast a shadow over us. I clutched

Jack and looked around. The emptiness was everywhere, close and far away, and it went on and on for ever. Even when it came to the end of the earth it didn't stop, because there was no way of knowing where the earth ended and the emptiness began.

Fortunately Mother wasn't gone long. Before I was completely overcome by the vastness around me she came hurrying across the grass, her long skirts blowing behind her, a pail of water in each hand. As soon as she was close enough she began to talk, as if she also felt lonely. 'So many wrigglers,' she panted. 'I think they get worse every day. Mary, go and get the strainer.' She put the pails down, went into the tent, and brought out the two white enamel bowls she had brought from England. 'Now help me,' she said, and put the strainer cloth over one of the bowls. 'I don't want any of these queer things to get among the clothes.'

We strained the water, then Mother built a fire and heated it. She washed in one bowl and rinsed in the other, and spread the clean clothes out on the grass to dry. She hadn't even a washboard to help her, only her two hands and a bar of royal crown soap.

When the washing was done Mother bathed us and washed our hair, and by that time the long day was almost over and it was time to milk the cow.

Mother had learned to milk while she was in England, but the English cows were far better behaved than the Old Cow. Dad had always tied her securely to the wagon wheel when he milked her, but the wagon was gone now, and there was nothing to tie her to but a stake.

She was staked out all the time, of course, but the rope was long so that she could feed. Mother tried to tie her feet while the rope was still long, but the Old Cow wouldn't let Mother get near her feet, and when Mother tried to shorten the stake rope the cow jabbed at her with the one good horn. 'You're more bother than you're worth,' Mother said as she struggled with the stake rope while I held a stick and tried to keep the cow from jabbing her.

Mother got the stake rope shortened at last, but that was only half the problem: the Old Cow's legs had to be tied. She wouldn't stand still, and every time Mother went near her hind legs she threatened to kick. But she had to be milked. If she wasn't she might get milk fever and die.

'You get on her other side,' Mother told me at last, 'and I'll throw one end of the rope under her.'

I did as I was told, but the Old Cow was suspicious of that trick, and kept moving around and swishing her tail. At last, however, Mother threw one end of the rope under her quite close to her front legs, and I managed to grab it. Then, each holding our end of the rope, Mother and I went to a point well behind the cow, and out of reach of her tail and feet. Mother took my end of the rope and slipped it through the loop at her end, then holding the rope as high as she could to keep the cow from stepping out of the big loop Mother gradually tightened it. Once the rope was snug around her legs the Old Cow gave up and milking her was reasonably easy, but Mother was nervous by that time, and her hands were trembling. The fresh milk did make the supper bannock taste better, but Mother said the struggle she'd had getting the milk almost ruined the flavour.

After supper Mother restaked the cow for the night, and in a little while darkness began to fill the great spaces around us.

We could no longer see the emptiness, but we knew it was there, and Mother's cheerful voice could not drive it away. Without Dad's confident smile and warm presence to reassure us we felt terribly lonely as the night closed in.

Usually we three children went to bed according to our ages: first Jack, then Lily, then me. That night, however, we all went to bed together. Mother washed our hands and faces and put on our night-gowns, then we sat up in bed while she put out the fire, brought in the axe, made sure the gun was close, and fastened the tent flap. When we were all snugly in bed Mother told us a story. Her voice was calm and cheerful, but when she paused for breath I could hear the tent-ropes creaking, and the impatient noises the cow made as she tugged at her stake rope.

We were up early next morning, and it was a good thing, for the cow had almost worked her stake out during the night. 'I might as well water her now,' Mother said when she discovered the loose stake. She untied the rope and started to lead the cow towards the slough.

The Old Cow, however, didn't wish to be led. She tossed her head and started for the slough at a fast trot, dragging Mother behind her. 'Whoa, whoa,' Mother called as she bobbed along, but the cow didn't seem to hear.

I ran to help, but Mother told me between gasps to go and look after Lily and Jack. I went reluctantly back to the tent, but I watched Mother until she and the cow bobbed over the little hill out of sight.

They were gone a long time, and when they finally reappeared Mother was carrying a stick, and both she and the cow looked angry. 'Bring me the axe,' Mother said, breathing hard. 'This dratted cow is more bother than she's worth.'

I thought Mother was going to hit the cow with the axe, so I brought it slowly, dragging it behind me.

'Be sharp,' Mother ordered, 'before this thing runs away again.' She took the axe from me, and to my relief began driving the stake into the ground. 'There!' she said when the stake was in and the rope tied. 'That's the last time I'm going to take her to the slough. She nearly pulled my arms out, and she didn't want to come back. I thought for a bit she was going to get away.' And dropping the axe Mother wiped her pretty round face that was pink with exertion, then she smoothed and repinned her ruffled hair.

The cow switched her long, curled tail and glared at us out of her crossed dark eyes, then she tossed her head disdainfully, but she didn't get to the slough again until Dad came home. Mother carried water to her. It was hard work, but much easier than getting the cow to the slough and back. The cow, however, had her revenge. She always managed to upset at least one pail of water.

And so the days passed. Mother washed and baked, repacked our things, carried water, and milked. I watched Jack part of the time, and played with Lily when Jack was asleep. We hunted for coloured stones, and picked the small buttercups that were beginning to bloom in a damp spot, but we never went far from the tent. We knew no bears lurked in the willows by the slough. Mother went there every day and came back without even a claw mark, but we had no desire to go and look at the water. The emptiness that surrounded us made us feel so uneasy that when Mother was out of sight we talked in whispers.

At night when the shadows rose from the prairie and came towards the tent we huddled near the stove and watched while Mother fried bacon and made tea. After supper we went quietly to bed without a word of argument. When Dad came home Mother told him how good we had been, but actually we were too overcome by the stillness to be naughty.

At least once during the night Mother got up and went out to look at the cow. Usually she had to come back for the axe and drive the stake deeper into the ground, for the cow was persistent, and never stopped trying to work the stake loose.

There were surprisingly few passers-by while we were camped by the trail. Those who travelled fast seemed to be well ahead, and the slower travellers like us had gone back for food. One afternoon, however, a team did come down the trail, but from the west instead of from the east.

'Must be somebody short of food,' Mother said, and shaded her eyes with her hand and watched the approaching wagon. 'Two men,' she said at last. 'I'd hoped there'd be a woman.'

The team stopped when it got to our tent. The horses lowered their heads and looked as if they would like to rest. They were thin, and their eyes looked dull and tired. The wagon had no cover, and from the way it swayed it seemed almost empty. Two dreary young men with narrow faces and pale hair and eyes sat on the wagon seat. The one who held the reins also held a whip.

The men made no effort to get down, so Mother advanced a step or two. 'Is someone ill?' she asked, glancing at the wagon box.

'No, we're going back, that's all.' The man with the whip sounded disgusted. 'There's nothing back there.' He indicated the trail behind him. 'No sugar, no butter, no milk.' He flicked the horses with his whip and they went on without another word.

'What did they expect in a new country?' Mother asked as she watched the wagon jolt down the trail. 'Milk in the streams, and butter on the bushes? They must be daft.'

One day, when all our clothes were clean, and all our flour made into bread, Mother took us for a walk down the trail.

It was a bright afternoon. The sky was blue and the wind gentle and sweet. I was sure we were going to meet Dad and skipped along happily, urging Lily to hurry. 'How far away do you think he is?' I asked when we got to the foot of the little hill over which Dad had disappeared.

'I don't know.' Mother looked startled.

'Just over the hill?' I asked, walking backward. 'Shall we see him when we get to the top?'

'I don't think so.' Mother's blue eyes looked tired. 'You mustn't be disappointed if he isn't there.'

I said I wouldn't be, but when we got to the top of the little hill and I saw the empty trail going on and on until it got lost in the grass I couldn't stop the tears from coming into my eyes. 'Let's go just a little farther,' I begged. 'Perhaps he's behind the next hill.'

Mother, however, said it was time to go home. Lily was tired and Jack, who had to be carried, was getting heavy.

'Please!' I begged when Mother turned to go back. 'Just a bit farther.'

'No, it's getting late.' Mother started towards the tent.

'Then let me go. I'll come back if he isn't there.'

'You'd get lost. Now be a good girl. Dad's nowhere near that hill.' Mother went down the little rise, her skirts bending the dry grass. I followed, but slowly and pausing often to look back. Dad, I was sure, wasn't far away.

'I do wish Dad would come,' I said when we got back to the lonely tent that stood like a white mushroom on the prairie. 'I don't like it without him.'

'I don't either.' Mother put chips into the stove and put the kettle on. 'But wishing won't do any good. We have to wait the best we can.'

⌁·CHAPTER TWELVE·⌁

W E had to wait three more days before Dad returned, then after he had rested a day we broke camp and started west. The sky was overcast that morning, and the wind seemed to be getting colder instead of warmer. 'It feels like snow,' Mother said when she climbed into the loaded wagon. 'I wonder if they ever have spring in this country?'

Dad said of course they did, but it was a bit late warming up this year, that was all. Mother said he had a right to his opinion, but she didn't agree with him. Here it was May and the leaves not out. There would be tulips in England. Dad said there would be flowers here soon, but next day it seemed as if Mother was right and there wasn't going to be any spring. In the middle of the afternoon snow began to fall.

It came down slowly at first in big, soft flakes that melted when they landed on the backs of the horses. 'It isn't going to be much,' Dad said. 'It won't bother us at all.'

In a little while, however, the air was full of snow, and the prairie, or as much of it as I could see from my place behind Dad and Mother, was white.

Mother thought we ought to stop and pitch the tent before the snow got deep and we got lost, but Dad was anxious to go on. We had already lost a lot of time. Besides, he argued, it was still early in the afternoon. The snow wouldn't last long. After all, it was May, practically summer. By rights there ought not to be any snow at all.

Mother said there wouldn't be snow in any civilized country. In England the leaves would be out, and the hawthorn in bloom. But this wasn't England, and there was no telling what might happen.

Dad argued that it wasn't a cold snow, and we were warm and dry, which was more than we would be if we camped on the wet ground. Besides, someone had told him there was a big Government tent ahead, and it would be far better to spend the night there.

Mother said 'Well, get lost if you want to,' and we jogged on. The wagon wheels creaked through the soft snow, and bumped hard over the ruts.

Instead of stopping in a short time the snow began to fall faster than ever. It covered the trail until there was nothing left of the two wheel tracks, and all the prairie was white. After a while even the tall dry grass was hidden, and snow clung to the branches of the willows, and lay thick on the backs of the team. 'If we aren't already lost we soon shall be,' Mother said. 'Then the bairns will freeze.'

Dad, however, refused to worry. He laughed and told Mother not to be so ready to throw cold water. He was sure we were going in the right direction, and the trail was as plain as could be if Mother would only look.

Mother said Dad could deceive himself if he wanted to, but he couldn't pull cotton over her eyes. There was no trail anywhere, only snow. Then she wrapped a shawl around herself and Jack, told Lily and me to get under a blanket, and settled down to wait for night.

Dad whistled to the team and told them to get up, and we went on and on. The soft daylight began to turn grey as the sun, only a pale silver ball, began to go below the white horizon. The team went slower and slower, and their dark heads seemed to sink lower with every step. And still there was no sign of a tent. Once we thought we saw it, but the high white patch turned out to be a clump of willows half hidden by snow.

We went around a little hill and skirted a clump of trees, then we went up a slope and through a narrow space between two small groves. Suddenly, when we came out of the trees, Dad sat up straight and peered ahead, and a slow smile spread over his thin face. 'Well, there it is, Sally,' he said happily. 'I allus told you you'd have nothing to bother about as long as you stuck with me.'

'Where's what?' Mother asked. She was short-sighted, and dusk was creeping over the snow.

'The tent.' Dad pointed with his whip to a patch of grey-white at the far side of a little depression. 'We'll be there in no time now. I told you we weren't lost.'

'You can't make me believe that tale,' Mother said. 'You were lost, and you know it.' But there was relief in her blue eyes.

Afterwards Dad admitted he hadn't been able to see a sign of a trail for a long time, but he didn't want Mother to be frightened, so he insisted the trail was there, and kept going in what he thought was the right direction. To make sure that the team, not liking to face the wind, wouldn't edge around he lined up landmarks—a clump of willows, a little hill, or even some extra tall grass—and headed for them, spotting new landmarks when he passed the old.

Dad rested the tired team at the top of the little rise, then we went down the gentle slope and started to cross the depression. The snow that covered it looked as harmless as a huge sheet spread on the ground to dry, and even the team didn't hesitate when they came to the flat expanse of white. The innocent-appearing snow, however, was deceiving. Instead of covering solid ground it hid a swamp, and before Dad realized what was happening the horses were up to their bellies in mud and slush. They plunged and struggled and did their best. Their dark shoulders heaved, and their tired flanks strained, and they tossed their heads and tried to find firm footing, but it was no use. The wheels were hub deep in the churned snow and mud.

Dad cupped his hands and shouted 'Hey, there!' in the direction of the tent, but no one answered or came to help us.

'Fine thing!' Mother said. 'We can stay here all night and freeze for all they care.'

Dad got down into the cold slush and went to the horses' heads and tried to lead them, and again they struggled. The wagon inched forward a little, leaned sideways, and stuck again.

The snow had stopped just before we got to the top of the little rise at the edge of the swamp, and now the clouds parted and the setting sun, a ball of pure gold, rested on the snow. The long, bright rays of yellow light gilded the edges of the grey clouds above us, and sprinkled the snow about us with gold. 'It looks as if it might be a nice day to-morrow,' Dad said.

'Much good it will do us if we freeze to-night,' Mother said.

Dad didn't reply, and in a moment the rent in the clouds closed. Once more we were surrounded by the unfriendly greyness. The horses hung their heads, and even the Old Cow looked cold. 'This is a fine thing to do,' Mother told Dad. 'You might as well get back up here where it's at least dry.'

Dad, however, was looking at the trail over which we had come. 'Somebody seems to be coming,' he said at last, and his thin, anxious face brightened.

Lily and I lifted the edge of the wagon cover and peeped out. A team of long-horned red-and-white oxen came slowly down the trail towards us, and sitting hunched in the uncovered wagon were two men.

The tired oxen stopped a little way behind us, and the men got down and came over to us. Their coats looked heavy on their shoulders, and their caps sagged. 'Stuck, eh?' the curly-haired man said.

'Well, a trifle,' Dad said, and smiled.

The tall, curly-haired man said maybe a push or two would help, and the other man, who hadn't spoken yet, heaved on the wheels. They heaved until their faces were red, and the team struggled until the horses got nervous and started to plunge, but it was no use. The wagon lurched sideways a little and that was all.

'It's damned queer them devils in the tent don't come and give us a lift,' the tall man said at last. 'A little more beef and we might make it. Hey, you!' he yelled. Nobody answered, and the tall man mumbled something about blighters who were afraid of getting their blistering feet wet.

We were all blue with cold by that time, and the horses were so tired they were trembling. The three men talked the matter over and finally decided to get Mother and us three children to the big tent, unhitch the team, untie the cow, and leave the wagon where it was until morning. The horses would be rested then, and maybe somebody who wasn't afraid of a little cold water might come along and give us a push.

The two young men decided to leave their wagon where it was also, rather than risk getting stuck, so while the tall man stayed with the teams the quiet man helped Dad get us to the tent. He carried Lily, Dad carried Jack, and Mother and I walked.

It was a hard trip. The snow and slush covered my knees, and I was afraid I was going to be stuck just like the wagon. It wasn't a pleasant prospect, so I tried to walk in the footprints the men made the way Mother was doing. She didn't seem to be having much trouble, but my legs were short. I stood sideways and put out a foot, and finally managed to straddle a hump of snow, but neither foot was steady, and I swayed dangerously before I managed to get both feet into the same footmark. I rested a moment, breathing hard, then I went through the difficult process all over again.

Naturally my progress was very slow, and in a short time I found myself in the middle of the swamp with nothing but empty footprints before and behind me. For a moment I was terribly sorry for myself, and lonely tears came into my eyes. Maybe if I waited somebody would come and help me, but Dad and Mother and the quiet man had disappeared into the tent, and the tall man was out of sight behind the wagon. I rubbed the tears away with a cold fist and went on.

Dad was building a fire in the stove when I got to the tent, and Mother was saying it was no wonder no one came to help us, nobody was there. The tent was completely empty.

We didn't have the tent to ourselves for long, however. Other wagons arrived late that night and early next morning, and the tent was soon crowded, but we had the warmest corner right next to the stove.

We stayed in the tent for a day or two until the snow went and the trail dried a little, then we moved on. Good land was going fast, according to the old-timers, and we ought to hurry if we wanted anything worth while. Someone told Dad there was fair land to be had on a side trail, and after talking it over with Mother Dad decided to go and take a look at it.

The land, however, turned out to be rocky and barren-looking, and Dad decided to go back to the main trail and continue west. Mother thought we ought to go back the way we had come, but Dad said that would be wasting time, and took a short cut across the prairie. There was no trail at all, and Mother said we were sure to get lost, but Dad was in a good mood and laughed and told Mother she hadn't a thing to worry about as long as she stayed with him. He knew we were going in the right direction, and saving ourselves several miles besides.

Mother said she hoped Dad knew what he was doing, but she doubted it, and we bumped on and on over stones and badger holes, and a little gully or two, but there was no sign of a trail. At last, when the sun was getting low, and one rise was getting just like another, dim and lonely and hostile, Dad decided to camp until morning. The horses and the cow, however, needed water, they hadn't had a drink since morning. 'Look for some willows,' Dad said. 'Where there's willows there's often a slough.'

We all looked as hard as we could, but there didn't seem to be a willow on the prairie. The red sun sat on the rim of the world for a moment, then it began to go out of sight, and the little wind that roamed the prairie began to sigh and rustle about as if looking for a bed. 'I think we're lost,' Mother said at last.

Dad said we couldn't be. We were only a stone's throw from the trail. Mother, however, was sure we were not only lost, but would never be found again. She was quite sure a whole army could disappear in such a wilderness and never be heard of again.

We bumped along a little longer, then Dad pointed to the right and said: 'Doesn't that look like a house to you?' Mother agreed that the brown slope did look like a roof. 'But what would a house be doing out here?' she asked.

'We'll soon find out,' Dad said, and turned the team in the direction of the large brown mushroom squatting close to the ground.

When we got closer we saw there was not one house but five, all huddled close to the earth as if they didn't wish to be seen. 'Someway I don't like the look of this,' Mother said in a troubled voice. 'Let's go on.'

Dad said you couldn't expect brick houses with chimney-pots on the prairie, and whoever lived in the low, sod-roofed houses would at least give us water. But even he looked nervous when three or four shaggy dogs ran barking towards us.

The team stopped when they saw the dogs, and before Dad could get them started again a huge man with a big fur cap on his head came out of one of the houses and hurried towards us, calling to the dogs in words we'd never heard before. 'It must be one of them Dukhobors,' Mother gasped. 'Let's be going.'

We had heard about the Dukhobors more than once as we came up the trail. They were strange people, we had been told, who lived in small villages, worked community farms, made their wives do the ploughing, and liked to be left alone. It was too late to leave them, however. The huge man was already leading the horses closer to the low houses.

'You've gone and done it now,' Mother told Dad in a low voice. 'We shall all be killed.'

'It isn't likely.' Dad tried to sound cheerful, but he looked uneasy. 'Water,' he called in a loud voice, and smiled at the huge man, and pointed to a horse-trough.

The huge man said something that sounded like 'Sure, sure,' and a row of big white teeth appeared below his fierce black moustache, then he began unhooking the traces.

'He's going to steal the team.' Mother's voice trembled.

Dad slipped off the wagon, went over to the big Dukhobor, and took the trace out of his hand. 'No water,' he said firmly and again pointed to the trough.

Afterwards Mother said she held her breath at that moment, not knowing what to expect, for Dad was only about half the size of the dark man.

'Sure, sure.' The Dukhobor smiled at Dad, waved at the trough and the haystack, then he looked at Mother and pointed to the ground. 'Him stay,' he said.

Dad hesitated, the unhooked trace in his hand. The big dark man looked friendly, but the black-and-yellow dogs still hovered in the background, and faces crowded the small window in the nearest house.

As if he understood Dad's hesitation the big man shouted at the dogs and they slunk away, then he turned towards the houses and shouted again and waved his arms.

The door of the nearest house opened, and four or five women popped out and came towards us. They were not tall women, but they were wide and strong looking, deep of bust and thick of thigh. Their long, shapeless dark dresses hid their legs, but their bare feet and ankles were as big as the feet and ankles of most men. If the women had been horses they would have been *percherons*: large, thick-chested animals, accustomed to hauling huge loads without any fuss or bother. According to the stories we had heard these women were also used to hard work. They toiled in the fields from daylight to dark; hoeing potatoes, weeding, and cultivating gardens, ploughing the fields, and if a horse got sick they were said to help pull the plough. Mother had always laughed at these stories, and said the old-timers were having us on, but when she saw these wide women, more like oaks than willows, I think she believed part of the yarns, at least.

The faces of the women were brown and weathered, and they had what in Yorkshire was known as a stolid look, but they were not dull. Their small, light blue eyes, set deep in sun wrinkles, were bright and intelligent, and their wide mouths were strong and firm. They looked contented and capable, and oddly proud, as if they enjoyed their lives and the work they did. Afterwards Mother said: 'You can't tell me anybody makes them women do anything. If they plough it's because they like ploughing, not because some man tells them to.'

'They came when the man called, didn't they?' Dad asked.

'They'd have come anyway,' Mother said. 'He only happened to call at the right time.'

Dad didn't agree, but the women did seem to have minds of their own. They came to within about five yards of the wagon, then they stopped and stood there looking at us.

The huge man pointed to them, said something we couldn't understand, and smiled, then he pointed at Mother and waved his hand as if he wanted her to get down off the wagon.

'What does he mean?' Mother asked, looking at Dad.

'I think the women are his wives, and he wants you to get down,' Dad said.

'Wives or not I'm not going to budge,' Mother said, and narrowed her blue eyes and pursed her red lips.

Dad said he thought the women looked friendly, and it might hurt their feelings if we were rude. After all, nobody had ever heard of the Dukhobors hurting anybody, and we did need food and water for the horses and the cow.

'Well, all right,' Mother said at last. 'When we're all murdered I hope you'll be satisfied.' She passed Jack to Dad and climbed over the high red wheel.

Dad lifted Lily and me down, and we all stood there not knowing what to do. The Dukhobor women pointed at Mother's good-looking dark blue hat and smiled, then they talked gaily to each other. When they had exhausted the hat they pointed to her fur and talked again, as if they were dividing her things, Mother said. Finally, a young woman with a smooth, unwrinkled skin and merry light blue eyes stepped forward, pointed at Jack, and said: 'Baby pretty.'

Mother looked startled for a second, then her round face glowed, while the distrust left her blue eyes and her tight lips smiled. 'Oh, do you think so?' she asked, and her voice was suddenly as warm and friendly as a June breeze.

The young woman may not have understood the words, but she understood the friendliness in Mother's voice. She nodded, and the smile on her square face widened. 'Boy?' she asked, and touched Jack's sleeve.

Mother said 'Yes' and smiled again, and as if they knew the ice had been broken all the other women crowded around us talking and smiling. They pointed to one of the houses and pushed us gently in that direction, and in a short time we were all in one of the little houses, and the plump young woman was holding Jack on her ample lap.

She was not the only one who admired him. All the others swarmed around. They exclaimed over his green coat and bonnet, his dress, his shoes, his soft fair hair, and his plump pink arms. With the help of signs they asked how old he was, and when Mother told them they exclaimed over that. Lily and I, feeling a little left out, edged forward for our share of the admiration, but the women were not interested in us. They smiled at us and touched our coats, but they didn't really see us. It was Jack, the man child, who was all-important, especially to the young woman. She felt his little fat hands, stroked his fluff of hair, and talked baby talk to him.

Jack responded beautifully. He clapped his hands, said 'Dad, Dad,' showed them how big he was, and pulled his shoes off.

While this baby worship was going on Dad and the huge man watered and fed the team and milked the cow, then they came into the house and we had supper. The food was plain, but very good. We had soup, hard-boiled eggs, the first since we left England, and large slices of sweet brown bread spread thick with butter.

The Dukhobors didn't eat with us. They waited on us, urging us to have more bread and another egg. When we couldn't eat another bite they pointed to the beds on a low platform, indicated with signs that the house was ours, smiled, and left us.

Actually it wasn't much of a house. The walls were low and made of clay, and the floor was only well-swept earth. Stools and a rough board table were the only furniture, even the fire-place was made of earth and stones, but to us it seemed wonderful. The feather-beds were soft and warm and clean, and the atmosphere was generous and friendly.

When we left early next morning the Dukhobors gave us food to take with us: big loaves of their delicious brown bread, potatoes, eggs, and butter. Dad tried to pay them for their hospitality and for the food, but the huge man shook his head, put his hands behind him, and smiled. Dad and Mother shook hands with everyone and thanked them. The Dukhobors smiled, and in broken English told us to come again; then the young woman gave Jack a last hug, and we left.

'Such wonderful people,' Mother said as we drove away. 'I wish we could have found land near them.'

'And you thought they were going to kill us. Sally, you just don't know people,' Dad teased.

'You were frightened yourself for a bit.' Mother tossed her small, neat head and tried to look scornful.

'Not me.' Dad chuckled and his eyes twinkled. 'I knew right off that they meant well. And that young girl that took such a shine to Jack! A man could do a lot worse than marry such a lass. She'd be a big help to a farmer.'

'Well!' Mother said, and glared at Dad out of cold blue eyes. 'If that's the way you feel maybe you'd better dump me and the bairns in the next slough and go back.'

Dad looked at Mother out of the corners of his happy eyes, and a teasing smile twisted the corners of his expressive mouth. 'No, Sally,' he said cheerfully, 'I promised your brother Sam I'd look after you, and I'm going to do it. You're only as big as tuppence, but you'll be all right as long as you stick to me.'

'Hmm,' Mother sniffed, and tilted her nose and turned her shoulder towards Dad. 'If you didn't want a little woman you shouldn't have married one,' she said coldly.

CHAPTER THIRTEEN

A few days after we left the Dukhobor village we came to the Eagle Hills. We had been hearing about the hills for some time: how steep they were, how narrow the trail, and how many accidents and near-accidents had happened on them. Nobody, as far as I know, had been killed on them, but according to the stories there had been some very close shaves.

The stories, of course, worried Mother, and the closer we got to the hills, the more anxious she became. 'If we were only over them hills,' she said as we bumped along the trail. 'I never did like steep places.'

'I bet they aren't half as bad as they're painted,' Dad said. 'And besides, people cross them every day.'

'I know,' Mother fretted, 'but we have the cow and she's contrary. She might upset the wagon. Canada, it seems to me, is just one trouble after another.'

'It won't be for long. The railroad will be through here before you know it, and you'll be riding across here in a first-class carriage,' Dad said.

Mother laughed unbelievingly. 'The railroad will never get to this god-forsaken place,' she said. 'And even if it does it won't do the bairns and me a bit of good if we're killed on them hills. I know they're big. Everything in this country is ten times the size it is anywhere else.'

Dad said he was quite sure nothing would happen to us, but even he was a little perturbed when we suddenly came to the rim of the deep cleft in the prairie.

The ground had been irregular and rising for some time, and Dad said if these knolls were the hills we'd heard so much about they were nothing at all, and wouldn't even frighten a rabbit. Mother agreed with him, and we were feeling quite safe and pleased with ourselves, then all at once the deep cleft was before us.

If there had been a fair road the hills and the creek at the bottom wouldn't have been bad, but there wasn't. Two wagon tracks, one higher than the other, constituted the road, and the tracks meandered down the hill so carelessly that we got the impression they would just as soon we fell off as not. They skirted boulders, slipped between trees, skimmed around shoulders, dipped, turned sharply, plunged downward suddenly, and now and then disappeared entirely.

Dad stopped the team at the rim of the steep hill, and looked down anxiously at the trees and shrubs below. They had come into leaf while we crossed the prairie, and their tops were fluffy and green in the sunshine. Looking down on a tree was a new experience for me, and I was so fascinated I didn't pay much attention to the way the trail tipped, so when Dad asked Mother if she'd like to get out and walk I was disturbed, and wondered what was wrong. 'Are we going to tip over?' I asked.

'No,' Mother said, but she didn't sound any too certain, and when she leaned far forward to get a better look at the trail she drew back quickly, and her round face turned pale. I leaned out as far as I could and looked too. Nobody, I was sure, could get down into that hole. The sensible thing as far as I could see was to go around it. I said as much, but nobody paid any attention. All Dad did was ask Mother once more if she wanted to get down and walk.

'What are you going to do?' Mother asked.

'I have to drive,' Dad said. 'I can do it better up here.'

'If you ride we'll all ride,' Mother decided. 'What would I do alone in a place like this?'

'Hold on then,' Dad said, and shook the reins and we started.

Afterwards Mother said if the team hadn't been old and steady we never would have got to the bottom of the hill alive, and I think she was right.

First thing we knew the heavy, overloaded wagon was right on the horses' rumps, and their collars were up behind their ears instead of on their shoulders. The wagon tipped sideways until it seemed to be hanging out over space, and the wagon tongue protruded far forward between the horses' ears. Most horses would have become nervous in such a situation, but Darkie and Nelly kept their heads. They stayed close to the bank, and in the steep places they sat down and slid on their haunches.

Half-way down the hill Mother turned sideways and put Jack behind the wagon seat with Lily and me. I expected her to turn and face forward again, but she didn't. She stayed bent over, one hand clutching Jack, the other the mattress. This left me a clear view ahead, and being too frightened to shut my eyes I saw everything that happened. The horses' rumps almost came into the wagon at one point, and their harness seemed about to slip over their heads. The wagon tongue tipped up and the trail tipped down, but the worst thing of all was the space before and beside us. The foot of the cliff and the treetops seemed to be a mile below. I was so frightened I'm sure I must have looked like a little owl, but I had to look. I saw rocks dislodged by the horses' hoofs go rolling down the hill, and a boulder that would have upset us if a wheel had gone over it, and the place where the trail seemed to go straight down. Every curve seemed worse than the last, and the hill seemed endless. When we got to the bottom, and Dad stopped the team and said 'All right, Sarah, you can look now,' I was stiff all over.

Mother sat up and opened her eyes, and Lily, who was too little to realize the danger, but didn't like sitting on a slope, righted herself and let go of the back of my coat. I tried to let go of the back of the wagon seat, but found I couldn't. My stiff fingers wouldn't move.

When he had rested a moment Dad got down and went to see how the cow had made out. There had been a drag at the back of the wagon, and Dad was afraid that the cow had fallen and been unable to get up. The cow, however, was a wise animal. She had kept her rope away from the wheel, and by hanging back had provided a brake of a sort.

Mother said Providence, and nothing else, had brought us safely down the hill, and she was thankful. I was sure Dad had done the driving, and said so, but Mother seemed to think otherwise, and said if only Providence would help us up the other hill everything would be all right.

Dad said the other hill was nothing to worry about, it was only a slope compared to the hill we had come down, and anyway we were not going to go up it until to-morrow. The team had done enough for one day and deserved a rest. He unhitched and pitched the tent, and tethered the horses and the cow in the long grass. Mother, however, wasn't really at ease again until we had climbed the other hill, which wasn't at all steep, then she said Providence had been good to us. I asked where Providence was, and Mother said it was everywhere, but though I kept a sharp look-out all day long I couldn't catch a glimpse of it.

Our next real rest after the Eagle Hills was Battleford. Like Saskatoon it was mostly a city of tents pitched on the prairie a short distance from one or two wooden store buildings, the livery barns where horses could be bought and sold, and the land office.

We were lucky enough to find space in the big Government tent, and while Mother went through the routine of washing clothes and baking bread, I amused Jack by putting him on the little folding chair and pushing him the length of the tent and back.

For safety he sat facing me, his chubby legs dangling over the edge of the seat, his fat little hands clinging to the chair back. The tent floor was rough and sometimes Jack must have been frightened by the jolts he got, but he never cried.

People watching us often asked if I wasn't tired, but I never seemed to be. I enjoyed the ride almost as much as Jack did, perhaps because of the constant element of danger. The folding chair often threatened to collapse. The tent-poles and other children were a constant hazard, and rough spots in the floor often tripped me.

Other children also seemed to think that pushing the chair and Jack was an interesting game. They often asked to be allowed to push a little, but I refused. Jack was our baby, and I meant to enjoy him myself.

While we were in Battleford Dad went to the land office and asked about homesteads. He was told the same story: there wasn't much good land left around there. A few fairly good quarter sections might still be vacant a little to the north, but the best land was farther west.

Dad and Mother discussed the matter and decided to go north first. Dad was anxious to get settled, and Mother felt that the sooner we stopped the sooner we would get back to England. In her opinion this long, hard trip was mostly a waste of time, but it was the only way she knew to convince Dad that Canada was impossible.

Most of the other women thought as Mother did, and endured the hardships of the trail for the same reason. 'Let 'em get a bellyful is what I say,' a big, red-faced woman said one day when a group were discussing the problem. 'It's the only way to satisfy the blighters. The worse it gets the better I like it.'

'But think of jolting all those miles again, and that train ride, and that ship,' a thin-faced woman said.

'What about it?' the red-faced woman asked. 'London will be at t'other end, won't it? I'd jolt a lot farther for a whiff of that fog.'

'So would I,' Mother said. 'I wouldn't care how far we jolted if the Spen Beck was at the end of it.'

The other women felt the same, but the men were not satisfied to go back. The trip was hard but they seemed to enjoy it, and most of them were still looking forward to the rich land they were going to find, and the fortunes they were going to make. They collected in little groups and talked about it. Battleford hummed with hope. All the good things the colonists had been looking forward to ever since they left England, the free houses, free schools, free meat, vegetables, and fish, were just around the corner.

We had to hurry, however, before all these good things slipped away, or other people found them, so early one morning Dad harnessed the team, tied the cow to the back of the wagon, and headed north. We travelled for a few days, but the farther we went the less Dad thought of the land. He said it was light soil, not the rich dark loam he wanted.

'Maybe all the land's like this,' Mother said hopefully. 'Old Barr was never out here, so how would he know what the land was like?'

Dad said the old-timers knew, and since they said the land farther west was much better it was only sensible to go and take a look at it, so we turned in that direction and headed for the ferry.

'What will you do if the land farther west is no better than the land here?' Mother asked as we jogged along.

'It will be,' Dad said confidently. 'The old-timers say the pea-vine in some places is knee high.'

'Them places might be gone by now,' Mother said.

Dad said that was what he was afraid of, and shook the reins to make the horses walk faster. He looked a little worried, and kept squinting his eyes and looking far off across the prairie, getting a little green by now. 'We ought to be getting to some fair land soon,' he said.

Mother agreed that we ought, but she didn't seem to mind the poor land one bit. As we rolled over mile after mile of thin grass a placid look came into her blue eyes, and a little smile tweaked the corners of her mouth. If Dad couldn't find good land, and became discouraged, we might be back in England much sooner than she had dared hope, perhaps even before the roses had finished blooming.

Dad, however, didn't discourage easily. He was short and slender, and still quite young, not yet thirty, and he had a wife and three small children to provide for, but there was always a smile on his lean face and a twinkle in his dark, ocean-flecked eyes. 'Just you stick to me, Sally,' he would say cheerfully when the going was difficult. 'You'll allus be all right.'

As we got closer to the ferry, however, Dad did seem a little worried by the increasing thinness of the grass and the poor earth in the gopher mounds. Like many of the Barr colonists he had asked for land with a river frontage, but so far all the land near the river had been poor and rock-strewn. 'Looks as if we'll have to forget about land near the river,' Dad said as we creaked along. 'I haven't seen any worth having.'

Mother said as far as she was concerned she could get along without the Saskatchewan River. What she had seen of it didn't impress her. It was far too big and wild. What she wanted was a friendly little river like the Spen at home.

Dad said rivers in Canada had to be bigger than the rivers in England. Canada was a much bigger country. Mother said that was just the trouble, and one reason why she didn't like it, and sometimes wished she'd married Edmond Bastow, as Uncle Sam had advised. 'I'd be safe in England now,' she said dismally, 'not wandering about in the middle of nowhere looking for land that isn't there.'

'You'd be living in Bradford, and smothered in soot,' Dad said cheerfully. He never took Edmond Bastow seriously.

Mother said she'd at least have had a roof over her head, and a bit of garden for geraniums.

'Don't you worry about a garden,' Dad said. 'We'll find land that will grow geraniums ten feet tall on the other side of the river.'

Mother was doubtful, but she wished we were across the river. She didn't like any sort of water, and Canadian water was worst of all.

We had crossed the Saskatchewan River at least once before, but the banks at the Paynton Ferry were much higher than the other banks had been. When we camped that night Dad said we were on the river bank, but we couldn't see any water at all: only treetops, and a greenish blur in the distance that I thought was part of the sunset, but which actually was the far bank. Next morning, however, we found the river in a hurry. The horses slid down a steep bank, and went around a turn or two, and there was the river, wide, serene, and smiling in the morning sunshine.

Saskatchewan means rapid river, or swift-flowing water. There was an Indian legend about the river that may or may not be true. It was said that when the Indians signed the treaty with the white people they stipulated that their treaty money was to be paid as long as the Saskatchewan River continued to flow. One year there was a terrible drought, and the river dwindled to a mere trickle. Alarmed, the Indians came from miles around and gathered on the river bank and prayed the Great Spirit to send rain. The Great Spirit heard their plea and sent a downpour, and the treaty money was saved.

There are two main branches of the Saskatchewan: the North Saskatchewan that rises in the Rocky Mountains, and the South Saskatchewan which is formed by the union of the Bow and the Belly Rivers. The two big rivers wind across what is now the province of Saskatchewan, but was in those days still the North-West Territory. The rivers finally unite near the city of Prince Albert, and as one big river they empty into Lake Winnipeg.

It was the North Saskatchewan River we were about to cross. There had been a lot of snow the previous winter, and the water was very high and fast. It was also very wide, almost like a lake, and small islands with trees growing on them were in the middle of the stream. At the end of one island a golden sand-bar glistened in the sun, and lying on the gold, their branches held out as if begging for help, were the bleached skeletons of several trees.

I was quite sure that the white wood was the bones of people who had died while trying to get the gold. One branch especially was exactly like a bent knee, and I urged Dad to go to the island and see if the rest of the person was there. Dad said the water was too deep, and what I took to be a knee was only a root, but I wasn't entirely convinced, and it was a long time before I stopped worrying about the knee in the river.

Although the Saskatchewan looked wide and serene, it was really very fast, and very treacherous. It created sand-bars overnight, then as quickly washed them away again. Sometimes it scooped out deep holes, and undermined the banks in unexpected places. Often the ferry had to be moved because of these tricks. Even in winter when the ice was several feet thick the river wasn't safe. A shift in the current, or a spring, would undermine the ice, leaving a thin spot. The old-timers said that more than one man had stepped on such a spot and never been seen again.

That morning, however, the river was in a friendly mood. It chuckled as it ran over the stones near the shore, caught the sunlight in its ripples and rolled it over playfully. It swirled around a boulder and threw a feather of white spray into the warm air, and far out in the main channel the broad expanse of deep blue water lay still and shining as if it wasn't moving at all. 'Did you ever see anything like it?' Dad asked as we waited for the ferry which was on the other side. 'That's a river that is a river. I bet it's near a quarter of a mile across.'

'The Spen Beck was big enough for me,' Mother said. 'I wish we didn't have to cross.'

'It won't take long.' Dad let the reins fall slack over the backs of the horses, and leaned out of the wagon and talked to the two or three other settlers also waiting to cross. They agreed that the Saskatchewan was quite a stream, but like Mother they were overawed by its size, the height of its banks, far higher than the banks of the Thames, and the untamed wilderness on every side. 'There isn't a bridge anywhere,' one man said, and there was home-sickness in his eyes and in his voice.

The ferry came slowly across the wide river. It left a streak of churned water behind it that the river quickly caught and carried downstream.

A quiet man by the name of Nolan operated the ferry. He backed it up close to the rough landing, then he and another man put out a sort of rough gang-plank and the loading began.

Some of the horses didn't want to step on to the swaying ferry, that was actually little more than a flat platform only a little distance above the water; and even our steady team tested it with careful feet before they walked slowly aboard. Only the cow objected strenuously to leaving land. She had to be pushed on board.

When the loading was finished the men pulled up the gang-plank, hooked a chain across the space, and moved slowly into the stream. 'What did I tell you?' Dad said. 'It's just like sitting in a chair.'

'We aren't across yet.' Mother regarded the water with suspicious eyes, and leaned away from it. She said it made her dizzy, and she didn't like the way the ferry swayed.

The island of gold strewn with the bones of dead trees drifted past, and we entered the swift, night-blue main channel. We were half-way across now, in a little while we would be going up the bank away from the river. Dad began to adjust the reins and Mother relaxed a little, then all at once the ferry jerked, swung around, and began slipping quickly downstream.

Excitement broke out everywhere. The men who operated the ferry hurried about and shouted to each other. They looked over into the water, and waved their arms, but the ferry continued downstream. Everybody began asking questions, but no one seemed to know what was wrong, not even the ferryman. He told us not to worry, we were perfectly safe, the ferry wouldn't either tip or sink, but we were all worried, and wanted to know where we were going, and what had happened.

Nobody really knew, of course, but everybody took a guess. Some said the paddle wheel had broken, others thought the rudder had fallen off. One man was sure we would be wrecked in rapids, another thought we were drifting out to sea where a storm would surely sink us, even if we didn't starve to death. Everybody thought the ferryman ought to do something, but there didn't seem to be a thing to do. The ferry simply drifted down the river until it struck a sand-bank, and there it stopped, swaying gently in the current. 'I knew something would happen to this thing,' Mother said, looking at the wild beauty of the green banks and the blue river. 'This awful country will kill us all yet.'

Dad said there wasn't a thing to worry about. The ferry would be fixed in an hour or two. We'd had an extra ride for our money, and had nothing to complain about.

The situation, however, was worse than Dad thought. We were stuck on the sand-bank almost four days. There was talk of taking us ashore in a row-boat, but there didn't seem to be a boat. Even if there had been the horses and wagon couldn't have been taken to shore, and without our teams we were almost helpless. So we stayed where we were. Mother was the only woman on board, and we were the only children. When night came the ferryman told Dad to put our mattress in the little boarded space where his stove was so that Mother might have a little privacy. The mattress more than filled the little space, but it was a place to sleep. Dad and the other men spent the nights in the wagons.

We were out of bread, and there was no way to make bannock, since the little stove had space on top for only a kettle, and no oven. Fortunately we had our old stand-by, crackers and cheese, and the little milk the cow gave. To help out Mother made tea with river water, which was a great improvement on the brown water in the sloughs.

The horses and the cow were far worse off than we were. There was lots to drink, but practically nothing for them to eat. We had a few oats, and Dad gave them a handful or two night and morning: that was all the food they had. The ferryman said they would be all right, but they did get very hollow looking. Mother said their sides almost touched. Fortunately the weather stayed warm and pleasant while we were stranded. A boisterous wind would have been very disagreeable.

The days on the river were uncomfortable, but there were happy moments, even happy hours. One hour in particular was pure joy for me. Dad showed me a sunset.

To most people Dad was a cheerful, hard-working, practical man, but there was another side to his character which he hid most of the time. He loved nature, and all the beautiful things of the earth. In England he had called my attention to the scarlet poppies in the golden wheat, to the snow of the hawthorn, the dandelion puffs, and the delicate fringe that grew on the tall seeding grass. Sometimes he picked the flowers and arranged them carefully, putting a little frill of ferns around the blooms. 'How's that?' he would ask, smiling at the flowers. When he thought they were arranged just right he handed them to me, and told me to give them to Mother.

There were few flowers in bloom while we were coming up the trail, for the spring was late, but when the flowers did appear Dad called my attention to them, and told me their names. And once many years later when we stood looking at a field of wheat Dad sighed and said: 'Do you remember how it used to be, Mary? All the trees! It's practically a desert now. It will never be the same again.'

But the night Dad showed me the sunset western Canada was new. Trees and willow grew on the banks of the river, and the ploughs of the settlers had not yet disturbed the prairie. There were no roads and no fences, only the prairie rolling on for hundreds of miles like a vast, still sea.

We leaned on the ferry rail, and Dad looked at the glowing sky, and then down at the water. 'What are you looking at?' I asked, and looked down also.

Dad smiled apologetically. 'At the sunset,' he said in a low voice.

I stood on my toes and leaned far over the rail. 'Down there it shivers,' I said.

'So it does.' Dad looked surprised. 'See that ship?' He pointed to the reflection of a glowing cloud.

I nodded and watched the cloud for a moment. 'It's melting,' I said at last.

'Everything changes. See those feathers?' Dad pointed to the long, softly curled pink streamers that extended from the horizon to the top of the sky. 'They fade a bit, and then they brighten, but they never brighten as much as they fade.'

'Will they go out after a while?' I asked. 'Like the fire in the fire-place?'

'Yes, everything goes out sooner or later.'

'But it will come again to-morrow?'

'For a bit, anyway.' Dad looked down at the purple water, and his thin face seemed sad. I moved a little closer to him and together we watched the pale aquamarine sky behind the pink feathers turn a tender amethyst. The little boat lost its golden frills, and purple shadows drooped low over the dark trees. The last of the sunset gold fell into the river, and floated a moment on the rims of the ripples. Then a little wind came out of the west and scattered the gold, and the earth and the sky became a warm purple-grey, and drew close together like two old friends who have much to talk about. The river went on its way alone, talking to itself in the gathering night. I slipped a cold little hand into Dad's warm palm, and we stood quiet for a while watching the darkness deepen and listening to the river, and after a while a star came out.

⌣·CHAPTER FOURTEEN·⌣

W HEN we finally got off the ferry we rested the team for a day, then we started west again.

Lily and I, snug in our nest behind the wagon seat, saw very little of the prairie. The wagon cover hid three sides, and Mother and Dad pretty well obscured our forward view. Sometimes I stood up and looked between the horses' ears, but the trail was so rough, and the wagon bumped so much, that I soon fell down again. Now and then I caught a glimpse of trees, but I had no idea what the country was really like.

Even at night we couldn't see much. Dad, anxious to find good land, didn't stop until the sun was low and the shadows long, and by that time both Lily and I were worn out by the long day of jolting, and could hardly keep our eyes open long enough to eat our bannock.

Although I couldn't see much, however, I could hear Dad's voice. Before we crossed the river he had sounded anxious, and sometimes really worried. Now, however, he became quite happy again. 'Look at that grass,' he said, and a little later: 'See them trees? I do believe, Sarah, this is about it.'

'The land may not be as good as it looks.' Mother didn't sound as pleased as Dad.

One afternoon Dad got off the wagon and looked at some dirt a gopher had dug up, then he got the spade and dug a little hole. 'It's even better than it looks,' he said happily. 'There's no end to it. I never saw such rich earth, and without any manure at all.'

'But there's nothing but land,' Mother objected. 'No houses, not even a tent.'

'We'll go a bit farther.' Dad climbed to the green wagon seat and we jogged on.

The trail dwindled until it was only two wagon tracks, and after a while Dad turned the team and we made our own trail around sloughs and bushes and little hills. The day was warm, and the wind sweet with the smell of young leaves and waking earth, and I found sitting behind the wagon seat unbearable. I stood up and exclaimed at the yellow flowers growing everywhere, and at the blue-and-yellow butterflies that fluttered over them. I wanted to get down and chase the butterflies and pick the flowers, and I urged Dad to stop. Dad, however, said we hadn't come to our farm yet. When we did I could pick all the flowers I wanted.

I hadn't seen a sign of a farm since we left the Dukhobor village, but if Dad said there was a farm out here there must be one, and I looked eagerly for it. 'Is that it behind that bush?' I asked, pointing to a small grove of poplars edged with willows and chokecherry just coming into leaf.

'We'll see,' Dad said, and shook the reins. But when we rounded the little grove there was no sign of a farm: no barn, no house, nothing but a stretch of flower-covered prairie dotted with clumps of willows, and gay with swarms of butterflies fluttering lazily in the warm sun.

Dad, however, seemed very pleased with the flower-strewn grass and the gentle roll of the prairie. He stopped the team and let the reins fall slack, and while the horses lowered their heads and cropped the new grass he leaned forward and looked eagerly in every direction. The warm spring sunlight warmed his thin face and was reflected in his happy eyes. 'What do you think of this, Sarah?' he asked, in a voice that throbbed with excitement.

'If it suits you it suits me,' Mother said, but her voice sounded thin, and her blue eyes were disappointed. 'It isn't a bit like Littletown, is it?' she asked.

'It's a lot better.' Dad slipped off the wagon bench and got out the shovel, and dug another little hole. 'Such soil!' he exulted, his eyes shining. 'Black loam as far as you can dig. This land will grow anything. There must be plenty of moisture, too, or there wouldn't be all them trees, and this thick grass.'

'Do you want so many trees?' Mother asked. 'I thought you wanted big fields.'

'The fields will be big enough,' Dad said happily. 'We can break forty acres right here before we grub out a single willow. I tell you, Sarah, we couldn't have found a better spot. There's water handy, too. From the noise them ducks are making there must be a slough beyond that rise. And did you ever smell such air? Not a bit of smoke or soot in it.'

'I could stand a bit of soot if a sink went with it,' Mother said.

'A sink!' Dad said, his face glowing. 'In three or four years you'll have more sinks than you know what to do with. With this land we'll be rich in no time, and I'll build you a house with a sink in every room.'

'Four years!' Mother's morning-glory eyes went bleak, as if a sudden frost had touched them. 'You said we'd only be here a year, or two at the most. You even promised your mother.'

'Sally,' Dad said happily, 'in a year you'll like Canada so well wild horses won't be able to drag you away from it. You'll have forgotten all about England.'

'Oh, no, I won't,' Mother said firmly. 'And I shall always want to go back.'

╰·CHAPTER FIFTEEN·╯

WHILE Mother and Dad pitched the tent and unloaded the wagon, Lily and I picked the yellow buffalo beans. I was supposed to watch Jack, but the flowers enchanted me. There were millions of them. They were like small sweet peas, and ten or twelve blossoms grew in a cluster at the top of the slender green stems. Shoulder to shoulder they were a yellow carpet over the prairie. They grew right up to the feet of the willows and poplars, and they hid the grass on the hills. I had never seen such profusion. The buttercups and daisies in the meadows at Castle Hill were a thin sprinkle compared to these flowers. I carried Jack out of the way of the team and the tent, sat him down among the flowers, and picked until my arms were full.

'You couldn't pick flowers like that in England,' Dad said. 'You'd have a gardener after you. This is a wonderful country and no mistake.'

'It looks nice now.' Mother glanced from the shining yellow prairie to the mass of flowers that filled her white enamel bowls. 'But flowers fade, and anyway you can't eat them.'

'No, but with land like this we'll soon grow a lot of things we can eat,' Dad said. 'Just imagine! A hundred and sixty acres, and it's all ours.'

Mother looked at the wide sweep of land around us and sighed. 'It's so big it frightens me,' she said. 'I could do with a hedge here and there, and walls dividing the fields the way it is in England. But all this land without even a cart-track! It's that lonely.'

'There'll be plenty of roads soon, and people, too. Land like this won't be vacant long.' Dad untied the horses, and holding a halter rope in each hand he led them to the nearby slough to drink. Between the big dark animals he looked very short and thin, but there was pride in his square shoulders, and exultation in his feet.

Mother, always neat, put the tent in order. She hung a clean towel on a nail driven into the tent-pole, put the iron kettle on the back of the stove, and set the box that held the pans behind the stove out of the way, then she began to slice bacon for supper.

The bacon had been in the supply box ever since we left Battleford. It was greasy and not too fresh, but it was all the meat we had, and

Mother said we couldn't afford to turn our noses up at it. She boiled it before she fried it, which freshened it considerably and took out a lot of the salt, but it still tasted queer, especially at the edges.

'We won't have to live on that much longer,' Dad said when he came back from the slough, his lean face one big smile. 'The water in that slough is black with ducks. We're going to eat like kings.' He ate his supper quickly and got out the old muzzle-loader.

Loading the gun was always exciting. A piece of rag had to be pushed through the barrel to make sure it was clean, then the charge was put in. It was a series of powder, paper, and pellets, then more paper, and everything tamped down carefully with the ramrod. A cap on the firing pin came last of all, then, except for cocking the big, gracefully curved trigger, the gun was ready. I always managed to help with the loading, though Mother said the gun was dangerous, and one of these days I should be killed.

I wanted to go with Dad to the slough, but he said I might frighten the ducks and hurried off alone. In a few minutes we heard a shot, then a loud, excited quacking, and a cloud of disturbed ducks flew over the little hill by the slough. 'Oh, he missed,' I cried as I watched the ducks stream away on quick, stiff wings. 'He missed, and they've all gone.'

Mother said nobody could help missing with that old gun, and went on washing the supper dishes, but every few minutes she paused and looked anxiously in the direction of the slough. 'I wonder what's keeping him,' she said at last. 'If he didn't get a duck he ought to come home.'

After a while Dad came slowly over the hill, and Lily and I ran to meet him. He was soaking wet, but he carried two big ducks. 'I had to wade after them,' he told Mother when we got home, 'and it was deeper than I thought, but aren't they beauties!'

Mother said one of them looked a bit small to her, and after this she hoped Dad would look where he was going when he waded for ducks. He could catch his death of cold getting so wet.

We had wild duck for dinner next day. It was the first fresh meat we had eaten in a long time, and it was delicious. 'What did I tell you?' Dad asked when the meal was over. 'I said there'd be all the free meat you could eat, but you wouldn't believe me.'

'When are we going to get to our farm?' I asked, still chewing a bone. 'And will there be a swing in the hayloft?'

'This is our farm,' Dad said. 'And pretty soon you'll have a swing that will take you to the moon and back.'

'This isn't a farm.' I stopped sucking the bone. 'There isn't a mistle, or even a house.'

'We'll build a house,' Dad said cheerily. I thought for a moment he was teasing me, but his thin face, though happy, was serious.

Live here! I was terribly disappointed, and tears came to my eyes. I had expected our farm, when we found it, to be like the farm in England: complete with a house, and mistle, and cows, and a swing if I was lucky. I had been looking forward to such a farm for a long time: on the ship, on the train, while we were toiling up the trail. Every hardship—the dirty train and the crowded bed, the cold days in the tent, the nights when the tent had threatened to fall down, even the tricks of the contrary Old Cow—had been tempered by the thought that when we found our farm everything would be fine, and we would be safe and comfortable again. There would be real beds to sleep in, a real fire-place to sit beside, a real rocking-chair to rock in. Instead of all these things there was nothing. Only the tent and the team and the prairie, no house at all. Suddenly I felt very lonely, and an emptiness that had nothing to do with hunger contracted my stomach. For the first time since leaving England I longed for Aunt Jane and Grandmother, and the little house by the Spen. The wide expanse of buffalo beans, the flitting blue-and-yellow butterflies, the tall poplars, and the stubby willows blurred before my unhappy eyes, and became a mixture of sickly green and yellow. 'There—there isn't even a house,' I said, and bit my lip to stop its shivering.

'No, but there will be soon, and a barn, too. We'll build them ourselves. You'll see,' Dad promised.

'When?' I asked.

'As soon as we find the corner stake.'

I wanted to go and look for the corner stake right away, but other things had to be done first. Mother wanted to open the bales containing our extra clothes and blankets. She thought they might be damp, and this was a good time to air them. Then a hole had to be dug at the edge of the slough for seepage water. Slough water wasn't good for the horses, it sometimes gave them swamp fever. Seepage water still tasted of grass and willows, but it wasn't as strong as the regular slough water, and the colour was pale amber instead of dark brown. A few wrigglers lived in it, and we still had to boil it before we could drink it. So Dad opened the bales, and dug a seepage hole about three feet deep, then one afternoon he and I went to find the corner stake, and locate the boundaries of our land.

It was one of those lovely days that often come after a late spring. The sky was a clear, tender blue, and the wind that wandered over the prairie was warm, and sweet with the smell of new leaves, sap, sticky catkins, young grass, slough water, and flowers. Together Dad and I walked through the yellow buffalo beans, pausing often to look at the rich soil the gophers had thrown up when they dug their holes, and to smell the warm sweetness of the wind.

We soon discovered that buffalo beans were not the only flowers growing on the prairie. In the shade of the poplars dark blue violets poked shy heads over their big heart-shaped green leaves, and a little deeper in the woods tall white violets lifted sweet pale faces. There were tender fern fronds half uncurled, and a rank tangle of young pea-vine. The warm air that hovered over these growing things was unbelievably fragrant. It was a pool of perfume, and Dad and I stopped and breathed deeply of it. But sweet and fresh as the air was there was a slight undertang in it: a trace of decaying leaves, a hint of frost and fall that seemed to urge us to hurry.

Dad looked at the rank-growing things and the dark rich earth and smiled. 'This is a wonderful country, Mary,' he said. 'We're lucky to have found it.'

I agreed with him. The sunshine was warm, my home-sickness had passed, and I skipped along through the grass and flowers, my hands full of violets, and my mouth full of questions. When were we going to find the corner stake? What would it look like? How big would it be, and what colour?

Dad said when we found the stake we'd know all about it. We walked back and forth across the prairie looking for something that even Dad wasn't sure would be there. At last when my short legs were getting tired we stumbled over it. Was I ever disappointed!

I had expected something large and important, at least as tall as I was, with red and white strips on it. The stake we found was only about a foot long, an inch square, and being of iron it was dark coloured. A very poor thing, I thought, and not worth half the trouble we had taken to find it.

Dad, however, thought the stake very important. He knelt down and looked at it from every angle, then he examined the little mound of earth in which it stood. There were some figures on the stake, and Dad found a pencil and paper and copied them carefully. Then he told me how lucky we were to find it. Surveyors, he said, had planted stakes in the middle of every section, but Indians had taken a great many of them away. I didn't know what surveyors were, and somehow I got the idea that the stake had grown right out of the little mound. Dad stood by the stake for a long time, then he walked away and came back. 'I think our quarter's the best of the lot,' he said at last. He told me the stake marked the middle of a section and our quarter was the south-west corner of section 14, range 25, township 49. I repeated it after him, and he told me to try to remember it. The stake we left where it was, but Dad told me to take a good look at it, I might never see another. I never did, and I am glad Dad impressed that one on my memory.

When we got back to the tent Dad told Mother about the stake and the numbers on it. 'Now you know just where you are, Sarah,' he said gaily. 'If you ever get lost all you have to do is remember them figures, and anybody can tell you how to get home.'

'Anybody!' Mother exclaimed. 'You know right well, Walter Pinder, that there isn't anybody but us in the whole of this wilderness.'

'There'll soon be plenty of folks,' Dad said cheerfully. 'Land like this won't be vacant long.' He untied the cow and took her to the slough to drink. As usual she tried to get away. She tossed her head and broke into a sudden trot when she thought Dad wasn't watching, then she swished her tail and did her best to get her rope tangled in the willows. 'She's a witch of a cow,' Dad said when she was safely staked again. 'She drank and was off so fast I near fell into the slough.'

'She's of a piece with the rest of this fearful country,' Mother said gloomily.

CHAPTER SIXTEEN

THE country, however, wasn't the least bit disagreeable at that time. The sun smiled, and the breeze was sweet with the fresh, clean smell of flowers and leaves. The ducks continued to float on the slough, and prairie chickens poked their long necks out of the thick grass.

Prairie chickens, we soon discovered, were much better eating than the ducks were. Their flesh was dark and their legs were full of tendons, but their breasts were thick and juicy, especially when rolled in flour and fried in bacon grease. 'Fit for a king, aren't they?' Dad said. 'You never had a meal like this in England.'

Mother admitted that the prairie chickens were good, but she still longed for a woman to talk to.

'There'll be all the women you want soon,' Dad promised, and sure enough a day or two later a couple of round white tents appeared on a little hill to the west of us. A grove hid them from us, and Dad saw the new tents for the first time when he watered the cow one evening.

He was almost too excited to tether the cow. 'There's tents on the hill just behind the bush,' he called. 'Let's go and see who it is.'

He harnessed the team, and Mother washed our faces and changed our pinafores, and away we went to see the newcomers. They turned out to be a newly married couple, Frank and Ellen Metherell, from London, and Bill, a boy of about eighteen, also from London.

I never knew Bill's last name. He was a quiet boy with big brown eyes, a nervous nose, and arms and legs that didn't quite fit, or had not been put on properly. They dangled a little, and often his feet seemed to get in his way, and his hands had a tendency to drop things. He didn't talk much, and he usually stayed close to Mr Metherell when they were out together.

Mr Metherell was only a few years older than Bill, but he looked as reliable as a tree. He was tall and strong, with straight black hair and friendly brown eyes. He was seldom angry, and he never hurried, but his long stride covered a lot of ground. He looked like a man not easily blown over.

Ellen Metherell was almost as tall as her husband, and in some ways as easy-going as he was. She had no hard and fast rules for doing things. She washed when the day was fair, and swept the tent when she felt like sweeping. She was not really a pretty woman. Her face was a little too long and thin, and her chin too narrow, for beauty, but she had ears as small and dainty as the star flowers that grew in the woods, and her eyes were as clear and green as fresh young leaves. Her figure, too, was perfect. Her clothes, of course, covered her from head to heel, but smothering as the styles were in those days they could not completely hide her lovely flowing lines. Especially the line of her back. She had one fitted dress that was especially becoming. When she wore it I know I stared at her outrageously, but I couldn't help it. Years later when I saw the Venus de Milo, serene and alone under her dome at the Louvre, something about her seemed familiar. I looked at her for a while, then I remembered: Mrs Metherell's back had once had the same grace.

Mrs Metherell's manner was as charming as her back, and she was one of the most generous people I ever knew, but the very nicest thing about her, in my opinion, was her gift for gathering news. She often said if she hadn't met her husband she would have become a nurse, and she was very good at removing slivers. Once she even performed a minor operation. Mr Claxton, another neighbour, gouged his hand with a chisel, and the cut refused to heal until Mrs Metherell straightened the skin flap. But it was as a reporter that Mrs Metherell really excelled. She could smell an approaching scandal the way some people can sense an approaching storm.

She wasn't the least bit selfish with her talent, either. She shared her news generously, and she made every item interesting. It wasn't what she told, but the way she told it. She could make a black eye seem more interesting than a murder.

Even tiny items gained in importance when Mrs Metherell told about them. A certain glance of her green eyes, and a tone in her voice, could make a conversation between a single man and a married woman—all women were married then—seem deliciously mysterious and wicked. Not that she was malicious, she wasn't. She told only the facts. But how interesting she could make them!

I'm ashamed to admit that when Mrs Metherell came Lily and I tried to make ourselves invisible. We played quietly and talked only in whispers, hoping we wouldn't be noticed until the most interesting part of her news was told. Usually, of course, we heard about most of the local goings-on—there isn't much privacy in a tent—but Mrs Metherell's version of a barked shin was far more interesting than anybody else's.

Mother always worried after one of Mrs Metherell's visits, even though she enjoyed them. Had she said anything she wouldn't want repeating, she wondered? Had Mrs Metherell noticed that her towels, washed in brown slough water, were turning dark? And why did Lily and I keep hovering about when she had company? Mrs Metherell would think we had no manners at all.

Mother, of course, wasn't the only one who worried about what Mrs Metherell might say. Even the men had a healthy regard for her ability to sense news, and it was good for them in more ways than one.

Without Mrs Metherell, or someone like her, life in those days would have been dull. There was almost nothing to read: most of our books had been left in England. The mail came only at long, irregular intervals; there was no school, no church, no shops, and no parties. The goings and comings of their neighbours were all the settlers had to take their minds off their loneliness, the distance to the doctor, and what might happen if the baby had croup. It was greatly to Mrs Metherell's credit that she could make small events seem important and interesting enough to be worth thinking about and discussing.

Besides providing entertainment, Mrs Metherell's news sense kept us law-conscious. Not that we were lawless people, we weren't, but with civilization so far away, and the visits of the Mounted Police rare, a slight relaxing of morals would have been only natural, especially if such lapses could have been kept under cover.

With Mrs Metherell about, however, nothing could be safely hidden, or even camouflaged. She knew the difference between a black mark made by a flying chip and a black mark made by a fist, and which bumps were natural and which weren't. She knew which bachelor went where, and exactly how long he stayed, who gave Mrs Johnson a ride, and how far they rode, and who threatened whom with the axe. She was a stimulating and exciting person, and we would have been lost without her.

The Metherells and Bill greeted us warmly, and Mrs Metherell made tea. They had arrived that morning, and they didn't know anyone else was about until we rounded the grove that hid their tent from ours. The men were as enthusiastic about the land as Dad was, and Mrs Metherell was enough of a backslider in Mother's eyes to say she thought it was a bit of all right, too.

We visited with the Metherells until the sun went down, then we drove home slowly through the gathering blue shadows.

Next day Dad went to look at the far side of our land, and came back full of excitement. There was a tent pitched on the quarter section to the east of us. 'What did I tell you?' he exulted. 'You'll have neighbours everywhere in no time.'

'I hope they have children,' Mother said as she pushed Jack into a clean dress.

We drove to the new tent full of anticipation. Surely these people would have at least one child. I wondered what she would look like, for of course she would be a girl about my age, and what her name would be. I favoured Nancy, but Lily thought Flora would be better. We almost had a scrap about it.

The newcomers, however, didn't even have a wife, but they were old friends. They were the two young men who had helped us when we were stuck in the mud and snow.

Mother and Dad were delighted to see them again, and there was much handshaking and a lot of talk, but Lily and I were disappointed. We hadn't seen any other children for a long time. The prairie, we were beginning to think, was populated only by old people.

Dad asked the newcomers what they thought of the land, and if they were going to stay.

Charlie Maule, the tall man with the merry eyes and tight-curled hair, said: 'Darned right we are going to stay.' He'd had enough of four walls and fog. Then he told us that in London he'd been a barber, and at least part of his work had been in a hospital.

Mother thought barbering a good trade, but Mr Maule said it was awful, and there was no future in it. All you could look forward to was one ragged head after another, and a lot of cranky customers who thought they knew more about cutting hair than you did. And after a while you got fallen arches and bunions. 'So I said the hell with it,' he said cheerfully, 'and came to Canada.'

Dad asked if he'd ever done any farming, or lived in the country.

'Not half I haven't,' Mr Maule chuckled. 'I've been out to Hampstead Heath half a dozen times.' Then he admitted he didn't know a ploughshare from a coulter, but at least half the Barr Colony didn't, either. 'But what does it matter?' he asked in a voice as robust as a spring wind. 'This land hardly needs ploughing. Any blighter with half a brain could grow things here. Just look at the way the wild things grow.' He waved a big hand at the yellow buffalo beans, then, his bright eyes flashing, he told us of the crops he hoped to grow, and the house he intended to build. His ideas were wonderful, and his way of expressing them unusual, and Mother and Dad talked more and laughed louder than they had for a long time. Later, when we were on our way home, they decided that Mr Maule might be a bit of a talker, but he was a rare good tonic.

The other young man, unlike Mr Maule, was so quiet we didn't even know his real name for some time. Mr Maule called him Willie, and so did I until Mother told me it wasn't proper for a little girl to call a man by his first name, and I had better call him Master Willie until we knew what his last name was. We discovered eventually that his full name was Walter Calvin Gardiner, but by that time we had become accustomed to calling him Master Willie.

Although Mr Maule did most of the talking you didn't forget that Master Willie was there. His few words, spoken slowly and in a deep voice, were to the point and worth listening to. He had steady dark eyes and a friendly smile, and was seldom excited. He wasn't as enthusiastic about Canada as Mr Maule was, but he thought something could be made of it.

'Looks like we have some fine neighbours,' Dad said as we jogged home through the soft blue dusk. 'I told you we wouldn't be by ourselves for long. We got here just in time. Another couple of weeks, and the best land will be gone.'

Mother said the prairie still seemed awfully empty to her, and it would be years before there was somebody living next door the way they did in England.

Although there was still a lot of vacant land, the good land went fast that summer. New settlers came almost every day. We didn't see them immediately, of course, the hills and groves and the distance hid their tents, but we heard of them, and as soon as they got their bearings most of them went visiting to see what their new neighbours were like.

Much to Mother's disappointment most of the settlers were bachelors. Alf Schoffom homestead the quarter section to the north of us, and two other young men, Jack Price and Lord Arthur, found land about two miles west.

Lord Arthur wasn't a real lord, but somebody gave him the nickname. He was a small, dapper man with a little dark moustache, and hands as soft and smooth as the hands of a woman. He always wore well-tailored clothes, and his brown eyes were always anxious.

Jack Price also wore well-made clothes. He was tall and lean, with dark hair and eyes and a quick, pleasant smile. He had spent some time in Australia, and told interesting stories of that strange land. He also played the accordion, and sang droll songs, and everybody was always glad to see him.

Gordon Watson was another young bachelor. He had been in the Boer War in South Africa, and sometimes told hair-raising tales about it. Jovial and good-natured, and full of vigour, he swaggered when he walked, and his laugh was a rumble deep in his broad chest. He always wore riding-breeches and brown leather leggings, and rode a brown horse. To me he was a fascinating figure, and for years I thought he had fought the Boer War all by himself.

There were also several other young men, among them Mr Whitely, Mr Ducker, and Mr Bromly. They seemed to be going one way or another all the time, and often paused at our tent and talked to Dad. I tried to talk to them, too, but most of them treated me as a pest about one degree worse than the mosquitoes.

Besides Mother and Mrs Metherell, Mrs Johnson was the only other woman anywhere near us. Her husband had brought her and their three children, two girls and a boy, to their land, then, after pitching their tent, he had gone off to earn extra money for the winter.

As soon as Mr Johnson left Mrs Johnson went to visit her neighbours. We were always glad to see her, though we were a little sorry for her children—Dora, the eldest, was only about eight—left at home alone. Mrs Johnson, however, said they were quite safe. Mr Barr himself had said there were no dangerous animals, and anyway she was always home at night. In no time at all, of course, Mrs Johnson knew everybody within a distance of ten miles.

She was also quite a talker, and a visit from her was an event, but she hadn't Mrs Metherell's knack of making small events startling.

Besides her other assets Mrs Johnson also had a pleasant singing voice, and a way of strutting when she sang that somehow gave the song more meaning than there was in the words. This trick made Mrs Metherell certain that Mrs Johnson had once been on the stage, but the stage being considered slightly indecent in those days Mrs Johnson never admitted it. So although Mrs Johnson wasn't exactly an ideal neighbour she was fun, and everybody enjoyed her accounts of the walks she took, and the deer and elk she saw.

She was not, of course, the only one who wandered over the prairie. Everybody seemed to be going one way or another, simply because they enjoyed their new freedom. The Barr colonists were not the grim, conquering type of pioneer. They were neither big nor raw-boned, and they didn't carry rifles or even shot-guns. They were anxious to find land, but having found it they were in no hurry to plough it.

Like Dad a few of the settlers had been farmers in England working for themselves, but most of them had worked for somebody else. They had stood long hours behind dry-goods counters in London, in fish shops in Blackpool, in hot cotton and woollen mills in Yorkshire and Lancashire. They had kept books in small, ill-lighted rooms, toiled in blacksmiths' shops, and swung picks in dark coal-mines near Leeds. They had been slaves to clocks and whistles all their lives. Now they were free.

And how they enjoyed their freedom! They slept late if they felt like sleeping. They hunted the ducks, prairie chickens, and rabbits. They explored the Big Gully, a huge slash in the prairie two or three miles to the north. They bathed in the sloughs, and swam in the lakes at the bottom of the Big Gully. But most of all they visited, especially the bachelors. They went to each other's tents and sat in the sun, laughing and talking, and telling each other what a wonderful country Canada was, and how much land they were going to break next year. Life for a while was a continuous picnic.

The weather also was in a holiday mood. Spring had been cold and late, but summer made up for it. Fresh flowers bloomed every morning. Before the buffalo beans wilted the chook-cherries came out. They were shrubs something like lilacs, and they grew everywhere; around the groves, on the hillsides, and in the hollows. The blossoms were in thick clusters, and the bushes were white with bloom. 'The prairie looks ready for a wedding,' Mother said.

Besides the chook-cherries there were also the white flowers of the Saskatoons, and the strawberries, and a host of other flowers whose names we didn't know. The air was so sweet with their perfume that the butterflies seemed a little drunk.

Before the chook-cherries withered the wild roses bloomed. We hadn't noticed the rose-bushes growing, the chook-cherries were so thick, but suddenly there were roses everywhere. Their dainty, five-petalled pink faces smiled from every bush and grove, and the air was heavy with their fragrance. 'Did you ever see such flowers?' Mrs Metherell asked, and pinned some in her dark hair.

As if the flowers were not beauty enough swarms of butterflies also appeared. The little blue-and-yellow ones were everywhere, and big black-and-orange monarchs also came. They sat on the backs of the horses, on the rim of the dishpan, on the stove if it happened to be cold, and on our hands if we kept still for a few seconds. Once when Mother emptied some wash water they covered the damp spot like a carpet. The huge black-and-yehow swallowtails were more timid and stayed in the trees, but there were numbers of them.

Dragonflies were almost as numerous as the butterflies. Their slender bodies, often three inches long, were like blue, iridescent jewels supported by gossamer wings. They hovered over the sloughs and the flowers, and skimmed around the tent, darting about like blue arrows in the sunshine.

Birds, of course, were everywhere. Meadow-larks warbled in the grass, blackbirds babbled in the willows, hawks soared overhead on wide, still wings, and tiny wrens and chickadees twittered in the trees and willows. There were also black-and-white woodpeckers, polished crows, brown-ruffed grouse, and quiet birds that we called mosquito hawks that skimmed through the blue twilight.

To people who had spent most of their lives in soot and fog, or shut in mines and shops, and crowded in narrow streets where the houses stood one against another, the flowers, birds, and sunshine of the prairie seemed like a preview of paradise. Most of us had enough flour for bannock, fuel was free, there was no rent, and meat could be had for the shooting. What more could anybody want?

The old-timers, people who had been with the Hudson's Bay Company, or had drifted west to ranch a few years before, warned that the good weather wouldn't last. They said there would be storms, and in a few short months frost and snow and bitter cold. Nobody, however, paid any attention to the warning. The old-timers had told us tall tales before. These yarns about fifty below zero, and snow so thick you couldn't see a foot in front of you, were probably just more of the same thought up to frighten us. Freeze your nose in fifteen minutes? Ridiculous! England was farther north than we were. As for the Gulf Stream, it couldn't possibly make all that difference. So the settlers spent long lazy days enjoying the fresh, sweet air, laughing and talking and visiting each other. The picnic, however, didn't last long. In a very short time the mosquitoes came.

We had heard about the mosquitoes, but we thought they were just another tale. Nothing could be as bad as they were supposed to be. They weren't, they were much worse.

The mosquito larvae, we had been told, grew in the sloughs as wrigglers, then they hatched and flew. They must all have hatched at once, for suddenly there were millions of them, and every last one was ravenous.

They swarmed about us in clouds, buzzing and hungry. In the day-time they were not unbearable, but at night or before rain they were terrible. Fortunately they were allergic to smoke, so we built smudges every night: one for the horses and the cow, another near the tent door for ourselves. The smoke reddened our eyes and made us cough, and Mother said she didn't know which was worse, the smoke or the mosquitoes.

We were soon a mass of itching lumps because of the mosquito bites. Lily, Jack, and I scratched the itching spots, we couldn't help it, and soon we were covered with small sores. Mother bathed the bites with soda solution, but it didn't help much, we soon had a lot of new bites. Mrs Metherell had us all green with envy: the mosquitoes didn't like her at all.

Dad, who had never used tobacco, decided to start smoking in self-defence. He hadn't a pipe, but someone loaned him one, and a filling or two of tobacco, and he lit up. He didn't smoke long. In about ten minutes he turned a queer green, and I thought he was going to die. Mother helped him to bed, and he felt better next morning. Smoking, he said, was only a matter of getting used to the taste of tobacco. Another try or two, and he'd be making so much smoke the mosquitoes wouldn't bother him.

He lit up again that evening, but he turned green sooner than he had the night before. He was so dizzy he could barely walk from the wagon to the tent, and he swayed from side to side like a tree in the wind. He lay down on the bed and Mother put a wet cloth on his forehead. 'You just aren't a smoker,' she told him. Dad groaned and agreed with her, and next day he returned the pipe and what was left of the tobacco.

The mosquitoes didn't put a stop to the visiting, but they did manage to curtail it considerably, especially in the evenings. Walking a mile or two with a humming cloud of ravenous insects around one's head was almost torture. Some of the men tried it, but even with a branch to beat with it was impossible to keep the mosquitoes from biting. They attacked from every side, and their barbed probes could even penetrate clothing.

The horses and the cow suffered as much as we did. Without a smudge they would have spent the nights walking through the brush in an effort to scrape their tormentors off, and even a thick smoke wasn't complete protection.

To circumvent the mosquitoes as much as they could the settlers tried to be at home, with their own smudges going, before the sun went down and the mosquitoes got up.

CHAPTER SEVENTEEN

D AD enjoyed visiting as much as anyone, but he did not do as much of it as most. He was anxious to break some land and plant potatoes so that we would have something to eat besides beans and bread in winter.

Between visits, and while the horses rested after their long trip up the trail, he assembled the plough, and one morning, soon after the mosquitoes came, he decided it was time to break the first furrow.

He looked the land over carefully and decided to plough a ten-acre patch not far from the tent. No trees or willows grew on it and he thought the work would be easy.

Furrows in England had always been straight, and Dad wanted the first furrow on the new farm to be perfect. He set up a line of stakes, sighting them carefully, and moving one or two that seemed a little out of line, then he hitched Darkie and Nelly, our two horses, to the plough.

Dad had often ploughed in England, but the earth there had been tilled for generations and turned easily. The new, unturned prairie sod resisted the ploughshare with root and stone.

Dad tugged the heavy plough into place at what he hoped would be the beginning of the furrow, then he tied the reins and slung them over his shoulder. Next he tilted the plough a little so that the bright share would bite into the earth, and told the horses to get up.

The horses went forward for about a dozen steps, then they swayed and stopped.

Dad jiggled the plough handles, shook the reins, and urged the team on again. They threw their shoulders into their collars, but they couldn't seem to move the plough. The sod was matted with the roots of grass, buffalo beans, late roses, and many other things, and breaking it as deep as Dad thought it ought to be broken was too hard for one team. Dad, however, didn't realize how tough the sod was, and thought Darkie and Nelly knew nothing about ploughing. He told me to get a stick and keep them going.

I did as I was told, and the horses made a little progress, but they didn't go straight as Dad thought they should. They wavered from side to side, and the furrow, instead of being straight, was a frightful zigzag. It went first east, then west, and in one spot it was almost a half-circle. 'A fine farmer they'll think me,' Dad fumed, and called to Mother to come and guide the team while he held the plough.

Mother had come to see the first furrow turned, but she knew nothing about ploughing, or even driving the team. She was, however, willing to help. She put Jack in the grass and told Lily to watch him, then she took the reins. Dad heaved the plough into position again, showed Mother the stake she was supposed to make the team head for, and ordered the team to get going.

I ran forward as instructed, and slapped the horses with my switch, and the willing animals tried again, but they wavered as badly as ever, and the plough was jerked first one way, then the other.

'Go right,' Dad shouted, and the team swerved sharply. 'No, no,' Dad yelled, 'that's too much. Go left.'

Mother tugged at the reins and the team turned, and Dad shouted again. 'Not so much, not so much. You're going in a circle. Hit for that stake.'

Mother tried hard. Her round face got pink with sweat and excitement, and the hairpins came out of her neat bun of hair. She told me not to frighten the horses so, and shook the reins and waved her arms, but the horses still reeled from side to side.

'Can't you even drive a team straight?' Dad snapped, and glared at her.

'No, I can't.' Mother's face was red by now, and she glared back at Dad. 'And I never had to before I married you. If I'd only had sense and married Edmond Bastow—here, you drive if you think you're so smart, and I'll hold the plough. You always did take the easiest job if you could.' She tossed the reins to Dad and took hold of the plough handles.

Dad said she wasn't strong enough to hold the plough, but Mother said she was as strong as he was if not stronger, and for him to go ahead and drive if he thought it was so easy.

'Well, have it your own way,' Dad said, and took the reins. 'Hold hard,' he warned. 'The plough jumps.'

Mother told him to mind his own business and tend to his driving, she could plough as well as he could.

Dad looked doubtful, but he shook the reins and told the horses to get up.

The horses were tired by that time, and they jumped nervously. The plough jumped too, and since Mother wasn't holding firmly it tipped over, pulling her with it. She was up before Dad had time to help her. 'You did that on purpose,' she said, her blue eyes flashing. 'I allus knew I made a mistake when I married you.' Then she picked up Jack, said she wished she'd never heard of Canada, or Dad either, and went to the tent. Lily followed her.

Dad sighed, rested the team a while, then gave me the reins. 'Now all you have to do is head for that first stake,' he said.

'All right.' I felt very big and important, and with the courage of ignorance I shook the reins and ordered the team to get up in a loud voice.

They were certainly good-natured animals. They put their shoulders into it and really pulled, but being more tired than ever they seesawed a lot.

Dad, also tired and excited, shouted at me and at the team, and in a few minutes I didn't know which rein I was pulling on, or where the stakes were. We ploughed a short furrow of sorts, but it was more crooked than any corkscrew, and the sod stood in humps.

Dad wasn't a bit pleased with the furrow, and shouted at me to go first right, then left. I tried hard, and so did the sweating team, but the plough wouldn't co-operate. At last, as if it, too, was tired of the struggle, its nose struck a stone and the handles flew high in the air, hitting Dad a smart blow on the jaw and, to use his expression, knocking him spinning into the middle of next week.

I was terribly frightened. The horses stopped, but the plough was on its side and Dad was sprawled on the grass. He looked as limp as a just-shot duck. His hands and feet drooped, and there was no strength in his neck. Panic prickled my knees, then a scream gathered inside me. But before the scream got to my throat Dad stirred and sat up. He looked around as if he didn't know where he was, then he shook his head and felt his jaw. 'Are you better?' I asked.

Dad nodded slowly, and in a little while he got up, took the reins, and turned the team towards the tent.

Mother was upset when she saw Dad's bruised and swollen jaw, but under her concern there was a noticeable trace of satisfaction. 'I told you this prairie was never meant to be ploughed,' she said as she put hot cloths on Dad's black-and-blue face. 'Even the Indians had more sense than to try it.'

'The Dukhobors ploughed it,' Dad mumbled.

'The Dukhobors are a lot bigger than we are.' Mother put water in the kettle and lit the fire. 'This country was never meant for little people like us.'

Dad, who still wore his cap, pulled it low over his eyes and said nothing.

Mother made tea, and Dad managed to swallow some, then he stood up and smiled a little with the side of his face that wasn't swollen. 'Come, lass,' he said to me in a queer, stiff voice, 'let's try again.'

'And let that plough kill you?' Mother asked. 'Isn't one accident enough?'

'If them Dukhobors can break this prairie so can I,' Dad said. 'Though I have heard tell the women do most of their ploughing.' And miserable as he must have felt there was a chuckle in his thick voice, and a twinkle in his good eye. The other was swollen shut.

'Well, if you brought me to this god-forsaken place to plough for you, you can send me right back to England, then you can have one of your Dukhobors,' Mother said, and, her pretty little figure stiff with indignation, she flounced into the tent.

Because he couldn't talk much Dad took my face between his hands and showed me where the stakes were, and told me to head for them.

I wanted to please him, of course, but I couldn't see what difference it made whether the furrow was crooked or not. There were no other furrows to bother about, and potatoes would grow just as well under a crooked furrow as they would under a straight one. Grown people, I decided, made a lot of fuss about things that didn't matter. But I shook the reins, chirruped to the team, and did my best to head for the stake.

The horses slewed from side to side just as they had before, and Dad, who was tired and in pain, lost his temper and said if I didn't do better he'd throw the plough at me.

I knew very well he couldn't even lift the plough, and being a little upset by that time I began to laugh. Dad looked startled for a minute, then he laughed, too, though his swollen face looked twisted, almost as if he were crying.

After a while Mother came to see how we were getting on. She told Dad he had done enough for one day and ought to give up, but Dad shook his head. He was going to have a straight furrow if it killed him. How long we would have worked if Dick Forest hadn't come I don't know. Perhaps till freeze-up.

Mr Forest was tall and broad, almost twice as big as Dad, and like most big people he had a calm voice and easy, effective movements that accomplished a great deal without any apparent difficulty. Unlike most of the settlers, who wore caps and rather tight trousers, he wore overalls without any creases, and a felt hat so out of shape it looked more like a sou'wester.

Finding no one at our tent Mr Forest came over to where we were trying to plough. 'How are you making out?' he asked in a voice that sounded as if it ought to have a beard.

'Not so well.' Dad looked at the twisting, humped furrow. 'Team doesn't seem to know much about ploughing. We can't get them to go straight.'

Mr Forest looked thoughtfully at the horses, then at the sod. 'Looks to me as if you're trying to plough a bit thick,' he said slowly.

Dad said the sod wasn't nearly as thick as the sod they turned in England. He thought it was a little thin if anything.

Mr Forest, however, said that breaking new land was much harder than turning land that had been ploughed before, and with only two horses you had to take it easy. Besides, this land was so rich there was no need to plough deep. 'What do you say we try it a bit thinner?' he asked.

Dad was quite willing, so Mr Forest reset the gauge wheel and clevis, glanced at Dad's stakes, that were still standing, draped the reins over his wide shoulders, took the plough handles in his thick wide hands, and clucked softly to the team.

Darkie and Nelly lowered their heads and humped into their collars as if to say: 'Here we go again.' But after they had taken a step or two their backs straightened and their heads came up. Instead of lunging from side to side they walked sedately straight ahead. Even the sod behaved better. Instead of falling in humps and hills it curled off the mould-board in a smooth, moist black ribbon that laid flat on the ground.

'I can hardly believe it,' Dad said, looking at the neat, straight furrow.

'You had it a bit too deep and too wide, that's all.' Mr Forest came to the end of the furrow, tipped the plough neatly, turned the team, righted the plough, and started again. He ploughed three or four rounds without any trouble. Nelly followed the furrow as if she had been ploughing all her life, and Darkie walked sedately beside her.

One or two blackbirds had hovered in the background when we were trying to plough, but the noise we made kept them from hunting. Now they swooped on the newly turned earth, and ran swiftly on their three-toed feet, their bright, bead-like eyes alert for worms and grubs. To my surprise they didn't eat the worms they found. They held them, a wriggling fringe, until their beaks were full, then they flew off to the willows near the slough.

The sun was low by now, and the horses were tired and so was I, and very glad when Dad said he thought it was time to unhitch and have supper.

Although we had a guest we ate outside as usual, for our tent was full of boxes and bedding, and even the stove was outside near the door. We had no table, but even Lily had learned to balance her plate on her small lap, so we managed very well. Dad and Mr Forest sat on the green wagon seat, Mother sat on her little folding chair, and the rest of us sat on the warm grass, and did our best to mind our manners, and keep the fried prairie chicken, bread, jam, and stewed apple rings from skidding.

After supper when the smudges were going Mr Forest asked Dad if he had filed on our land yet. Dad said he hadn't, he thought there was plenty of time, and the filing could wait until he had some ploughing done, and potatoes planted.

Mr Forest, however, thought Dad ought to go to Lloydminster, a new town that had just come into existence, and file on at once. Good land was getting scarce, and even though we were living on our quarter section someone else could file a claim to it. He had just come from filing on his land, and the land office was very busy.

That night before they went to sleep Dad and Mother discussed the matter. Mother was sure there was plenty of time. Besides, why pay a filing fee when we were not sure we were going to stay? It would be money wasted.

Dad argued that the filing fee wasn't much, and if we decided at the end of the year that we liked Canada, we'd look pretty silly if we'd lost our land.

'But you can't plough the land, so what is there to stay for?' Mother asked.

Dad said of course he could plough. Now that the gauge wheel was set right he'd turn furrows as smooth as any Dick Forest turned, if not a little smoother.

'You know very well you can't,' Mother said sharply. 'You aren't anywhere near as big as he is, and it takes big people to best this place. We're only little folk. You were nearly killed to-day. There's no telling what might happen the next time the plough jumps. We could be back in England by fall. I'm sure Arthur will let you have the farm at Castle Hill.'

'I think we ought to stop a bit longer,' Dad said. 'We haven't really given Canada a chance yet. Ploughing's easy enough once you get the knack of it.'

'Well, if you're bent on killing yourself,' Mother said. 'But don't say I didn't warn you.'

Dad said he wouldn't, and went out to see how the smudge looked. I wondered unhappily how a dead person could say anything.

Next morning Dad was up so early the tent shadow was still long on the grass, and even the cow was asleep. He brought in the horses and put the harness on, and right after breakfast he hitched them to the plough. Sure enough he could plough just as well as Mr Forest could, and just as straight. 'What did I tell you, Sally?' he exulted, though his face was still swollen and stiff. 'Size means nowt. It's knack that counts.'

Since the land was ploughed Dad decided to plant the potatoes before he went to Lloydminster. We had only about a bushel left, and the temptation to eat them instead of saving them for seed was often more than we could bear. Dad, however, said if we ate the potatoes now we wouldn't have any for next winter, but if we planted them they would multiply, and we would have all the potatoes we needed.

Before planting, the potatoes had to be cut into pieces, leaving about two eyes in each piece. Cutting looked fascinating work, and I was sure I could do it. I coaxed until Dad finally gave me a knife, but I wasn't much help. I had to ask Dad about every cut to make sure it was right. Planting was more fun. We simply tucked pieces of potato under the sod about two feet apart. It was dirty work, but I enjoyed it.

As soon as the potatoes were planted Dad went to Lloydminster to file on our land.

Filing on, as it was called, did not mean that the land was ours. It merely gave us a priority. Before we really owned the land we had to build a house and barn, and plough about ten acres a year for three years. We also had to spend part of each year living on the homestead. At the end of three years, if all requirements had been met, we could prove up. This meant proving that all the requirements had been fulfilled. We then got the deed to the land, and it was ours to sell or keep as we pleased.

Claims could be jumped if the land was not lived on, or the required improvements were not completed in the specified time, but as far as I know no one ever jumped a claim. It was generally considered a low trick.

Dad was away about three days. When he came back he brought mail for everyone who lived near us, and some baking-powder and tea. Lily and I had hoped for candy, spice we called it, but Dad said there wasn't any. All the food had to be brought by wagon from Saskatoon, and there wasn't room for luxuries. 'But I did manage to get some mosquito-netting,' he said proudly, and unrolled several yards of green mesh.

Mother said she didn't know what to do with it, she'd never seen a mosquito-net, so Dad showed her how to make one. It looked like a large onion bag open at one end and gathered at the other. Mother made several, and we put them on over our hats, caps, and bonnets. They looked queer, but they were quite a help. Not that the mosquitoes were defeated, far from it. Their probing stingers could go right through cloth and stockings, but they much preferred uncovered flesh.

CHAPTER EIGHTEEN

OON after Dad returned from Lloydminster we had our first real storm. We had had rain and snow while we were coming up the trail, but the old-timers said they were mere sprinkles and dribbles. 'Just wait till a real one blows up,' they warned. 'And be sure your horses are well tied. If they break loose they'll run before the wind, and you may never see them again.'

Dad asked if such storms came often, and the old-timers admitted they didn't, but there was at least one humdinger every summer, and we had better be ready for it. 'When you see it coming see that your team's sheltered by a bush, and your tent-pegs are tight,' they told us.

We were at the Metherells' when our first storm gathered. It didn't look the least bit like a storm, it was simply a large puff of white cloud far down in the west. A few clouds at sunset were not unusual, but that one, though white and soft as whipped cream, did look rather dense, and when the sun went behind it the light rays did not filter through it. The fluffy edges of the cloud turned pink and gold, but the colours soon faded, and the cloud leaned against the darkening sky like a huge white-crested dark wave thrown up by some great wild ocean just below the horizon.

Dad glanced uneasily at the cloud as we drove the short distance to our tent. 'That lower part does look a bit dark,' he said, as we rounded the little grove that hid our tent from the Metherells'.

'Perhaps it's just darkness coming early,' Mother said. She didn't like storms. In England when the lightning flashed she had always darkened the bedroom and buried her face in a pillow.

Dad may or may not have liked storms, I never heard him say, but he always watched them, sitting in the open door from the first flash to the last, unless he happened to be in bed. Mother always said she didn't know how he did it, because once he was struck by lightning as he was wheeling the big milk can. The shock knocked him down, and he was unable to get up for at least an hour.

Dad glanced at the towering cloud as he unhitched and hobbled the horses. The wind, quite strong, was blowing into it, and he thought the cloud might veer north and follow the river about ten or twelve miles away, but just for the sake of safety he drove the tent-pegs, and the stake the cow was tied to, a little farther into the ground.

We sat near the smudge for a little while, but the uneasy waiting all about us was a little frightening. Instead of being blue and velvety as usual, the gathering night was tinged with green, and the leaves of the poplars, stirring in the wind, were a ghostly white, as if fright had made them turn their light sides outward. The willows, too, seemed to tremble and huddle close to the ground, and homing birds darted quickly into the trees as if in a hurry to find shelter. Having found perches they did not flutter about and chirp cheerfully as usual. They were still and silent, as if they also feared the threat in the green light. The night insects all seemed to be crouching quiet in the grass, and there was no friendly croak of either frogs or peepers from the slough. Even the mosquitoes did not hum as loudly as usual.

'Guess we might as well go to bed,' Dad said, his voice unusually loud in the surrounding quiet.

We three children went to bed first, and pulled the blanket over our heads, then Dad brought a shovelful of smudge into the tent to drive out the mosquitoes. When they were all out he and Mother hurried into the smoke-filled tent, closed the flap, and got ready for bed in the dark. A light attracted mosquitoes.

Careful as Dad was, however, one mosquito always seemed to survive the smoke, and the minute we were quiet its hungry whine began. That night was no different from any other, there was one mosquito left. We slapped at it for quite a while, and at last Dad got up and caught it, and we went to sleep.

The next thing I knew the world that had been so quiet a while ago was full of screaming wind and crashing thunder. The tent canvas strained and shuddered, and lightning, so bright I could see it with my eyes shut, filled the tent. One flash was a weird and ghostly green, followed immediately by a dazzle of bluish purple, then forked lightning like a pale snake slithered down the tent-pole, leaving a queer smell like sulphur matches behind it. I pulled up the blanket and tried not to look at the lightning.

The flashes, however, were too bright to be ignored, and they were almost constant. There was also continuous thunder: great booming crashes that shook the earth, crackles as if all the glass in the world were breaking, and bangs like the firing of huge guns. The whole world was full of sound. One crash followed another just as one blaze of green or purple light came on the heels of the glare just gone.

When it seemed as if the world must fall apart hailstones began to fall. They thudded furiously on the tent, bounced, and thudded again. Rain in torrents followed the hail. The tent swayed in the wind, and glistened in the lightning flashes. 'It's going to come down,' Mother said in a frightened voice.

'I'll have to loosen the ropes.' Dad got out of bed.

'You can't go out in this,' Mother told him. 'Them hailstones...' But Dad had found his coat and gone. In a minute he came back dripping wet.

'The ropes are that tight I can't get even one loose.' He picked up the axe and began chopping a hole at the foot of the tent-pole. 'If I can let the pole down a bit it will help,' he said as he scooped away the earth. He got the foot of the pole into the small hole, but the canvas was already overstretched, and the next thrust of wind was too much. The tent-pole went through the top of the tent, and the canvas, a wet, soggy mass, fell on us.

'Walter!' Mother cried in a thin, frightened voice, and pushed the wet mass up a little and got out of bed.

'Sarah!' Dad's voice, muffled by the wet canvas, and smothered by the noise of the storm, seemed very far away.

'Where are you? Where are you?' Mother's voice was also muffled as she crawled under the wet tent looking for Dad.

'Are you hurt?' Dad called.

'No, but you...' Mother's voice was carried away by the wind. I didn't hear any more for a while, the rain and the wind were everywhere. Then suddenly Mother said 'Oh, there you are,' and both she and Dad laughed with relief.

Soon after the tent collapsed the storm, as if satisfied with the damage it had done, went away into the east. The thunder still banged, but it was muffled and tired, and the wind stopped screaming and began to sob, as if sorry for the trouble it had caused. The rain, too, stopped, and the world that had been so full of noise and confusion a little while ago was comparatively quiet. A box at the head of the mattress kept the wet tent off my face, and in a little while I fell asleep.

When I opened my eyes next morning I thought the storm must have been a dream. The canvas of the tent sloped above me, and sunlight warm and bright came streaming through it. I looked at the tent-pole. There was a small hole at the foot, but it was upright. I looked at the top of the pole: surely it had gone through the top of the tent last night! But there was no hole there now. Instead, upside-down on the top of the pole was the small-sized chamber-pot.

'How did that get up there?' I asked.

'Dad put it up there,' Mother said, spooning oatmeal into Jack.

'What for?'

'To fill the hole, of course. Now eat your porridge, and don't ask so many questions.'

I ate a spoonful of oatmeal and looked around for the milk. There wasn't any. Thunder had soured all that was left from last night, and there was no fresh that morning. The cow had at last realized her ambition and got away. Some time during the storm she had pulled her stake and gone. Mother gave me a little extra sugar to make up for the lack of milk, and I finished the oatmeal, but without milk it was sticky.

As soon as the bed and blankets had been put out in the sun to dry we went to see how the Metherells had fared. Their tent had blown down, and they had spent part of the night under the wagon, but they were not hurt, and their oxen, Billy and Curly, had not strayed.

People, of course, came to see how we had survived the storm, and the first thing they noticed was the chamber-pot. The polite visitors blinked and turned pink, then tried to pretend they hadn't noticed it, but some were better pretenders than others.

Mrs Johnson's brown eyes bulged and her mouth fell open when she saw the chamber-pot, then she choked and coughed and all her generous curves began to shake. 'I think I've swallowed a fly,' she gasped, and wiped her eyes. Mother, who always put the kettle on when visitors came, handed her a cup of tea. She drank it fast and said she felt better, but every time she glanced at the tent-pole she began to shake all over again. After a while, when Dad had gone to look for the cow, she laughed outright and pointed at the pot. 'Why did you put it up there?' she asked.

Mr Maule, who never pretended about anything, said what he thought about the chamber-pot. 'What the hell?' he asked, glaring at it. 'That's a fine place for a chamber-pot! It isn't even decent. How d' you expect the kids to grow up right when you stick pots on poles? You ought to have more sense.'

'It was the only thing we could find in the dark,' Mother explained.

'Well, you don't have to leave it up there, do you?' Mr Maule asked. 'You could take it down.'

'We haven't had time.' Mother's round face looked hurt, and there were tears in her soft blue eyes. She wasn't used to being scolded.

'I don't see anything wrong with it, Mrs Pinder.' Master Willie's deep voice had a chuckle in it, and there was a little smile on his serious lips. 'Charlie's in a bad mood to-day, that's all.'

Mr Maule said his mood was all right, but the pot was a bad example for the kids, and he thought it ought to come down.

'And him always so broad-minded,' Mother said to Dad when Mr Maule had gone. 'It does look a bit indecent, doesn't it? Maybe we ought to take it down.'

Taking the tent down and repitching it, however, was a lot of work, and besides there were more pressing things to do. Water had got into our clothes, and the boxes had to be opened and aired. Some of the flour had got wet, and though we tried to dry it, most of it caked and we had to throw it away. The cow also had to be found, and so far we had heard nothing of her. So Mother stood on a box and pinned a cloth around the pot, and although Mr Maule looked at it suspiciously every time he came, he didn't say anything more about it.

Along with the difficulties, the storm brought us one great satisfaction. It proved to Dad and Mother that they were equal to danger. It was perhaps the first real difficulty they had ever had to face without any help from anyone, and they were very proud of the way they had handled it, and of each other.

'The way you handled that pole,' Dad said, his grey, ocean-flecked eyes shining. 'And saying you were scared of lightning! I wish Sam could have seen. He'd never be bothered about you again.'

'Don't try to soft soap me.' Mother tossed her little head, but there was pleasure in her blue eyes, and a smile on her lips.

'I'm not soft soaping you at all,' Dad said. 'I'm just telling you the truth. You have plenty of pluck, and Canada had better look out.'

'You didn't do so bad for a little man, either,' Mother said.

'Size doesn't matter, as I've allus told you,' Dad said. 'It's guts that counts.'

Mother told him not to use such language, the bairns were listening, but her voice was gentle and her eyes were smiling.

CHAPTER NINETEEN

A s soon as the bedding and clothing were dry, and the tent in order again, Dad went to look for the cow. He had already walked around every grove within a mile or so of our tent; now he decided to ride one of the horses and really trail her.

The Old Cow had always resented being tied to a stake. She had been born on a ranch, and had been used to her freedom. She was also used to a herd, so Dad decided she had probably made for the nearest ranch, several miles to the east.

There was also the possibility that her stake had caught in a stump or a bush, and if that had happened she would be in danger of starving to death or dying of thirst. 'I'd sure like to know where she is,' Dad said, 'even though she is dry.' Mother thought the search was a wild-goose chase. The prairie was so big it was impossible to look behind every bush, and if her stake had caught the coyotes would most likely have eaten her.

Dad was sure the Old Cow was equal to any coyote, perhaps even two or three, and decided to go and look for her. The hunt sounded like fun to me, and I asked to go with him.

Dad said he was going a long way, much too far for a little girl, and Mother said I wasn't old enough,, but I pleaded and coaxed.

If Dad was going to ride Nelly why couldn't I ride Darkie? And I wasn't a little girl. I'd driven the team, and helped Dad plough. Sitting on a horse was no different from sitting on a chair. And I'd eaten my porridge every morning for days and days.

Finally Dad, who always liked company, said: 'Well, I think she'd be safe enough on Darkie. He's very quiet.'

'That big thing?' Mother looked startled. 'She'll fall off and break her neck.'

'No, I won't,' I insisted. 'I'll hang on with both hands.'

Mother gave in at last, though reluctantly, and Dad put the bridles on the horses. We hadn't any saddles, but Dad folded a coat and put it on Nelly's back. I wanted a folded coat, too, but Dad said it would slip off and take me with it. I had either to ride bareback or stay at home. That, of course, was out of the question, so I gave in, and Dad lifted me up and put me on Darkie's back.

He was a lot higher than I had thought. The green grass, and the harebells sprinkled through it, looked miles away, but I took his dark, coarse mane in both hands and made him walk a few steps, and by the time Dad climbed on Nelly's back I was beginning to feel like an old hand at riding, and quite brave.

'Well, here we go,' Dad said gaily, and turned Nelly towards the rising sun.

It was a sparkling morning, perfect for a ride. The sky was the colour of forget-me-nots, the wind was warm and soft as a kiss, and sweet with the smell of growing leaves and opening roses. Dew diamonds twinkled in the grass, and on the lace the spiders had made. Dad gave Nelly a tap with the stick he carried and away she trotted, her dark haunches swaying gracefully, and her long black tail waving.

I tried to make Darkie trot, but he wouldn't. A sedate walk was all I could manage. I slapped his big shoulder with my small hand, and tried to kick him with my little heels. He paid less attention to me than he would have paid to a mosquito.

I was furious, and bitterly disappointed. A horse that wouldn't trot when trotting looked such fun! I pulled at his mane and shouted.

Dad and Nelly came back to see what was wrong.

'I want a stick,' I said crossly. 'I want a stick like yours. I want my horse to run.'

'Well, all right, but hang on,' Dad said, then he gave Darkie a tap with his stick.

Darkie was startled and outraged. He leaped forward, snorted, swung around, and galloped back to the tent.

I bounced up and down, and from side to side, but I didn't fall off. When Darkie stopped at the tent I was clinging to his mane with both hands and crying.

'I knew she wasn't big enough to ride that thing,' Mother said when Dad arrived close behind me. 'Lift her off before she's killed.'

'No,' I said firmly. 'I want a stick of my own. Dad hit my horse and he ran too fast, that's all.'

'I didn't expect him to jump so,' Dad said. 'But the way she hung on she'll do fine.'

'All right, but don't blame me if she's killed.' Mother looked uncertain and worried.

'I want a stick,' I insisted. 'I want a stick of my own.'

Mother handed me a small stick, and told me to take care of myself, then Dad and I started again, riding side by side. 'Now don't you hit my horse any more,' I told him as we jogged along around the corner of the slough. 'I can make him run by myself.'

Dad laughed and said I was strictly on my own, and we had a pleasant ride. I coaxed Darkie into a trot, but I didn't enjoy it as much as I expected. I bounced up and down, and Darkie's back was hard.

Dad didn't care to trot much, either, so the horses ambled more or less at their own pace through the grass and pea-vine. There were no signs of the cow, but the prairie was full of interest. We lost count of the speckled prairie chickens that flew up in front of us and sailed away on stiff wings, and we didn't even try to count the ducks floating lazily on the sloughs. Gophers, of course, were everywhere. They sat up on their haunches, their little forepaws hanging, and watched until we were close, then they flipped their impudent tails and popped into their holes.

I tried to imitate the bubbling song of the meadow-lark, but no matter how tight I screwed my lips a thin tweet was all I could manage.

Dad was as interested in the birds as I was. He called my attention to the little yellow canaries darting among the tall black-hearted sunflowers, and the red-topped woodpeckers that seemed to slide from one tree to another. There were black-and-white birds that Dad called whisky jacks, and once we saw a bird that was all red. Now and then the shadow of a soaring hawk glided silently across the grass and flowers.

'Just smell that breeze,' Dad said as we rounded a little grove. He inhaled deeply, and I did the same. The warm air was both sweet and sharp: a delightful mixture of wild honeysuckle, roses, wild sweet peas, green grass, sap, tall slough plants, rich brown earth, and the yeasty odour of the silver wolf willows. 'It's fair wonderful, isn't it?' Dad said as we jogged along again. 'Just like God's own garden.' We came to the top of a little rise, and Dad let Nelly stop. Darkie stopped, too, and we sat there for a while and looked at the beauty around us: at the poplars and willows both silver and green, and at the roses, wild mint, and harebells that were everywhere.

'Take a good look at it, Mary,' Dad said quietly. 'You'll never see it this way again.'

I did as I was told. I looked at the tall grass, and the pea-vine, and the soft green silk of the wild barley, but the sad note in Dad's voice puzzled me. How could the prairie change, I wondered. I did not realize then what an instrument of change a plough is.

The trees and willows are gone now, grubbed out and burned, and the roses and wild mint have been ploughed under. Wheat now grows where the chook-cherries and the violets bloomed. The wind is still sweet, but there is no wildness in it, and it no longer seems to have wandered a great way over grass, and trees, and flowers. It now smells of dry straw and bread. The wild, keen fragrance the wind knew in those days has gone for ever.

After a little while we went down the hill and across a little valley. The grass was so tall that the horses could eat almost without bending their necks, and their hoofs made a pleasant swishing sound. The long grass seemed to restore Dad's cheerfulness, and he began to tell me of all the wonderful things we were going to have when we got the farm going. I asked if I could have a swing, and Dad said all the swings I wanted, and a pony, too, all for myself.

'Will it have a saddle?' I asked, for Darkie's back was warm, and I was thin and beginning to feel sore. I was also hungry and thirsty, and tired. Dad was also tired, and when we rounded a grove and saw a tent, white in the sun, we were both thankful.

The man who owned the tent, Harry Bligh, was at home, and glad to see us. He had just finished his midday meal, but he got out his frying-pan and cooked another meal for us: the usual bacon, bannock, tea, and jam.

Dad asked Mr Bligh if he'd seen anything of the cow. He hadn't, but he said there was a big ranch farther east in the Big Gully, and suggested the cow might have gone there.

After we had eaten Dad and Mr Bligh talked for a while, mostly about what a wonderful country Canada was, then Dad said he thought he'd go and see if he could find the ranch and the cow.

I was half asleep by that time, but I wanted to go, too. Dad, however, said I was too sleepy to ride, and he wouldn't be gone long.

I argued as much as I could. Mr Bligh was a stranger, and I didn't want to stay with him. I was also afraid Dad would get lost, and never find Mr Bligh's tent again. Dad said he knew just where the tent was, and he'd be back before sunset, sure, so I finally gave in and agreed to stay where I was.

Mr Bligh was a young man, not more than twenty, and taking care of a little girl must have been a new experience. There was a mattress in the tent, and after Dad left Mr Bligh told me to take a nap on it. I stretched out and would have gone to sleep, but for some reason Mr Bligh thought he ought to keep an eye on me. He stayed outside the tent, but every few minutes he came to the tent flap and looked at me.

I was instantly suspicious. Why was he watching me? It wasn't as if I was a little girl. I could stir the porridge and not let it burn, take care of Jack when Mother was busy, dress myself, even the buttons, help Lily into her clothes, and drive a team and ride a horse. Nobody had to watch me. I could take care of myself. Maybe I ought to keep an eye on Mr Bligh.

The next time he looked into the tent I glared at him and told him to go away.

He looked surprised and a little worried. 'Aren't you going to go to sleep?' he asked.

I didn't answer, and after a moment he let the tent flap fall. But I wasn't fooled. I knew he hadn't gone far, I'd heard his feet stop. I lifted the tent wall a little and peeped out. Sure enough, Mr Bligh was over by the woodpile sharpening his axe.

I dropped the tent canvas and shivered. I knew my 'Jack and the Beanstalk.' Mr Bligh didn't look quite like a giant, but you never could tell. I sat in the hot tent and worried. If I tried to run away he would surely catch me, and if I went to sleep he would steal into the tent and chop off my head. Dad was my only hope.

I sat in the hot tent all afternoon. Mr Bligh crept to the flap and looked in now and then, and I glared at him. Sweat rolled down my face and prickled my skin, and sleep pulled at my eyelids, but I didn't dare let my eyes close. Once, after a long quiet spell, I looked under the tent wall, hoping Mr Bligh had gone, but he was still over by his woodpile.

At last the sun began to go down. Where was Dad, I wondered miserably. Perhaps lost. What would Mr Bligh do if Dad didn't come? I remembered that the Giant had hoped to cook Jack in his oven. Mr Bligh didn't have an oven, but he did have a big frying-pan. I began to cry.

The noise, of course, brought Mr Bligh. He asked what was wrong, and when I wouldn't answer he tried to amuse me, first by talking, then by making what he probably thought were funny faces. To me, however, they were horrible, and I was quite sure he was an ogre. I stopped crying so that I could watch him more closely.

Looking relieved, but still puzzled, Mr Bligh offered me some bannock.

I was hungry, but too frightened to eat. I knew the axe, a big one with two cutting edges, was just outside the tent.

After a while Mr Bligh stopped trying to amuse me. He went outside and lit a fire in his tin stove and put the kettle on. I sat in the middle of the bed and watched the tent flap, and listened to the crunch of Mr Bligh's feet until Dad came back just after the sun had set. The minute I saw Dad I dissolved into tears, and cried so hard I couldn't even tell him what was wrong.

After I had sobbed for a while, and frightened both Dad and Mr Bligh, I finally managed to tell Dad about the axe, and the way Mr Bligh had watched me.

Dad laughed, but Mr Bligh looked quite provoked. He said he'd only been grinding his axe because it needed sharpening, and he thought he might as well do it while he was watching me. 'I thought she was sick, or something,' he said crossly, and went out to make some tea.

After we had eaten Dad and I went home. He hadn't found the cow, but Bill Banks, who lived near the Big Gully, said he had seen her heading for Inkster's ranch that morning. He had tried to catch her, but she was going fast and was out of sight in no time.

I don't remember much about the ride home, or even getting home and going to bed. Dad took me in front of him on his horse and led mine, and I think I fell asleep immediately.

Next day I told Mother about the axe and Mr Bligh. She said it was silly of me to be frightened. Mr Bligh wouldn't have hurt me for anything, and was only trying to be good to me. I didn't argue, but I wasn't convinced. If Mr Bligh wasn't an ogre, then he was akin to one. In a day or two I was quite sure he had horns, and when I told Lily about my experience I gave him horns a foot long.

Mother asked Dad what he was going to do about the cow, and he said he thought he'd leave her where she was. 'She'll be dry by now anyway, and she'll only get away again if I bring her back,' he said. 'I'll talk to Inkster about it when I see him.'

'That's a good idea,' Mother said happily. 'Maybe Mr Inkster will buy her when we leave here.'

⤚·CHAPTER TWENTY·⤙

SOON after we returned from our unsuccessful hunt for the cow Dad decided to go to Battleford. We were almost out of food, and Dad was still a little worried about the cow.

Mother didn't like the idea of being left alone on the prairie, but there was nothing else to do. The Metherells, of course, were fairly close, but, as Mother said, if anything happened in the night they would be no help. She couldn't shout loud enough to wake them at such a distance.

Dad said nothing could possibly happen, and anyway he wouldn't be gone long, not more than a week. 'Just keep the gun handy,' he warned, 'and take the axe to bed with you.' Mother didn't think much of the gun, and said so, but she agreed to keep the axe near.

I listened quietly to the plans Dad and Mother made, and tried to get up courage to ask the question I'd been turning over in my mind ever since I heard about the trip, but it was almost bedtime before I managed it. 'Dad,' I said at last in a low, pleading voice, 'can I go with you?'

Both Mother and Dad looked startled, but a gleam of pleasure flickered in Dad's ocean-flecked eyes. He never liked to be alone, even for a short time, and this trip would take several days. 'Well...' Dad said and glanced at Mother.

'Where would she sleep?' Mother asked.

Dad was going to sleep in the wagon box, and I said I could sleep there, too. Mother said a wagon box was no place for a little girl to sleep. And if I went who would take care of Lily and Jack when she was busy?

I said I could sleep in the wagon box just as well as Dad could, and I wouldn't be any bother at all, but Mother said I was better off at home. She didn't want me left with strangers any more. Dad agreed with her, and so, overruled, I stayed at home. Dad left early, before I was awake, so that I wouldn't be upset.

The tent by the grove seemed more like home than the tent by the trail had been, but without Dad the prairie still seemed terribly wide and empty. The Metherells were only about a quarter of a mile away, but we couldn't see their tent from ours, and it might as well not have been there at all as far as I was concerned. Without Dad I felt as if I didn't belong, and the prairie became alien and strange.

The sunshine was clear and bright, but some of the gold was missing, and the prairie was no longer friendly. It seemed to have turned its back towards me, and closed its eyes. Even the wild flowers— the tall fireweed, the smiling marigolds, the purple mint, and the regal tiger-lilies—didn't seem to know me.

There was always something very independent about those beautiful Canadian wild flowers. No one planted them or cared for them. They simply grew by themselves, and for their own pleasure. They belonged to the wilderness, and the wilderness was theirs. We had not brought them with us, and if we left we could not take them away. They belonged, and we were strangers. They could manage very well without us.

Only the potatoes, pushing spindly sprouts through the sod, were really dependent on us, and among the robust wild flowers they looked anaemic and out of place.

As soon as Dad left Mother began repacking all our things. 'Then if we leave everything will be ready,' she said as she wrapped pieces of lace around her small fingers, and tucked the little skeins neatly into a tin box.

She also washed everything washable, including the blankets. The slough water was brown and darkened the light things, and that worried Mother. 'What a dirty washer they will think me when we get home,' she said.

Mention of home always made me think of Aunt Jane and Grandmother, and the little house by the Spen. I seldom talked of them, but I thought of them often, especially at night when I was in bed and a little lonely. I never wondered what they were doing, or how they looked. To me they were always the same, beautiful and kind. The little house, too, was always warm, and often I drifted to sleep sitting in my little rocker by the fire.

Going to sleep was often hard in the tent. The sun seemed to stay up all night, for the days were long at that time of year. Mother, who sometimes woke in the middle of the night, said there was always a glow in the northern sky, even at three in the morning.

It couldn't have been more than four o'clock when I woke up three or four days after Dad left. The light was still dusky in the tent, and the birds were asleep. Mother, however, was wide awake. Still in her white cotton night-gown with the little frills at the high neck and long sleeves, she stood by the tent flap peering out at the prairie. I held my breath and watched. Something about her taut neck and her fingers that clutched the edges of the tent flap frightened me. 'What's the matter?' I whispered at last, when the suspense got too much for me.

'Shhh,' Mother said, without turning her head.

I slipped out of bed and went and stood beside her. The morning was blue-grey and cool. A few long clouds in the east were trimmed with pink, and the top of the sky was light, but there were no shadows. The trees were dark and still, and the willows hung their heads in sleep, but the shadows which ought to have been spread out on the grass were all rolled up and put away.

I glanced at Mother's face. Little worry wrinkles pulled at the corners of her eyes and puckered her mouth. She was looking at the grass.

I wrinkled my eyes and puckered my mouth, too, then I looked at the grass near the tent. It was blue-green and silvered over with a heavy dew, but in some spots the dew had been disturbed by big feet. The trail the feet had made went up the hill just this side of the slough and disappeared. 'Who was it?' I whispered.

'I don't know.' Mother backed into the tent and closed the flap. 'The cow must have come back for a while and gone again. Go back to bed, and don't wake Lily. It's too early to get up.'

I crept back into bed, but I didn't go back to sleep for quite a while. The cow had little hoofs, but the trail in the grass had been huge.

The blackbirds were singing, and the world looked so ordinary when I woke up again that I almost thought I had dreamed about the queer tracks. Mother didn't look the least bit frightened, either. She wore her usual dress: a plain dark skirt, long and four yards wide around the bottom, and a fitted bodice with a row of little buttons down the front. Her hair was combed and neatly coiled, and she was humming a little tune.

Black-and-orange monarch butterflies sat on the rim of the dishpan, a bee buzzed fiercely as it sampled a pink star flower. The fire in the little stove crackled, and the tent threw a long friendly shadow across the grass. I looked at the little hill by the slough. The dew diamonds had gone, and so had the large clumsy tracks. 'Come and stir the porridge, Mary,' Mother said. 'I don't want it to burn.'

I went to the stove and stirred the bubbling mass. When I learned to stir porridge I was very proud of myself; it was proof that I was a big girl. But now I hated the job. My face always felt roasted, and my hands half broiled. How I envied Lily who was still little, and had nothing to do but sit on the wagon bench and try to put on her shoes.

After breakfast Mother usually went to the slough for water, but that morning she put off going until almost noon. She had looked at the slough often, but she made no effort to pick up the water bucket until the shadows were short, and it was almost time for our noon meal. Even then she didn't hurry. She tied her little shawl under her chin, then she untied it and smoothed her hair, kissed Jack, and knotted her shawl once more. 'Stay near the tent, Mary,' she said as she turned towards the slough, 'and if I don't come back in half an hour take Lily and Jack and go to the Metherells'.'

I always enjoyed going to the Metherells', so I promised quite cheerfully to do as I was told.

Mother walked slowly across the little field, and up the small hill that hid the slough. At the top of the hill she paused a moment and looked back, then she went quickly down the other side and disappeared.

Lily, Jack, and I sat on the wagon bench and waited. I wondered how long half an hour was, I couldn't tell time, and if I ought to go to the Metherells' now or wait? Before I had time to make up my mind, however, Mother came hurrying over the hill. She walked very fast, and when she got to the tent she sat down and fanned herself with her little shawl before she lit the fire for the noon tea.

I was quite disappointed about not getting to go to the Metherells', and after we had eaten our bannock and jam, and Jack had had his nap, I began teasing to go. Mother didn't need much coaxing, so as soon as we had washed our hands and faces we started.

Mr Metherell and Bill were away, but Mrs Metherell was glad to see us. She found a box for Mother to sit on, then she lit the fire and made tea.

While they sipped the strong, hot brew Mother and Mrs Metherell talked in low voices. 'It walked around the tent and sniffed the ropes, then it put its nose near the tent wall and grunted,' Mother said.

'It was probably a badger.' Mrs Metherell smiled.

'It couldn't have been, it was too big.' Mother's blue eyes looked slightly offended.

'How do you know it was big if you didn't see it?' Mrs Metherell asked.

'It sounded big.' Mother pulled Jack close to her. 'And it was big. It pushed hard against the tent, and you ought to have seen the footprints. I think it was a bear.'

'Stuff and nonsense.' Mrs Metherell laughed. 'There are no dangerous animals in this part of the country. I bet it was a coyote, and they won't hurt you. All you have to do is make a noise and they'll run.'

'A coyote wouldn't have made a track anywhere near that big,' Mother insisted.

'The track probably looked bigger than it was because it was half dark when you saw it.' Mrs Metherell sounded slightly supercilious. 'But we'll see what the men think. Hi, Frank,' she called to her husband who was coming up the hill on which their tent stood 'Mrs Pinder thinks she heard a bear.'

'She does?' Mr Metherell's brown eyes laughed, and his even white teeth gleamed. 'There aren't any bears around here,' he said. 'It must have been a badger.'

'Yes, badgers make quite a noise,' Bill said, as if backing up Mr Metherell.

'It wasn't a badger,' Mother said firmly, but her blue eyes looked disappointed. She wasn't one to imagine things, and she hadn't expected to be laughed at. She drew her shoulders up proudly, and turned her head and stared at the little hill that hid the slough, while the Metherells, and Bill, drank their tea, and speculated about the tracks Mother thought she had seen.

Suddenly Mother leaned forward, and her round little figure stiffened. 'Look, look!' she cried hoarsely, and pointed a shaking finger at the hill by the slough. There, ambling along in the late sunshine, was a big black bear.

'I'll be damned!' Mr Metherell's cup fell with a crash, and his eyes opened wide in surprise, then gleamed with the anticipation of adventure. 'I'll get the gun,' he said, and dived into the tent. Bill dived after him. They were out in no time, and running in the direction of the bear.

'Do be careful, Frank,' Mrs Metherell called.

Mr Metherell didn't seem to hear, but the bear did. It paused a moment and looked in our direction, then it streaked over the hill into a grove of trees that grew beside the slough.

Mr Metherell and Bill went after it. Mrs Metherell stared at the spot where they had disappeared, and said how nice it would be to have a bear skin. Mother folded her dainty hands to keep them from trembling. Lily and I jumped up and down, we were so excited. Only Jack remained calm. He sat on the grass talking to himself, and playing with a handful of white chips. Bears and bear skins meant nothing at all to him.

'I do hope they find it,' Mother said after a while.

'They will.' Mrs Metherell sounded quite confident. 'Frank is a good shot.'

Time, however, drifted by and nothing happened. Mother and Mrs Metherell stared at the hillside. Lily and I stopped jumping.

A shot banged loud in the stillness, then another. 'There, Frank got it. I knew he would.' Mrs Metherell looked proud. 'I think I'll put the skin by my bed. It will make a wonderful rug.'

'Yes,' Mother said.

'I do hope it's a big one,' Mrs Metherell said happily. 'They ought to be bringing it out any minute.'

The minutes slipped past, but the men didn't appear. The little hill and the trees near it drowsed in the late sunshine, looking as if they had never been disturbed by either bears or men. 'I bet it's too big to carry, and they're skinning it,' Mrs Metherell said.

'Yes, that's it,' Mother agreed.

There was a long, anxious silence. We all stared at the hill and the trees that had swallowed the men and the bear. Mother's round face looked pale and worried, and she began to twist her hands. Mrs Metherell's thin face looked tight, and she also began wringing her hands. 'That animal must have killed them both,' Mrs Metherell said at last in a choked voice. 'I wish you'd never mentioned it.'

Mother didn't say anything. She just sat there looking smaller than ever, and knotted tight with fear. I felt tight, too, and even Jack stopped playing with his chips, and crawled over to Mother.

We were still for a long time. Mrs Metherell bit her lip and looked at her hands. 'If they'd only make a noise,' she whispered. But there wasn't any noise at all. There was only the great stillness that got bigger and bigger as the sun went down.

At last, when the quiet and the emptiness seemed about to crush us, the two men suddenly came over the top of the little hill. 'Oh, there they are!' Mrs Metherell cried. 'It must have been a big bear. But what have they done with the skin?'

'Maybe they hung it up to dry,' Mother said.

Mrs Metherell didn't answer, she was watching the men. 'Where is he?' she called as soon as she thought they could hear her.

The men said they hadn't even seen the bear after he galloped over the hill.

'Then what were you shooting at?' Mrs Metherell asked.

Mr Metherell said he fired the shots to frighten the bear when it was plain they were not going to find him, and he rather thought they had, because even though they looked everywhere, all through the grove, and in the slough, they hadn't seen a trace of him.

'All that work for nothing,' Mrs Metherell said. The men, however, didn't seem to think the time had been wasted. They looked and sounded as if they had enjoyed the chase, even though they didn't find the bear.

Mrs Metherell made more tea, and everybody sat on logs and boxes and talked. They were sure the bear must have been six feet long, perhaps even longer, and his head was as big as the head of a cow. And the way he ran! Like a streak.

'I knew he was a big thing when I heard him last night,' Mother said proudly.

'He sure was.' The men smiled approvingly at her. 'I bet he had good claws, too,' Mr Metherell said.

I listened to the excited talk and fear grew inside me. Katie Daw had read 'Goldilocks' to me. Bears didn't like little girls. Suddenly I felt very small, and wished I wasn't the one who had to sleep near the tent wall. 'Don't bears eat little girls?' I piped when there was a lull in the conversation.

The four grown-ups looked at one another and then at me. 'Not this bear,' Mother said quickly. 'This was a friendly bear, like the dancing bears in England.'

'Then why didn't it have a muzzle on?' I asked. 'And what was it doing all by itself?'

Mother said its muzzle had probably caught on a branch and come off, but I wasn't to worry, the man who owned the bear had probably found it by now, and put on another muzzle.

I pretended to accept the explanation, but I was still very uneasy. I hadn't heard of a single dancing bear in Canada.

The mosquitoes were beginning to hum and the blue shadows were creeping out of the woods by the time the tea and talk ended. Mother looked uneasily at the hill where the bear had been, and said she thought it was time to go home.

'You won't have a thing to worry about to-night,' Mrs Metherell told her cheerfully, 'but if you hear anything, shout.'

Mother said she would, then she picked up Jack, who was half asleep, told Lily and me to come along, and started home.

As long as we could see the Metherells' tent perched on its little hill we didn't feel quite alone. But when we rounded the grove that hid their tent from ours we felt practically lost.

In the blue light our tent looked very frail and small, and very lonely. Mother's feet slowed a little as she approached it, and no wonder. Until she came to Canada there had always been a house next door, and she had a stone house to live in. Except in a zoo, or muzzled and on a chain, she had never seen a bear. Now there was a wild bear loose in the woods, or in the tent waiting for us.

Mother glanced at the axe near the chopping-block, but she made no effort to get it. Perhaps she realized it wouldn't do her much good if the bear was waiting, for she was only a little woman with soft round arms and small hands, not the axe-swinging type at all.

The green wagon bench was outside the tent, Dad hadn't taken it with him, and Mother put Jack on it and told me to watch him, then she went to the tent flap and opened it. Except for a mosquito or two the tent was empty, and Mother sighed with relief. 'Can you undress Jack while I get the supper?' she asked as she lit the fire. I said I could and began pulling off his shoes and stockings.

We had bread, jam, tea, and stewed prunes for supper, then Mother gathered some green grass and put it on the fire to make a smudge, and as soon as the mosquitoes were out of the tent we went to bed.

Afterwards Mother said she didn't sleep much that night, but the bear didn't return.

Dad returned a few days later. We couldn't wait to tell him about the bear, but much to Mother's annoyance, and my disappointment, he took the story lightly. 'It couldn't have been much of a bear,' he said, smiling. 'There are no dangerous animals around here. The pamphlet said so.'

'The pamphlet may not think bears are dangerous,' Mother said sharply, 'but I do. I always told you this was no place for women and children, and if you have any sense you'll take us away before something happens to one of us. And if you don't believe it was a bear we saw, just ask Frank Metherell. He saw it, too.'

'He may have thought he saw a bear,' Dad said cheerfully, 'but Londoners don't know much about such things. I bet it was nowt but a big coyote.'

'So I'm a liar, am I?' Mother's blue eyes flashed, and an angry pink spot appeared in her round cheeks. 'You know very well it was a bear, but you won't admit it. You won't admit there's anything wrong with this god-forsaken country, no matter what. One of these days we'll all be eaten in our beds, then I hope you'll be satisfied.' Mother set down Dad's mug of tea so hard that some of it splashed over on to the wagon seat.

Dad sugared and stirred his tea slowly, and smiled placatingly at Mother. 'If you think you really saw a bear,' he said soothingly, 'I think we ought to build a house, then you'll feel safe.'

'I don't want a house.' There was disappointment in Mother's voice, and tears in her blue eyes. 'I don't want a house in this country. I want to go home.'

D AD stopped stirring his tea, and all the happiness went out of his thin young face. His smiling eyes became bleak like the ocean on a cold day, and his lips looked pulled together and desperate. He lifted the spoon out of the strong brown tea, and held it above the mug and watched the drops as they fell off the end of the spoon back into the mug. 'I'd go back in a minute if there was owt to go back to,' he said slowly and quietly. 'But there isn't.'

'There's your folks and mine,' Mother said, 'and your club. You allus seemed to enjoy it.'

Dad's face brightened for a moment, then he frowned. 'But how would I make a living?' he asked. 'The farm's gone now, and it never was so much.'

'You'd find something.'

'In a mill or a pit. Ten hours a day shut up, or underground. Even a foreman doesn't have it so easy. And besides, we said we'd try this country for a year. If we go back now everybody will call us quitters.'

'I don't care what they call us,' Mother said. 'They don't know what this country's like. Why waste a year here when we already know it's no fit place for anybody?'

'If everybody else left I wouldn't care so much,' Dad said, stirring his tea again. 'But to be the only one to run out! I'd be nowt but a laughing-stock. I tell you what we'll do. We'll build a house, and then see how you like it. I know this tent isn't much. We ought to have built sooner. What do you say?' Dad smiled hopefully.

'Well...' Mother hesitated.

'We'll start first thing to-morrow,' Dad said quickly. 'We'll have a real window and a door, and I'll put up a shelf, and make a table.'

'If you think the bairns will be safe in it,' Mother said.

'I'll make the walls a foot thick,' Dad promised. 'They'll be safe as birds in a nest.'

Mother didn't think nestlings were any too secure, but she agreed to try Canada a bit longer.

We started building next morning. Dad had already found what he thought was a good location. It was at the far corner of our quarter section diagonally across from the tent. Dad said the grove by the tent wasn't big enough to protect a house and barn from the winter winds, and the land was a little low.

The new location was at the top of a little rise beside a big grove. A huge poplar grew at the edge of the grove, and Dad planned on building close to the tree. He looked at the ground carefully, then he paced off what he thought would be about the right size for a house. Next he drove in four pegs, one at each corner of the proposed house, and tied a string to them to give us some idea of how big the house would be, then he asked Mother what she thought of it.

Mother took one look at the space Dad had tied off and her lips quivered. 'That won't be a house,' she said. 'It's only a bit bigger than a handkerchief. It isn't even big enough for a doll's house.'

Dad told her how big the house would be compared to the house in England, but Mother said he was all wrong. 'Even the tent is bigger than that,' she insisted. 'There won't even be room for the bed in such a small place.'

'You just wait and see,' Dad told her. 'This square looks small because the prairie's so big, but you'll be surprised. You'll have more room than you know what to do with.'

Mother said she very much doubted that, but to go on and build the house, and she'd do her best to squeeze into it until we went home.

To please Mother Dad made the house a little longer, but he couldn't increase the size much. Tall poplars were hard to find, and we had only the one little stove for winter heat, so a big house was out of the question.

Before we could start building we had to cut the logs and haul them out of the brush, and finding logs that were just right wasn't easy. There were plenty of trees, but if we found two or three straight trees in one grove we were lucky. To see if a tree would do Dad stood at the foot and squinted up at it from all sides. If it suited he chopped it down, lopped off the branches and the top, hitched Nelly to one end of it, and dragged it out of the bush. When we had hauled eight or ten logs to where the wagon waited we loaded them and took them to where we were going to build. Dad, of course, did the loading, but I kept him company and thought I helped. The rose thorns and the twigs scratched my hands and face, and I fell over the underbrush many times, but I enjoyed getting out logs. The sun was warm and bright, the woods smelled of sap, and pea-vine, and decaying leaves, and helping with the house made me feel very big and important.

Jogging back and forth to the woods on the wagon frame—Dad had taken off the green box—was also pleasant. The red frame wasn't comfortable to ride on. It was hard, and I had to sit near the back wheels so that if I fell off the wheels wouldn't go over me, but I got the full benefit of the bumps, and there were plenty. In spite of the hard seat, however, I enjoyed the rides. I watched the flowers going by below me, breathed the wild sweetness that I called the smell of the prairie, and listened while Dad talked.

Up to that time Dad, like everybody else, had usually talked to me the way grown-ups talk to children, but on those trips Dad began to talk to me as if I were much older than my six years. Actually he was really talking to himself, but some of the things he said made quite an impression on me, and I began to see Canada as he saw it.

To Dad's young eyes Canada was not a grim, harsh place. It was the land of opportunity, and his dreams for the future were bright and rose-tinted. 'Just think of the wheat this will grow, Mary,' he said as we jogged along. 'We won't be living in a log house long. I intend to build your mother a house ten times as big as the house we had in England. And one of these days I'm going to buy a quarter section for each of you, then you'll never have to work for anybody else, and you'll never be dependent on anybody, either. There's nothing like being independent. It's the best thing in the world. And everybody can be his own boss here.'

'When we have a house will there be pansies in the garden?' I asked, thinking of the garden at Castle Hill.

'Yes, and roses, too, and maybe a greenhouse with our own grapes in it. There's no limit to what will grow here. One of these days we'll be shipping wheat by the car-load. We'll have everything they have in England, and a lot more besides.'

Mention of England reminded me of Aunt Jane and Grandmother, and the little house by the Spen. 'When are we going back?' I asked.

Dad was silent for so long I thought I had made him angry, and I looked anxiously at his thin face. Some of the glow had gone out of it, and his eyes, looking at the far distance, were troubled. 'Mary, lass,' he said at last, 'you can't ever go back.'

'Why can't we?' I asked, for going back to England seemed simple to me. All we had to do was jolt to Saskatoon, take the train to St John, and the ship to Liverpool.

'Because the place you left isn't there any more,' Dad said slowly. 'It's changed just as you have, and you can't even find it, and if you could you wouldn't like it. Don't ever try to go back. Allus go for'ard. Once you turn back you're done for.'

A little later, while he was busy cutting logs, I gathered some tiger-lilies that grew near the grove. They were gorgeous flowers: deep orange-red with black spots in their throats. I had picked a handful in one patch and was going on to the next when Dad suddenly said: 'Don't pick them all.'

'Why can't I?' I asked, surprised. 'We aren't coming here any more.'

'Maybe not,' Dad said. 'But you should always leave some for seed. Other people will be coming some day. You shouldn't ever take everything. Allus see that you leave a bit for them that come after.'

I didn't understand what he really meant until years later, but I did as he told me, and left dozens of the lovely lilies still blooming.

As soon as we had hauled a supply of logs we started building the house. It was quite a job, and I thought Dad was terribly smart because he knew just how to do it. The logs that had looked straight when they were growing in the groves all curved one way or another when cut down, and they had to be turned this way and that so that the walls would be as even as possible, then the logs had to be notched and fitted one to another. When the walls were low the fitting and turning wasn't too hard, but the higher the walls grew the harder the fitting got, mostly because we could no longer do it standing on the ground.

The green logs were also quite heavy, and Dad lifted first one end then the other a little at a time. When they were finally hoisted to the top of the partly built walls the notching began.

Dad straddled one wall, I straddled the other, then Dad fitted the log. Next it had to be turned over and notched. The log, of course, never stayed still, it rolled first one way then the other. I did my best to steady it while Dad chopped, but it always seemed to tip a little. The first notches were seldom right, and the log usually had to be turned several times. The blows of the axe sent shivers up and down my thin arms, and often I almost fell off my precarious perch, but I was never hurt.

Sometimes in the afternoons Mother helped with the building. She put Jack on a blanket well out of range of the flying yellow chips, and Lily and I played with him until he fell asleep, then we gathered wild flowers, or tried to catch the blue butterflies that hovered over them. Often we pretended the house was ours, and arranged chips and stones for chairs and tables, and poured imaginary tea.

Those days of play, however, were exceptions. Often when Mother helped with the house I had to help also. Mother couldn't straddle the walls the way I could. Her long skirts got in her way, and since no decent woman exposed her ankles in those days she couldn't do a thing about them. She tried sitting sideways on the walls, but that didn't work very well. She couldn't balance both the log and herself, so the log slipped, the notch was wrong, and the whole thing had to be done over again, which irritated everybody. 'We just aren't big enough to build houses,' Mother said as she struggled to hold the log and keep her balance. 'It isn't as if we're going to stay here. We could just as well leave now, and save ourselves all this trouble.'

'I started this and I'm going to finish it,' Dad said grimly. 'You go back to the tent if it's too much for you.'

Sometimes Mother took Dad at his word and went back to the tent, taking Lily and Jack with her. When that happened Dad always chopped viciously for a while, and I kept quiet no matter how much the log rolled and the axe tingled my arms. After such a day, however, there was always a better than average supper waiting for us, and Mother often said she wished she was a bigger and stronger woman.

But she never wished she liked Canada, there were too many hardships, though sometimes it almost seemed as if she was glad of the difficulties and the irritations. Every new obstacle was another good reason for going home.

The other women reasoned the way Mother did. 'No, I don't care how bad the deer-flies get,' Mrs Johnson said one day when she dropped in for a cup of tea. 'I don't care about the sand-flies, or the spear grass, either. The worse things are the better I like it. I wouldn't mind if it rained pitchforks, and the mosquitoes were as big as wolves. The harder this place is the sooner Will Johnson's belly will be full of it, and we can leave.' And she mopped her pink, perspiring face, drank her tea, and told us how horribly a neighbour was acting. 'Jaws from morning to night,' she said, her brown eyes flashing. 'And all because he hasn't any tobacco.'

'How awful for his poor wife.' Mother refilled the tea-cups. 'Can't he borrow some tobacco from somebody?'

Mrs Johnson shook her head and her eyes twinkled. 'He's too proud.' She tilted her head and wiggled her shoulders, imitating a proud person.

'Then why doesn't his wife borrow a little? Anything's better than living with a bad-tempered man.'

'Yes.' Mrs Johnson lowered her voice. 'And it wouldn't surprise me if he landed her one now and then, as well as shouting at her. But she says she doesn't care, and she isn't going to try to get tobacco. The madder he gets the better she likes it. She thinks if he goes off his trolley a bit he might go home.'

'Poor woman,' Mother said thoughtfully and rubbed her smooth cheek. 'But it might work at that.'

'I'd hit him back if it were me.' Mrs Johnson licked her full lips. 'But some women just haven't any spirit.' She put down her tea mug, and said she had to be getting on if she wanted to get home before the mosquitoes came out.

Mother told her to come again, and Mrs Johnson said she would, then she walked off towards the Metherells', her wide, full hips swaying invitingly.

'I bet she made at least half of that up,' Mother said as she emptied the tea-leaves and washed the mugs. 'But if one would go the rest might follow. It's being the first to give up that's hard.'

'Who was she talking about?' I asked. 'And where's the trolley?'

'There isn't any,' Mother said. 'And little girls shouldn't ask questions.'

I never found out who the jawing man was, but he must have got some tobacco somewhere, for nobody was arrested for wife-beating, and nobody went off their trolley, which was a little disappointing to Mrs Johnson. The next time she came she said some women just had no pride. As for men they had bellies big enough to stomach anything. They didn't seem to care about ants in the jam, mice in the flour, or even sudden storms that put the fire out and ruined whole batches of bread.

Mother said she didn't think such things bothered men. They liked being their own bosses and doing as they pleased. They could work or not just as they wanted, and if they wanted excitement they went to the gully and shot ducks. With a woman it was different. All she could do was stay at home and worry, especially when she had bairns. Canada was a man's country, and if the women were sensible they'd leave.

Personally I thought Canada was as hard for Dad as it was for Mother. Building the house wasn't easy, I'd far rather mind Jack. As for shooting ducks, it was the worst thing I could think of.

The big ducks had left the sloughs by that time. The settlers frightened them, and their young, that hatched in nests in the grass near the sloughs, were now able to fly, so away they went to the quieter lakes in the Big Gully, and if we wanted duck for supper Dad had to scramble up and down the gully banks, about half a mile each way.

One evening I went duck-hunting with him. Going to the gully was fun, but when Dad left me with the team my troubles began. The mosquitoes came in clouds, and the horses got so restless I finally decided to go home. Dad got two mallards, but he had to walk all the way home, about two miles, through a mist of mosquitoes.

⌣·CHAPTER TWENTY-TWO·⌣

THE day after the duck hunt we returned to the hard task of house-building. The walls were quite high by that time, and lifting the logs was really difficult. Mother told Dad he wasn't big enough for such work, but Dad said size didn't mean anything, and went on lifting. At last, however, the walls were high enough and we started putting the roof on, hurrying a little, for the days were much shorter than they had been, and sometimes there was a feeling of fall in the air. The mornings and evenings had a new crispness, and the grass under our feet sounded dry.

The work on the house hadn't gone as fast as Dad had expected. Rains had kept us from building, and when the rain stopped and the sky cleared all the bedding had to be carried out into the sun to dry. The horses, though hobbled at night, had wandered away once or twice, and time had been lost looking for them. Actually it was only August, and late roses were in full bloom, but the old-timers were already talking of fall.

We did not actually see many old-timers, but their stories circulated. Every time we went to the Metherells' they told us some story they had heard, and whenever one of the many bachelors dropped by they told us of something we ought to do if we expected to live through the coming winter.

Put two layers of sod on the roof, they warned, you'll be a lot warmer when it's forty below, and bank the walls with earth to keep the frost out. Be sure to dig a deep hole or cellar for the potatoes, or they'll freeze. And above all plough a fire-guard as soon as you can. The prairie's ripe for a rip-roaring fire, and unless you have a guard you'll be burned out. Neither Dad nor Mother could believe in the cold. And as for the fire, who would be silly enough to set fire to the grass? But we hurried to finish the house. There would be some kind of winter, though we were sure it wouldn't be anything like tales the old-timers told.

Putting the roof on the house was even more difficult than raising the walls. The two end walls had to be built up to get the proper slope, and the beams and ridge-pole had to be long, straight logs. When they were in place Dad cut slim young poplars and laid them side by side, one end on the wall, the other on the ridge-pole, until the roof was covered. Hay went on top of the poplars. Dad cut it with the scythe he had brought from England, raked it by hand, and hauled it to the house in the wagon box. Sods were then laid over the hay.

To get the sod Dad ploughed several furrows, cut the turned sod into foot-long pieces, piled them in the wagon box, and hauled them to the house. Then Dad got on the roof and Mother handed the sods up to him, and he laid them more or less like shingles. It was hard, dirty work, and to get it over with as soon as possible Mother and Dad worked all day long, then, black and hungry, we got into the dirty wagon and went home.

We were returning to the tent after a day of sodding when we saw the second bear.

Dad had always pretended not to believe our story about that first bear, but when we saw the second he had to admit there might be dangerous animals in Canada.

We were jogging along home when suddenly Mother leaned forward, her blue eyes wide. 'Look there,' she said, pointing at the tent. 'Isn't that a bear?'

Dad stared for a moment, and blinked as if he didn't believe his eyes. 'I'll be damned if it isn't,' he said in a thin, excited voice. Then he tossed the reins to Mother and jumped out of the wagon. 'Where's them big bullets?' he called over his shoulder.

'In the blue box,' Mother shouted, then she pushed the reins in my direction, jumped out of the wagon, and followed Dad.

The bear, of course, had loped off into the little grove by then, but Dad began loading the old muzzle-loader. He was excited and he put things in by handfuls, and packed the whole down with the ramrod. 'You're overloading that gun,' Mother warned, but Dad didn't seem to hear. 'Get me some caps,' he said as he rammed down the last of the paper, then he dashed off into the grove. Mother dashed after him.

Lily and I, startled at being left alone, looked at each other, then without a word we huddled on the wagon seat with Jack between us and stared at the spot where Dad and Mother had disappeared.

Excited sounds came from the grove. Branches snapped and under-growth groaned as feet crushed it. Mother called to Dad. A gun banged.

The horses pricked up their ears at the noise, but Dad often shot prairie chickens from the wagon, so they were not really frightened, and the shot wasn't loud. Lily's eyes were as big as brown eggs. Jack buried his face in my shoulder.

A shout or two followed the shot, and there was more crashing of underbrush and twigs, then suddenly there was silence. The little grove and the wide prairie were still and silent. The white tent crouched close to the shadowy grass, and darkness like a stalking cat crept out of the woods and stole across the open spaces. Lily said 'Look' and pointed to a clump of dim willows. I couldn't see anything except twigs and leaves blotched by darkness, but Lily whispered that something moved. 'I sink it's a bear,' she said.

I leaned forward and looked hard. A shadow was all I could see, but suddenly I felt very small, and the prairie seemed terribly big and awfully quiet. 'Let's go to the Metherells',' I whispered, remembering we had been safe there when the first bear came.

Getting Jack out of the wagon was a problem: he was big and heavy, and he couldn't walk; but somehow I lifted him down, and staggering under his weight we started off. We had gone only a few steps, however, when Mother suddenly came hurrying around the grove. She didn't look at all like the quiet mother I was used to. She was young and excited, a Diana enjoying the chase. Her cheeks glowed pink, her blue eyes sparkled, her lips smiled, even her knot of hair that had slipped a little looked adventurous. A long bramble clung to her skirt, but she didn't seem to notice. 'Where are you going?' she asked as she came towards us on light feet.

'To the Metherells',' I said. 'The bear might come back.'

'No, it won't, and the Metherells aren't at home. They're after the bear, too. Stay in the wagon. You'll be all right.' She lifted Lily and Jack to the wagon seat. 'I'll be back directly.' She ran back the way she had come.

I climbed into the wagon and sat down on the seat. Mother's coming had reassured me a little, but I was still worried about the bear. The thickening darkness didn't help, either. It turned the trees and willows into blobs of night, and made the open spaces look bigger and more mysterious than ever, like long tunnels of darkness through which anything might come. I made myself as small as possible as I crouched on the wagon seat, and looked anxiously into the night. After a while excited voices came out of the emptiness; they seemed a long way off and strange, but after a while Mother, Dad, Mr and Mrs Metherell, and Bill came around the corner of the grove.

They were all talking and laughing, and for a moment they seemed like strangers, then Dad lit the lantern and lifted Lily and Jack off the wagon seat, and I felt comparatively safe again. In a little while a smudge was going, the fire was crackling, the kettle was on, and everybody was sitting close to the stove discussing the bear. Nobody had seen him after he disappeared into the grove, but everybody had enjoyed the hunt, and agreed that they had thoroughly frightened the bear. The Metherells were sure he was much smaller than the first bear, but he was still plenty big, and might be dangerous if hungry.

' Now do you believe me?' Mother asked triumphantly when the tea had been drunk, and the Metherells and Bill had gone. 'You said the first bear was nowt but a coyote, but you saw this one with your own eyes. You have to admit that this is no place for bairns and women with things like that about.'

'Well,' Dad said slowly, 'it really wasn't so much of a bear. And the way it ran! I doubt if it would hurt a flea. Why, even Jack could scare a thing like that.'

'I thought you'd have some excuse.' Mother dumped rolled oats into boiling water. 'You'll never be satisfied to give up until one of us is killed. And be sure you put that gun in a safe place. The way you loaded it, it might go off and kill somebody.'

Dad put the gun behind the big box, and warned both Lily and me not to go near it, but neither he nor Mother were easy about it. It was still loaded, the shot we had heard had been fired by Mr Metherell, and there was no way of unloading it short of firing it.

Mother wanted Dad to shoot just to get the charge out of the gun, but Dad said he was short of bullets and didn't want to waste any. He took the cap off the firing pin and assured Mother the gun was quite safe, but he handled it with great care when we went to work on the house next day. 'Keep an eye out for a prairie chicken,' he told me as we bumped along.

We didn't see a sign of a prairie chicken that day or all the next week. There were meadow-larks and blackbirds, sparrows, crows, and hawks, but no prairie chickens at all. 'Aren't you ever going to get us any meat?' Mother asked.

'I thought you didn't like prairie chicken,' Dad said.

Mother said she preferred beef, but you had to take what you could get in this country, and she would like some sort of meat before she forgot what it tasted like. 'You'll have to fire that gun some time,' she said. 'I told you it was overloaded.'

'I'll get a chicken soon,' Dad promised, but days passed. Either there were no chickens or Dad preferred not to see them.

One morning, however, I spotted a chicken. 'See, there's one,' I whispered excitedly, and pointed to the brown neck sticking up out of the grass.

'It looks like one all right,' Dad said, but he didn't sound pleased, and he was in no hurry to stop the team.

The chicken made no attempt to fly away. It just stood there in the grass looking the other way. 'Maybe I'd better have a go at it,' Dad said doubtfully and handed the reins to me, then he got out of the wagon and picked up the gun.

'Where are you going?' I asked, for the chicken wasn't far away, and neither the horses nor I minded the noise of a shot.

'Just over this way a bit,' Dad said, and walked a good way from the chicken and knelt down in the grass.

What was wrong, I wondered. Dad had always fired either sitting or standing. And what a long time he was taking about aiming! He fitted the gun to his shoulder, then refitted it, and settled lower in the grass. If he didn't hurry the chicken would fly before he was ready, and I wouldn't blame it. I'd almost lost interest in the business myself.

I lolled on the wagon seat and watched while Dad went through the process of aiming again, but I was fast losing patience, and half-wishing the chicken would fly, when suddenly the loudest bang ever heard in those parts rolled over the prairie. It shattered the air it was so loud, and even the staid old team almost jumped out of their harness. But far more frightening than the terrible noise was the flash of rainbow flame that spurted from the gun barrel. It was so bright it even dimmed the sun for a moment, and it pulled the gun right out of Dad's hands, and rolled him over backwards.

He lay quite still for a while all spread out on the grass, then he sat up and looked around and blinked. His face was a queer white, his mouth was open, and his eyes looked flat, almost as if he couldn't see. After a moment he felt his right shoulder, then he rubbed his eyes and got up. The gun was a little distance away, and he staggered over to it and picked it up, then he came towards the wagon. 'Aren't you going to get the chicken?' I asked.

'Eh?' Dad asked.

'The chicken,' I insisted. 'Aren't you going to look for it?'

'Which way did it go?' Dad shook his head and rubbed his eyes again.

'I don't know,' I told him, 'but it must be somewhere.'

'Yes.' Dad got into the wagon and drove to where the chicken ought to have been, but there wasn't even a feather. 'Guess it got away,' he said, and turned the team towards the tent.

'Aren't we going to build the house?' I asked, for there was still mudding and chinking to be done.

'Not to-day.' Dad sagged in the seat, and his face still looked queer. 'I think I'll rest a bit first.'

Mother came out of the tent when she heard the wagon. 'Walter, what is it?' she asked when she saw Dad's pale face.

'The gun kicked a bit.' Dad got out of the wagon and sat down on the little chair.

Mother unbuttoned Dad's shirt. 'You might have been killed,' she said when she saw the huge black and blue mark where the gun butt had been. 'I told you that gun was overloaded. Go and rest a while. I'll unhitch the team.'

'I think I will.' Dad walked unsteadily into the tent. Mother put a pillow under his damaged shoulder, then she put the kettle on for tea.

After he had had some strong tea and a rest Dad told Mother how the gun had acted. 'It hit me like a ton of bricks,' he said, smiling thinly. 'I tell you, Sally, I thought I was done for. And when I came to everything was spinning.'

'This country will do for all of us if we stay here much longer,' Mother said.

Dad spent the rest of the day in bed, and for a week his shoulder was stiff and sore.

The accident, of course, delayed the house. Dad tried to nail chinks in the spaces between the logs with one hand, but it was hard, slow work.

As soon as the chinking was finished mudding began. Mudding wasn't quite as bad as sodding had been, we weren't completely covered with dust, but it was still dirty work. Dad dug the clay in the nearby slough and hauled it to the house, then he mixed it with chopped grass and water. The grass was supposed to keep the clay from cracking and give body to the mud.

The cracks in the wall had to be filled with mud both inside and out, and the job took several days. I helped at first. I had always enjoyed making mud pies, but after three days I was no longer interested, and by the time all the cracks were filled I was sick of the sight of mud. Mother said she had always felt sorry for the Israelites when they had to make bricks for Pharaoh, but until then she had never fully realized what a truly miserable job they had had.

While we waited for the mud to dry Dad made a door out of some boards. For hinges he used pieces of leather, and a piece of wood with a nail through it kept the door closed. We hadn't a lock, but nobody in those days ever locked their door. Dad also made a frame for the little window. He had been warned not to have much window space. Glass was expensive, and windows let in a lot of cold, so our little window was only about two by two, and divided into four small spaces.

'What do you think of it now, Sally?' Dad asked proudly when the house was finished. 'Looks plenty big enough, doesn't it? And it's all ours. No rent to pay to anybody.'

'It turned out better than I thought.' Mother's lips smiled, but there was home-sickness in her blue eyes.

I, however, was as proud of the new house as Dad was. I thought it the most wonderful house in the world, and I found something new to admire every time I looked at it. The bulges in the walls were perfect shelves for my collection of small stones. I thought it pure magic that the ridge-pole stayed up. As for the door, I opened and closed it so often Mother finally told me to stop or the leather hinges would be worn out.

But the most wonderful thing about the house was the fact that we had built it. Not so long ago there had been nothing at all on this spot, and now our house stood there. We had caused it to grow. With our own hands we had put it together using the things we had found on the prairie, and I had helped. I had held that log while Dad notched it, and I had stuffed clay into that crack near the floor. How smart Dad was to know just how to build such a perfect house! I looked at his thin young face, and wonder and pride filled my small chest. My dad, I was sure, knew everything.

Having a real house of our own added greatly to my sense of security and belonging. Ploughing the land and planting the potatoes had given me an interest in the land, but when we moved into the new house I realized for the first time that this land out of all the land of the earth was actually ours. The prairie stretched wide and empty in every direction, but this spot, this hundred and sixty acres, belonged to us. It was our plot of earth, and no landlord could tell us to move. We could dig holes in it, clear through to China if we wanted, and no one could stop us. It was ours.

Although the house was small it seemed big after the tent. The bed didn't have to be rolled up every morning. The stove was permanently inside, and we could make porridge even when it rained. There was no glass in the window, and no floor except the bare earth, but to have four walls around us again was wonderful, especially at night.

Our furniture, of course, didn't take up much room. All we had was the stove, the little folding chair, the blue box, and the big packing-case. Dad built a bedstead soon after we moved in, and put up some shelves, and made an arm-chair. He also brought in the wagon seat and put it in front of the stove.

The brown walls and floor were still very drab-looking, and to brighten them Mother brought out a pink and white spread for the bed, and draped an antimacassar over the glassless window. 'That does it and no mistake,' Dad said when he saw the bed-spread. 'Sally, this is the nicest home on the prairie.'

When Mrs Metherell saw the antimacassar she said it was far too lovely for a log shack. It ought to be put away and saved for a better house some time in the future. Mother, however, said she had plenty of antimacassars and she was going to enjoy them while she could. The future might never come. And how sensible she was!

Mother had crocheted the antimacassars before she was married. They were a little over a yard long, and about two feet wide, and hours of work had gone into them. I used to marvel at the pattern, and at the number of stitches in them, for though I couldn't crochet I could knit, and knew the tedium of hand work. 'How long did it take you to make one?' I asked, and when Mother told me I knew she was just as clever as Dad. Beauty, however, wasn't the antimacassars' only virtue, they were something nobody else had. The Metherells' house had two rooms, and Mr Gardiner's little house had a pole floor, while the Claxtons' house was said to have two windows. None of them, however, had antimacassars, or even curtains. That hand-made lace draped so gracefully over our little window made our house unique, and gave it a touch of elegance even the bachelors noticed. 'You have a nice place here, Mrs Pinder,' they said, looking around the little room. 'It's real homelike.'

'It isn't much,' Mother said, but she looked pleased. Dad, of course, always looked proud when anyone admired the house, and told the bachelors they ought to get married and have a home, too.

The bachelors said there was nobody to marry, which was quite true, at least where we were. Dad, however, always told them about the Dukhobors, and what fine strong women they were. 'They'd be a rare help to a man,' he said, his eyes twinkling. 'And they aren't as plain as you might think, either. That one young lass was fair bonny.'

'If that's your idea of beauty,' Mother said with a toss of her little head, 'why didn't you marry a woman the size of a horse?'

'I wasn't thinking of myself,' Dad said, still smiling. 'But for a man that's going to live here one of them girls would be all right. He wouldn't have to turn a hand unless he wanted to. They say them women do all the work. All the men do is manage a bit.'

'What a shame!' Mother pressed her lips together. 'I should think with a bit of training the women could be taught to do the managing and save the men even that.'

'I wouldn't wonder,' Dad chuckled. 'But even though the Dukhobor women can't do everything, a man could do a lot worse than marry one of them.'

' Well, when you get rid of me you might try it,' Mother said. 'But I'll bet you'll be disappointed. They looked as if they had minds of their own to me. If you married one you might find you had to go her way more than a bit.'

The bachelors thought so, too, and they were sure the Dukhobor women wouldn't know how to make a home the way they wanted it.

Dad said the Dukhobor houses were very comfortable, and he was right. The one we had stayed in was both snug and warm, but the beds were covered with dark blankets, and there were no curtains at the windows. Women who worked as hard as they did had no time for frills.

Mother, of course, worked hard, too, but she had a knack for home-making. Wherever she lived that place was always cheerful, partly perhaps because it was always clean and tidy. Our beds were never left unmade until noon, and unwashed dishes never cluttered our packing-box table. The paper on the shelves, scalloped with the scissors, was always clean and straight, and the little stove never looked grey and neglected. Mother polished it every week even when it stood outside. The blue teapot never held old damp tea-leaves. It was emptied after every meal, washed, and put away. We had no broom, but Mother made one out of willows and swept the dirt floor every day. The home-made broom wasn't very effective, and Mother often got down on her hands and knees and swept with the little handbrush she had brought from England, but the willow broom was not thrown away even when it became dry and frayed. A broom to Mother was a symbol of home. Once it came into a house it belonged there, and it was bad luck to take it away. If you left the house you left the broom also.

As soon as we were settled in the house Dad built a barn. It was much easier to build than the house had been: the logs were thinner and smaller, and it had a flat roof. Dad said we couldn't have much use for it, horses, he had heard, could live outside, but a homestead had to have a barn. It was one of the requirements.

A fire-guard came next. Dad ploughed a big one all around the house, the barn, and the grove. The fire-guard served two purposes: it was a protection from the prairie fire the old-timers said was sure to come, and it provided sod for banking the house.

Mother, who was afraid of fire, said she couldn't understand why there was so much danger this year when the prairie hadn't burned last year, or the year before.

'It's these greenhorns,' one old-timer said. 'They don't know anything about fires, and they aren't careful. One of them's going to drop a live match one of these days as sure as shooting.'

Fire, however, wasn't the only danger the old-timers warned us about. They said the coming winter was going to be a regular humdinger. The musk-rat houses were huge, bigger than they had been for years, and that was a sure sign of extreme cold. They also said our clothing wasn't right for a Canadian winter, even a mild one. Cloth coats, caps without ear tabs, and thin gloves were not nearly enough protection. We needed coats lined with sheepskin, caps that came down over the ears, leather mitts with wool mitts inside, and long wool underwear. They also told us our feet would freeze in leather boots. We ought to have moccasins such as the Indians wore.

'I simply can't believe such tales,' Dad said when the old-timer had gone. 'It doesn't get that cold at the North Pole.'

A few days later, however, Bill Banks, a bachelor who lived about three miles east, came by and told us a similar story. He had just come from Battleford, and everybody had told him to buy long woollen drawers.

'They're having you on, Bill,' Dad said, for everyone knew that Bill was good-hearted and did not mind a practical joke.

'No, they aren't,' Bill insisted. 'Everybody said so.'

The Metherells, however, agreed with Dad. They said the old-timers were only pulling our legs. 'Stuff and nonsense,' Mrs Metherell said. 'They want us to leave, and they're trying to frighten us away. Forty below zero! Who ever heard of such cold? Just look at the map.

England's farther north than we are, and it doesn't get that cold there, or anywhere near.'

Mother mentioned the Gulf Stream that was somewhere near England, but nobody thought a mere stream could make all that difference.

'All right,' Bill said, offended by their attitude. 'But when you're all frozen stiff don't say I didn't tell you. Laugh all you like, but have some wood close to the house. They say the blizzards here are so bad you can't see a finger in front of you, and you're apt to freeze to death just going to the woodpile.'

Everybody laughed and said that was a tale that topped them all, except perhaps the one about the musk-rats. How could they know how cold it was going to be? It didn't make sense, and proved that the old-timers were stringing us.

Just to be on the safe side, however, Dad dug a deep hole under the packing-box that served as our table. 'The potatoes, when we dig them, will be out of the way there,' he said. 'And if it does get a bit cold we won't have to bother about them.' He hauled a lot of wood for the same reason, and piled it near the door so that it would be handy. When he finished, the woodpile was much larger than the house. The Metherells said we had enough wood to last the rest of our lives, and even Master Willie, who seldom laughed at anything, asked Dad if he expected to live for ever. None of the settlers, of course, realized how bitter cold the winters in northern Canada could be.

CHAPTER TWENTY-THREE

WHILE we were busy finishing the house, moving in, and gathering wood the days had been getting shorter and shorter, and the mornings and the evenings had become quite crisp and cold. Without any real warning autumn had stolen over the prairie.

It was, however, a pleasant season that year. There were no long, dreary days of drizzling rain, and no sudden snowstorms. In the mornings we were glad to sit by the stove while we ate our porridge, and in the evenings the smell of wood burning in the little stove was welcome, but the afternoons were mellow and warm, and everything seemed a little sleepy. The bees stumbling about on the golden-rod were only half awake, and there was a minor note in the song of the grasshoppers. The mosquitoes had gone by then, and so had the butterflies. A meadow-lark warbled now and then as it paused for a while on its way south. We were hardly aware of it, but sleep was stealing gently and softly over the prairie.

The great arch of the sky, that had been a bright and polished blue, was now slightly golden even at noon, and in the mornings and the evenings a thin blue haze like the ghost of a forgotten fog dimmed the horizon. The round leaves of the poplars and the long, slender leaves of the willows turned a deep and heavy green, then the frost touched them and they glowed red, orange, yellow, brown, and gold. The grass died and turned a pale silver beige that shimmered in the sun, and small rose-bushes that dotted the prairie became spots of deep maroon.

The sunsets and sunrises, though dimmed a little by the thin veil of mist that hung from the sky, were still beautiful, though the colours were much softer than they had been, and at night the stars blinked sleepily, and even the moon seemed to yawn.

There was still plenty of tall golden-rod by the groves, but there was a thin dust on it, and the wild asters, small blue flowers that grew in big clusters on long stalks, looked like the blue eyes of infants, wide but sleepy.

'You know,' Mother said one morning, 'I haven't seen a canary or a crow for a long time.'

Dad said he hadn't, either. Most of the birds had gone, slipping away quietly as if they did not want us to miss them. The blackbirds, however, made sure they would be missed. They had been everywhere during the summer—in the groves, and sloughs, and around the house—but when fall came they gathered in large flocks, hundreds of them in one grove, and trilled their throaty song from morning to night for about three days, then as if one of them had given the signal they left, and all at once the trees and willows were silent and lonely.

The sleepy silence that was settling over the prairie pleased Dad a lot. 'This is wonderful harvest weather,' he said as he and I hauled wood for our ever-growing pile. 'I tell you, lass, this is God's own country. All the seasons are fair perfect. The spring's not too hot, good growing weather in the summer with plenty of rain, and now this sunshine at harvest time. One of these days there'll be wheat fields here as far as you can see.'

Bill Banks, who was the unofficial mailman—he hated to be alone and bringing the mail gave him a good excuse to visit—warned us that this wasn't a typical fall.

'The weather isn't like this every year,' Bill warned. 'Nolan, who runs the ferry, says this is the best summer for years. And wait till you see what the winters are like. Nolan says your breath freezes before it leaves your nose, and first thing you know you have icicles in your head.'

'How awful!' Mother's blue eyes widened in horror. 'Maybe we ought to leave before winter sets in.'

'They're only trying to frighten us,' Dad said. 'They haven't been killed by ice in their heads, have they? We're just as tough as they are. No, this is a great country. What if it does freeze a bit now and then? Wheat will grow just the way the pea-vine grows. I tell you, Sarah, in five years we'll be rolling in money, and never have to turn a hand again unless we want to; then we'll go home for a good long trip.'

'I thought we were going back to stay,' Mother said. 'And in a year, not five.'

'In a year you won't want to go back and stay,' Dad said easily. 'You won't be used to the soot, and it will smother you, and you'll feel squeezed in them narrow houses next door.'

'I could do with a bit of soot, and I like a house next door,' Mother said. 'As for this dryness, I wish it would rain like it does in England in the autumn, then we wouldn't have to bother about prairie fires.'

'We won't have to bother about fires once we get some ploughing done.' Dad finished his tea and went out to harness the team for another afternoon of wood hauling.

Dad had taken the box off the wagon, we could haul bigger loads without it, and on our way to the woods we perched on the frame between the front and back wheels. Dad's swinging feet almost touched the dry grass, but my short legs couldn't even reach the tall wild mint that was now brown and dry. As we jogged along through the warm sunshine Dad talked of the advantages of Canada, a subject he never tired of. 'It's so rich you can't even believe it,' he said, 'and there's that much of it. It isn't only the wheat it will grow, but the things they might find underground. Jack will be rich some day.'

'Aren't we going back to England?' I asked wistfully after a while, for I still missed Aunt Jane and the happy, carefree life I had enjoyed in the little house by the Spen. Not that I wasn't happy in Canada; I was, but I was getting tired of being a big girl. It had been fun for a while, but being little and helpless had its compensations. When I was small my time had been my own. I could skip rope, and swing, dress and undress my doll, even be a pest now and then. Now, being big, I had to help Dad haul wood whether I wanted to or not, take care of Jack at least part of the time, set the table for meals, and help Lily with her buttons. Worst of all, I couldn't cry when I felt like it. Big girls of six didn't shed tears.

'There's nothing to look for'ard to in England,' Dad said slowly, and his thin face became serious and thoughtful. 'Nothing at all. A working man makes a bare living, and that's it. Some folks don't care. They can't see beyond the pub on Saturday night. But everybody ought to look for'ard to something. Them that's satisfied never amount to much.' He shook the reins and Darkie and Nelly trotted a few steps. 'Allus fix your sights on summat,' Dad went on, slipping into the Yorkshire dialect, 'and be sure it's worth summat, too. Three meals a day, a place to sleep, and a bob a week towards a funeral is nowt.'

'Yes,' I said, though I hardly knew what Dad was talking about.

'If we stop here you'll have a chance to amount to something, especially Jack. There'll be schools one of these days, and a man with an education can be anything he wants here. Canada won't always be like this, big and empty. There'll be big towns, and happen mines. You never know. They haven't even scratched this country yet. I won't live to see it, and maybe you won't, either. I wish your mother liked this place better, and I think she will after a bit if she'll give it a fair trial. I hope so at any rate. I fair hate to think of leaving.'

'But if we aren't going to see the towns,' I said, my imagination caught and frightened a little by the idea of dying, 'if we're going to die before they come why should we stay?'

'We'll see the beginnings and help with them, too,' Dad said, 'and that'll be something.'

I didn't relish the idea of dying before the towns were built. Schools didn't matter so much. I had never cared about going to school in England, but towns with candy shops and streets were different. I liked them, and I saw no reason to build them for somebody else. If I wasn't going to live to enjoy them why bother with them? It seemed far simpler, and more sensible, to go to a town that was already built.

'You don't understand,' Dad said when I told him how I felt. And being only six years old, of course, I didn't. But I tried hard. I listened patiently while Dad talked, not only that day, but many other days as we continued to gather wood. For although the season was getting on, and our food was low, Dad couldn't go to Battleford for our winter supplies until we had rain, snow, or a prairie fire.

We did not hurry with the wood gathering, we thought we had enough to last for two winters at least. We jogged happily through the warm afternoons, talking and dreaming. Dad, of course, was talking more to himself than to me, but I was very flattered that he told me of his plans, and I tried my best to understand them, though my ideas of wealth were not like his. Prosperity to Dad meant miles of wheat, belonging not only to him but to other people as well. You couldn't be rich alone. He dreamed of huge granaries, fat cattle, large barns, snug homes, and a Canada no longer thinly populated and poor, but a rich and prosperous country—a power in the world.

I thought his ideas wonderful, of course, but to me a new dress, preferably blue with some white lace somewhere, represented wealth.

Dad said I could have two or maybe three dresses as soon as he got the farm going, but he was never willing to stay long on the subject of clothes. The future was all-important. He talked of the railroad, and wheat trains a mile long, of good roads, and paved streets, and perhaps some day gaslight in the houses. 'It may not be in my time, but one of these days Canada will have everything England has and a lot more,' he would say. 'And we'll have been in on it. We'll have helped get it going.' There was a glow on his thin face, and awe in his voice, but I was worried. If Dad wasn't going to enjoy the towns what good would they do him? Why not let the next generation do their own hard work? As far as I could see it wasn't up to us to pave the street for people we didn't even know.

Dad, however, didn't agree with me. 'You have to look beyond the end of your nose if you're ever going to amount to anything,' he told me, trying to put his thoughts into words I could understand. 'You can't reap everything you sow, and you oughtn't to expect to. You should plan on leaving things a bit better than you found them for them that come after. If you do that you'll end up a bit better yourself. It's them that tries to see beyond to-morrow that keeps things going for'ard.'

'Yes,' I said, and tried to look as if I understood.

'It's going to be hard for a while.' Dad's wide forehead wrinkled a little. 'But there's something to work for besides bed and board. And when Jack grows up things will be easier for him and his children.'

'Yes,' I said, and kicked at the tall spears of dry mint that slipped past my dangling feet, but I couldn't help wondering why Dad seemed so pleased to be working for something he would never enjoy. As far as I could see it was a complete waste of time. Years later, of course, when my son was born, I understood how Dad felt, and why he did not mind, even enjoyed, laying the foundation for something that would not be full-grown in his time. Children extend time, and the present is only important because of the effect it has on their lives in the time beyond to-morrow.

CHAPTER TWENTY-FOUR

W E did not, of course, always talk of the far future as we jogged over the dry, crisp-smelling grass. Often we talked of the things around us, and I asked innumerable questions. Where had the birds gone? Why did the sky just above the red-and-gold trees look like thin milk? Why were the rabbits turning white?

Dad told me the birds had gone south for the winter, the sky was white because of the haze, and the rabbits were turning white so that they would match the snow when winter came.

Sometimes we talked of Aunt Jane and the little shop, and I longed for a lucky packet: a paper bag that held a whistle, a bit of liquorice, and a few hard candies, and cost only a penny.

'You wouldn't like Littletown now,' Dad told me. 'All that smoke, and them narrow streets, and no grass to play on.'

I didn't disagree with him, at least out loud, but I would have liked seeing Aunt Jane very much. As for the smoke, there seemed to be quite a bit of it, or something like it, right here. The haze was very thick, and my nose itched the way it did when the stove smoked.

'What shall we do when the prairie fire comes?' I asked, and rubbed my eyes. 'Shall we run away?'

'We'll be all right,' Dad said, but his eyes narrowed the way they did when he was worried, and he glanced uneasily at the grass. It was very thick and dry, and the gold and orange leaves that still hung on the trees were quite brittle. All the sap had gone out of them, and when I picked a leaf and rubbed it it broke easily. 'We have a good wide fire-guard,' Dad said as if trying to reassure himself. 'Sometimes I think there isn't going to be a prairie fire this year after all. It's near time for snow according to Bill Banks. Another week or two and we'll be safe.'

I hoped Dad was right, for we had heard some frightful tales about prairie fires. Sometimes, we had been told, they came at night, and people were burned in their beds. Sometimes the smoke smothered them. And they always came fast before you had time to run. 'Be sure you have everything ready,' the old-timers warned. 'Some sacks with hay in the bottom to give them weight, and a barrel of water to wet the sacks in. You won't have much time once the fire starts. There's always a wind, and it comes fast.'

We didn't always have a barrel of water, or even a wash-tubful. The slough was almost dry, and we had to get our drinking water from the Metherells. There were sacks in the barn, and hay, but they were dry. As far as I could see the fire-guard was all we had to depend on. It was twelve furrows wide, but prairie fires, it seemed, had a way of jumping.

Mother, who hadn't been sleeping well at nights because she was worried about a fire, always said she would run away when the fire came. She never said where she would run to, but I thought she had a good idea, and intended to run with her.

I was thinking of how my legs would fly through the grass as I outraced the fire when Dad suddenly leaned forward and tightened into a knot. 'Look there, Mary,' he said, and pointed over the ears of the horses. 'Isn't that smoke?'

A puff of yellow cloud was rolling upward behind the distant trees. I stared at it, fascinated. 'I don't know,' I said.

Even in that small space of time the cloud had grown much bigger, and the lower part of it had turned brown. 'It is smoke,' Dad said in a queer, tight voice. 'The prairie's on fire. Hang on,' and he whipped the team and turned them towards home.

'What are you doing back so soon?' Mother asked anxiously when we clattered into the yard.

Dad tried to smile though his face looked pale. 'There's a prairie fire coming,' he said.

'Where?' Mother looked around. 'I can't see any fire.'

'You can't see it for the bush,' Dad said. 'But it isn't far off.'

'Well, then, don't stand there looking gormless,' Mother snapped. 'Let's go and put it out.'

'It's too big for that.' Dad began taking out the heavy iron pin that held the double-trees to the wagon. 'But I'll go and plough a wider guard. You stay in the house with the bairns. You'll be all right.'

'The bairns can stay by themselves,' Mother said. 'I'm going with you.'

Dad told her she'd be better off in the house, but Mother paid no attention to him. 'Where's them sacks?' she asked, and she ran into the barn and got them.

I helped hitch the horses to the plough, then Mother told me to take Lily and Jack and go into the house.

'You'd better go with them, Sarah,' Dad said. 'You'll be better off there. All I have to do is start a back-fire.'

'Then let's get on with it.' Mother's round face looked frightened but firm.

'Well, all right.' Dad shook the reins, and Dad and Mother and the team went around the grove and out of sight.

I took Lily and Jack into the house, and we huddled on the wagon bench for a long time, but the four walls seemed to press in on us, and the unnatural darkness in the middle of the day frightened us. Also, we couldn't see a thing. The fire might be eating up the grove, and we wouldn't know it. I got off the wagon bench, and we all went outside and climbed into the wagon box, and crouched in a corner. We couldn't see any fire, or what was going on at the other side of the grove, but the world was still terrifying.

Rolling clouds of black and brown smoke filled the sky, and stung our noses and eyes. The friendly sun had become an angry red ball that glared at us. Darkness seemed to be closing in, though it was still early afternoon. The wind was hot, and it dropped ashes on us, and skeletons of leaves, and blackened grass. Lily held out her hand and caught a leaf, but it was warm and she dropped it.

I brushed the ashes out of Jack's fair hair, but more kept falling. The whole sky seemed full of ash, wind, and smoke, and we were alone in the turmoil. Mother and Dad had forgotten us.

After a while Lily began to cry, and even Jack, who was only about a year old, looked pale and frightened. Had the fire burned Dad and Mother? I recalled some of the stories I had heard. Prairie fires often jumped fire-guards and burned houses and people. Perhaps this fire had burned Mother and Dad and was now coming to burn us. The smoke was much thicker than it had been, and the wind hotter. 'Let's go to the Metherells',' I said, remembering that once Mother had told me to go there if she didn't come back from the slough.

Lily said 'All wite' and dried her eyes with her fists, and we scrambled out of the wagon box. It was supported on two or three logs, and was quite a drop for Jack, but he made it without any trouble.

I took one of Jack's little hands—he could walk by then—and Lily took the other, and we started off. We followed the little path that went around the grove, rubbing the smoke out of our eyes, and fully expecting to be safe and out in the friendly sunshine again once we were away from the trees that seemed to be holding the smoke and wind. But when we rounded the corner of the grove a terrible sight met us. Flames were everywhere. They stretched from grove to grove, jagged rows of fire much taller than I was, and all an angry orange-red. While we watched open-mouthed, the flames leaped high into some trees and licked at the bright leaves, turning them into black ash, then they dropped back to the cringing earth, leaving the trees bare and smoking, and began gobbling up the underbrush and the late asters.

The wind was almost as vicious as the fire. It tossed burning branches high in the air, fanned the flames into a wild dance, and hurled the smoke at us. It stung our eyes, and scraped our throats and made us cough, but worst of all it felt like a hot hand close on my face.

Lily and I stood still in the little trail and looked at each other. We were too frightened to speak. The whole world seemed to be on fire. We didn't know what to do.

Suddenly, as if she knew we needed her, Mother came out of the smoke, but she looked so unlike the pretty mother we were used to we were almost afraid of her. Her face was black, and her eyes were red. Her hair was singed, and so were her eyelashes and brows. 'Where are you going?' she called.

'To the Metherells' away from the fire,' I shouted.

'There's fire at the Metherells', too. You'll be burned to death if you try to go there. Go back home, and be quick.' And without waiting to see whether we obeyed or not she went back into the smoke.

We were more than glad to do as we were told. Hurrying as fast as we could we returned to the wagon box, climbed in, and crouched there too frightened to even move, and at last the fire came around the corner of the grove.

Driven by the wind a spear of flames began to eat up the grass in the little glade between our grove and the one nearest to it. The flames bent before the wind and took a bite of grass, then they straightened up for a moment, and weaved and swayed as they swallowed their mouthful. It was a terrible but fascinating sight. Lily's brown eyes, just above the rim of the wagon box, bulged, and her little face was white under its film of ash.

I suppose my face was white, too, and I know I shivered though I wasn't cold, but I made no effort to go into the house or even speak. I simply stood there practically paralysed with fear and fascination.

Jack huddled between Lily and me and didn't whimper even when hot ash fell on his face. Most of the ash and skeletons of leaves was warm by then, and once or twice a smoking twig fell in the wagon box, but fortunately they did no damage. What we would have done if Dad and Mother hadn't come I don't know: probably stood there watching the fire until we burned to death.

Dad and Mother, however, came around the grove while the fire was still some distance away. They were half hidden by smoke, and they looked like dolls in some terrible dream. Mother was driving the team and doing very well at it. She was running and her long, wide skirts streamed out behind her, and so did the little shawl tied around her neck. When they came to the edge of the fire-guard Dad righted the plough with a jerk, and the excited horses paused for a second, then, their backs bent and their legs stiff, they plunged forward.

There was only time to plough two furrows between Mr Gardiner's fire-guard and ours before the fire came dangerously close, but Dad and Mother didn't stop fighting even then. Dad tipped the plough on its side, snatched a handful of grass, lit it, and started back-firing. Mother drove the team close to the house, then, without even taking time to tie the horses, or glance at us, she ran to help Dad with the back-fire.

A back-fire is set along the edge of a fire-guard, a road, or some other obstacle. Having to burn against the wind it does not burn as fast as the wind-driven fire, and is much easier to control. The flames next to the guard are put out if they threaten to cross, the other side burns towards the oncoming fire, and they finally meet and burn out.

Dad and Mother had to work quickly, but they had to be careful, too. The wind was strong, and the two furrows only a narrow guard. Dad dragged a handful of burning grass for three or four yards, then, with their weighted sacks ready, he and Mother watched it. If the flames began to blow across the guard they beat at them until they went out. As soon as they had burned one little strip they started on another. It was exciting work. Dad tried to start each little section of fire when there was a lull in the wind, but a sudden gust sometimes caught the little back-fire and whipped it into a blaze. At times Mother and Dad were lost in smoke, and often the flames seemed to lean over and touch them. Once the fire leaped the guard, and Dad and Mother beat frantically until they got it out. They couldn't, of course, put the main fire out. All they could do was save our house, the grove beside it, and a little grass for the horses to eat.

Dad and Mother watched the fire until it had passed Mr Gardiner's fire-guard, then, when they were sure his little house was safe, they came slowly home, dragging their blackened sacks. Lily, Jack, and I were still clinging to the edge of the wagon box too stiff to move, even though we knew the danger was over. Afterwards Mother said she would have laughed when she saw us if she hadn't been so tired, and so glad we were safe. She said we looked so queer: three little noses, three pairs of eyes, and six little hands was all she could see above the rim of the wagon box.

Mother and Dad looked queer, too. Their faces were black, they had neither eyelashes nor eyebrows, and they were covered with ash from head to foot. The only clean thing about them was their eyeballs, and they looked like pale, red-rimmed marbles. Mother got quite a shock when she tried to hug Jack. He didn't recognize her and clung to me and cried.

But terrible as Dad and Mother looked, the prairie looked far worse. The grove beside Mr Gardiner's house and the one beside ours were still there, plus a little grass between, but all the rest of the prairie as far as we could see was charred and black. The trees that had been so lovely in their red and gold leaves were stark and bare. The tall blue asters and the golden-rod were only burned sticks, and the grass that had been a thick grey carpet and soft to walk on was now black and smoking ash. It seemed incredible that the prairie, lovely in its fall colours only this morning, was now a dark and dismal desolation. I looked at the poplars naked against the sky, at the shivering willows, and the consumed rose-bushes, and tears washed the ashes off my cheeks. 'Everything will grow again in the spring,' Mother said when I told her why I was crying, but I wasn't comforted. Spring seemed a long time away.

Dad and Mother had barely wiped the ash from their faces when the Metherells and Bill came to see how we had fared. They brought us some water because they knew we hadn't much, and Dad lit the fire, and Mother filled the kettle. While we waited for the kettle to boil we sat outside on the woodpile looking at the smoking desolation and the far-away fire that still winked in the gathering twilight.

I didn't see Mr Gardiner come, but after a while he was there. Everybody seemed to talk at once in happy, excited voices. The Metherells had saved their house and barn. It had been touch-and-go once or twice, but they had won. Dad and Mother had won, too, and they looked at one another with a new light in their smoke-reddened eyes, and a new pride on their smeared faces. The old-timers, who had predicted that the greenhorns would be burned out when the first prairie fire came, had been proved wrong. 'There's good stuff in the Barr Colony no matter what they say,' Mrs Metherell said proudly.

'Especially in the women,' Dad said, his thin face one big smile. 'You ought to have seen Sarah lambasting that fire. The way she swung that sack! I was glad it wasn't me she was hitting. And telling me she was scared of fire! She fair laid into it.'

'It wasn't because I wanted to,' Mother said, but she smiled happily. 'I beat because I had to, and I hope I never have to do it again.'

'Nell did a good job.' Mr Metherell smiled at his wife. 'As a matter of fact she told Bill and me what to do.'

'I did not.' Mrs Metherell's green eyes sparkled. 'I only told you to get the blazes out of the house when I saw the fire coming.' 'Well, we know now that we don't have to bother about the women,' Dad said, his ocean-flecked eyes sparkling. 'If they say they're scared we'll know they're having us on. The way Sarah tackled that fire, I bet she could best anything. And she thought she wasn't pioneer stuff.'

'And I'm not,' Mother said firmly. 'And I'd rather be where there are no prairie fires to fight.'

'Same here.' Mrs Metherell tilted her chin a little, and she and Mother went into the house to make tea.

After they had washed the ashes out of their throats with several cups of tea, and discussed the fire at length, our visitors went home, but they did not take the happy exultation with them. It filled our house, and lived with us for a long time, and while it was there Mother never mentioned going back to England.

CHAPTER TWENTY-FIVE

A BOUT a week after the prairie fire Dad went to Battleford for our winter supplies, and Mother and we three children were alone again.

We missed Dad, of course, the house always seemed quiet without his cheerful voice, and the great outside always seemed a little bigger and emptier when he was away; but with four stout walls around us we felt much safer than we had in the tent. We had a real door to shut, and even a bear wouldn't dare open it. At night when the lantern was lit the corners of the house were dark and mysterious, but the spot near the stove was snug and warm.

The days were still pale blue and gold, but Mother did not trust the sunshine. Most of the ducks had gone south, and there was a feeling of frost in the mornings. 'First thing we know it will freeze hard,' Mother said. 'And them potatoes still in the ground. I think I'll dig them.'

The potatoes hadn't done as well as Dad had expected, and we had eaten quite a few while they were still young and tender, but Mother didn't want to lose what were left. They were the only vegetable we had, and a pleasant change from porridge, bacon, and bread. The only trouble was that Mother couldn't take the three of us with her when she went to dig the potatoes. The patch was over half a mile away, close to where the tent had been, and although Jack could walk Mother thought the trip would be too much for him, and she couldn't carry both him and the potatoes.

'There's nothing that could hurt you,' Mother worried. 'You're just as safe without me as with me, and I would like to surprise Dad. Do you think you could manage for an hour or two, Mary?'

I had no idea how long an hour or two was, but I said I could manage fine, so Mother tied her little brown shawl under her chin, took a pail in each hand, and started for the potato patch.

The house and the grove seemed awfully quiet, but the sun was bright and we played outside for a while, then time began to drag. I had thought that two hours would be about the distance from the house to the barn, but apparently it was much longer, it had already gone over the far hill and out of sight. The shadow of the grove stretched long over the grass, and we got tired of the woodpile and went into the house.

I don't know who got into mischief first, or who opened the blue box, but Jack had a wonderful time pulling towels and pillow-slips out of it. Lily dragged out most of the pans and scattered them over the floor, then we discovered that the enamel bowls made good drums. When Mother came home we were pounding and shouting, and the house was practically upside-down.

'What an awful mess.' Mother stood in the doorway, a pail of potatoes in each hand, and dismay on her round face. 'And all the way home I was thinking how nice it was that you're a big girl, and then you do a thing like this.' She sat down on her little chair and wiped her perspiring face and looked as if she would like to cry.

Next day Mother couldn't make up her mind whether to leave us again or not. 'There's no telling what you might get into,' she said uneasily. But she wanted to dig the potatoes as a surprise for Dad. 'Do you think you can behave a bit better this time?' she asked. I said we would be just as good as gold, so after a little more worrying she put on her shawl and picked up the pails.

I herded Lily and Jack outside. Nobody was going to get into mischief to-day. We made a house with four pieces of wood, and built a fire-place with some stones, then, when the shadows began to creep far over the grass, I decided to be extra good and surprise Mother with a cup of tea when she got home.

I found some red haws and gave them to Lily and Jack to play with, then I went to the chopping-block and filled my pinafore with dry chips, and took them into the house. The stove lids were heavy, but I got them off and put my chips in the firebox, arranging them carefully, the small thin ones first, then the bigger ones. Lighting them was quite difficult. The matches were on the shelf out of reach, but I stood on the little chair and pushed at the match-box with a piece of wood until it knocked it on to the floor.

The matches had sulphur in them, and when I struck one it flared green and yellow, and the smell and smoke made me cough and brought tears to my eyes. I had to light quite a few matches before I coaxed my chips to burn, then the little flame had to be nursed carefully to keep it from going out. Finally I got a good blaze, put in some real wood, and replaced the stove lids. I knew I couldn't lift the iron kettle when it was full, so I dragged it to the hottest part of the stove and filled it with an enamel mug.

At that moment Lily came to the door and announced that Jack was choking. I ran outside and found he had filled his mouth with rose haws. I scooped them out with my finger, pounded him on the back, gave him a drink of water, and went back to my tea-making.

This being a special occasion I found a small white table-cloth and spread it over the top of the big box that we used as a table, then I set out the spoons, the enamel mugs, and the sugar. I had quite a time with the bread. It was soft, and the knife was dull, but I managed to hack a few lop-sided slices off the loaf. The jam didn't spread well, either, but I managed to get most of the bread that didn't crumble covered, then I put on more wood and went outside to watch for Mother.

I didn't have long to wait. In about five minutes she came around the corner of the grove. She was carrying a pail of potatoes in each hand, and her round face looked hot and tired. Her little shawl had slipped to her shoulders, and a small strand of hair had come loose and lay like a feather in front of her ear. I skipped into the house and poured the boiling water into the blue teapot, and announced proudly that tea was ready.

'Tea!' Mother dropped the pails of potatoes, and her face turned pale. 'You lit the fire?' Her voice was sharp.

'Yes. I had to light it to boil the kettle. I—I thought you'd like some tea.' I couldn't understand why she seemed so upset when I thought she'd be pleased, and tears of disappointment came to my eyes.

'Yes,' Mother said quickly, 'of course I would. I was just thinking when I came around the grove how nice some tea would be.' She moved towards the stove, but slowly as if she was rather limp.

'Let me pour it,' I said, and picked up the teapot.

'All right, but be careful.' Mother sat down on her little chair.

I tipped the teapot carefully and began to pour. To my horror a stream of clear water came out of the curving spout. I had forgotten to put tea in the pot.

Mother said she didn't mind weak tea at all, in fact she liked it much better than any other kind, and to prove it she drank three cups of hot water.

'How did you get the matches?' Mother asked after tea was over and she had rested a while. I told her, and she looked thoughtful for a while, then she told me to be very careful and never let Lily or Jack touch them.

A day or two after my failure as a tea-brewer Mother began teaching me what to do in case of fire. 'If a spark ever sets you or the others on fire, don't try to run,' she warned. 'Roll on the floor, or roll yourself or the others in a blanket. But one thing I want you to remember: don't play with the matches, or let Lily or Jack play with them.'

I promised never to touch the matches again until she said I could, and it was an easy promise to keep. The matches smelled horribly, and I had no desire to strike them. Rolling, however, was another matter. It sounded like fun, especially rolling Lily or Jack, and I asked a great many questions about it, and wanted to try it, but Mother said that wasn't necessary, and would only dirty a blanket. Since I couldn't try rolling I soon lost interest, especially when Mother repeated her instructions several times as if she feared I might forget. 'Yes,' I said in reply to her questions, and escaped to play as soon as I could. Instead of being fun, putting out a fire got to seem like a very dull business, and I didn't want to be bothered with it. So when, as sometimes happened, a hot spark fell on me or the other two I put it out with my fingers before it had time to grow into a blaze.

Soon after the potatoes were dug and stored in the little cellar under the big box Dad came home. We all ran to meet him and asked what he had brought. He laughed and said he had brought himself, and what more did we want? The wagon, however, was full to the top. There was bacon, tea, syrup, canned milk, jam, yeast, dried apples and prunes, Navy beans, baking-powder, a hundred-pound sack of sugar, five gallons of coal oil, and moccasins for all of us (they smelled of calves and were soft); a pile of letters and paper, a glass lamp, very wonderful I thought, and twelve hundred-pound sacks of flour.

Mother gasped when she saw the twelve sacks. 'Whatever made you bring so much?' she asked.

'I don't know.' Dad looked a little sheepish. 'They tell such tales. The musk-rat houses are bigger than they've ever been. They say we're in for a bad winter. I thought I'd be sure and bring enough.'

'You certainly did,' Mother sighed. 'That flour will last us for ever. Where are we going to put it?'

Dad suggested piling it in the corner opposite the bed. He laid some dry poles on the earth floor, then he piled the sacks crisscross on top of them. The pile reached almost to the rafters, and visitors asked Dad if he was going into the baking business, or expected to feed an army. And why, if he intended buying all the flour in Canada, hadn't he built a bigger house?

The flour did take up a lot of space, but when the white drifts were as high as the eaves, and Mr Gardiner's thermometer registered fifty below zero, the stack of white sacks with the blue and gold emblems on the sides became a symbol of security. No matter how long the winter lasted we knew our flour would last longer, and while we had flour we had food.

After he had stacked the flour Dad rested a few days, then he harnessed Darkie and Nelly and went on another trip.

We were always sorry to see Dad go away, but this was an especially sad departure. Darkie and Nelly were not coming back, Dad was going to sell them.

I was heart-broken when Mother told me. Darkie and Nelly had been good and loyal friends. Coming up the trail they had pulled us through many streams and tough places. They had brought us safely over the Eagle Hills, been stranded with us on the ferry, endured the mosquitoes and the flies, pulled the plough when the first furrow on our farm was turned, hauled the logs for our house and barn, helped combat the prairie fire, hauled our wood, and brought us our supply of food for the winter. Unlike the cow they hadn't deserted us at the first opportunity. At night Dad had hobbled them so that they couldn't wander far, but morning usually found them standing near the tent, head to tail, swishing at the flies. Except for the dapple-grey in Saskatoon they were the nicest horses I had ever seen. I thought of them as part of the family, and I expected them to stay with us for ever.

Dad didn't want to part with the horses, either, but a Mr Chisholm, an old-timer, had advised him to sell them. We hadn't enough hay to feed them through the winter, and they were getting too old to paw through the snow for their food. Besides, this was going to be a long, hard winter, and the horses would be better off in a good warm barn. 'We'd be in a bad way if we lost them,' Dad said.

'But they'll come back in the spring, won't they?' I asked hopefully. The crows, I had been told, would come back, so surely the horses could come back, too.

'Perhaps,' Mother said. 'But say good-bye to them for now.' There were tears in her blue eyes.

We patted Nelly's faithful brown head, and stroked Darkie's silky ears, and I talked to them, and told them how much I loved them, then I kissed their warm velvet noses, and hugged them as well as I could, and gave them some sugar. They nibbled my hand gently and blew through their noses, then Dad got into the wagon, and smiling with his lips but not with his eyes he drove away. We waved and blew kisses until he was out of sight.

A few days later Bill Banks brought Dad home. I knew Nelly and Darkie were not coming back, but when Dad returned without them I was disappointed. I had hoped he would change his mind about selling them. Dad, however, said the horses were well off. He had sold them to a nice fellow who had a good barn.

Soon after Dad came home the geese began flying south. Huge V's of them streamed across the sky. Some were as high as the clouds, some barely cleared the treetops. They passed almost constantly day and night, and their voices, though loud, still seemed lonely in the great stillness that had come over the prairie. 'Good-bye, good-bye,' they called, and their voices sounded sad and a little home-sick, as if they were sorry to go, and feared they might never return.

The passing of the geese and their wild, sad cry made Mother feel lonely and home-sick too. 'I wish we could fly away with them,' she said one day. 'This place is making me nervous. Everything seems to be going: the ducks and the blackbirds, and now the geese.'

'They'll all be back in the spring,' Dad said cheerfully, 'and singing louder than ever.'

'Yes, but what's going to become of us?' Mother asked despondently. 'Seems to me if everything else goes we ought to go as well.'

'The rabbits haven't gone,' Dad pointed out. 'Surely to goodness we're as tough as they are.'

Mother said we were not rabbits, and anyhow they were not noted for their brains.

The geese had barely gone when the first snow fell. One afternoon the sky became overcast, the wind fretted as it rounded the corner of the house, and a little later snow began to fall. The white flakes were big and soft, and they slipped down gently and quietly, and before sunset all the burned ugliness left by the prairie fire was hidden under a clean white sheet.

Lily, Jack, and I were enchanted with the snow, and eager to go out and play in it. 'You'll get your fill of snow before winter's over,' Mother told us, but she helped us into our coats and we ran outside.

The air was so cold our breath made clouds in front of our faces, and we ran about shouting 'Look, I can make smoke' and trying to outdo each other, and see who could make the biggest cloud.

Some of the soft snow lodged in the tree branches, and we found that if we shook the tree a shower of snow fell on us. We ran from tree to tree, shaking them and shouting until we were tired out and soaking wet.

The snow and the cold, squaw winter, as the old-timers called it, lasted for about a week, then the sun came out, the snow melted, and we had Indian summer.

The days were faded blue and gold, and it was like fall all over again except for the tremendous silence. There was neither movement nor sound. No gophers sat on their hind legs and flipped their saucy tails, no blackbirds trilled in the willows, no geese honked, no grasshoppers rattled their stiff wings. The woods were so still even the bare trees seemed to be holding their breath. The rabbits had no more substance than shadows. Everything seemed to be waiting, not daring to breathe.

As if to make up for the silence of the days a great brilliance appeared in the night sky. As soon as it was dark the northern lights began to flicker and dance.

The summer lightning had been gorgeous, but these lights were far more breath-taking. They did not flash and disappear as the lightning did. They rippled across the sky for hours. The lights stretched from the horizon to the zenith: great curtains of shining purple and gold that swayed and shook as if a giant hand were moving them; then they rearranged themselves and marched slowly and with great majesty as if in some solemn parade. At other times they were huge spears that darted down as if jabbing at the earth with their gleaming points. When they tired of teasing the earth they whirled across the sky in a wild and abandoned ballet. And always they glowed: purple, gold, silver, and green, and an odd, unnatural blue. But beautiful as the colours were there was always something weird about them, the purple had a greenish cast, and the green was unlike any other green. There was a touch of sulphur in it, and sometimes a splash of red. Though not as vicious as the lightning the northern lights were not friendly. They were aloof, impersonal, and cold. And they were also silent.

Watching those towering lights, that in some strange way seemed to have a life of their own, we felt very small and insignificant: little people who had invaded a vast land reserved for giants. Was this great place getting ready to crush us, brush us aside like annoying gnats? We did not know. But after watching the lights for a while we felt no taller than the dried grass, and just about as helpless. 'They make me feel so little, someway,' Mother said uneasily. 'And sometimes they look as if they don't like us, and would jab us if they could.'

'They're harmless,' Dad said, 'nowt but lights.' But even he seemed awed, and no wonder, for now that the birds had gone, and the bees and the humming things were stilled, the prairie was a vast pool of loneliness. And besides the emptiness there was a sense of menace. It was in the steel-edged wind, and the red sunset, and in the bare trees that did not even moan. Laughter, or any other noise, seemed out of place, and Bill, walking from the Metherells' to Mr Gardiner's, said he couldn't help glancing over his shoulder now and then even though he knew nothing was following him.

Indian summer, and its waiting quiet, did not last long. The wind that had been sharp-edged suddenly turned biting cold. Snow, dry and crisp, fell from the harsh clouds, and the earth, that up to now had been soft, froze stiff and hard.

Even when the wind stopped blowing and the snow stopped falling the sky did not clear. A cloud ceiling, grey as slate, hung so low it seemed to rest on the treetops. Through it the sun was only a fogged silver disk even at midday, and at night the starless dark was thick and close. It was during this first savage onslaught of winter that the coyotes began to howl.

We had seen one or two coyotes during the summer. They were about the size of an average dog, with pointed noses, slender legs, sharp ears, long bushy tails, and untidy-looking beige-grey fur. When they saw us they did not vanish quickly like most animals; instead they hovered nervously for a while, advancing a few steps as if they wanted to be friends, then retreating almost as if they wanted us to follow them. We had been told they had a hair-raising wail, but until we heard it we could not believe that such a despairing sound could come from such a friendly appearing creature.

The cry began with three short, sharp barks that stabbed into the stillness, then it became a long thin needle of agonized sound that went up and up until it reached and pierced the dome of the sky. All the hardships of the wilderness were in that wild wail. It was homeless, cold, hungry, and lost. When it ended the silence seemed deeper and more threatening than ever.

'Whatever's that?' Mother asked when the coyote's cry first sliced the stillness. She was cutting bread for supper, but she stopped half-way through the loaf and stared round-eyed at the window.

'It's only one of them coyotes,' Dad said. 'They're harmless.'

'It can't be,' Mother said incredulously. 'One of them little things could never make all that din. It's a timber-wolf, and you know it.'

Dad insisted that it wasn't, but when the lonely cry came again, from another direction and much closer, he looked uneasily at the door.

'I wish we were in Lloydminster,' Mother said as she spread jam on the bread. 'We should at least have company.'

'I thought you said you never wanted to see a tent again,' Dad reminded her.

Mother went on spreading jam as if she hadn't heard, but her lips puckered in distaste. She knew, as Dad did, that cold as it was many of the people in Lloydminster had only tents to live in.

Cheered by the sunshine and flowers, and the new sense of freedom, the Barr colonists, though home-sick at times, had enjoyed the summer, but when the cold came and the coyotes began to howl the wilderness frightened them. Most of them had come from large and crowded cities. They were accustomed to lighted streets, pavements, people next door, trams, trains, the corner pub, and noise day and night.

The emptiness and the stillness of the prairie troubled them. They had built shacks of either logs or sods, and bought provisions, and gathered wood, but when the water in the pails froze, and their breath was a cloud even in the house, they began to be afraid.

Maybe the old-timers were right about the cold and snow. Perhaps they hadn't enough wood. And if their food gave out how would they get more? Lloydminster wasn't much of a town, but at least they would have neighbours, and a doctor. If they were ill in the wilderness they might very well die before they had time to get a doctor.

First one packed and moved, and then another. Those who had sold their oxen or horses asked a neighbour a mile or two away to give them a lift. The Claxtons were the first to go from our vicinity. Their baby, Ted, was only a little over a year old, and they were expecting another baby any time.

When they arrived in Lloydminster, however, there was no place to stay. The town was swamped with homeless people. There wasn't even floor space. Men and women and little children had to sleep outside in wagon boxes and even on the cold ground. It was a frightening situation.

They couldn't go back to their lonely shacks, for they knew by now that they hadn't food enough to last the winter, or wood enough, either; besides, Mr Barr had promised to look after them. Why hadn't he warned them about the cold and snow? His pamphlets hadn't even hinted at how bad it would be. Where were the free houses he had promised? Shivering and angry the men gathered around their camp fires and talked.

They went to the land office, but no one there had any suggestions.

Surely they weren't going to be left to freeze to death? They looked at the cold grey sky and buttoned their thin coats against the bitter wind. Where was old Barr, anyway? He had got them into this, it was up to him to get them out. Their wives and children were blue with cold, soon they would die of pneumonia even if they didn't freeze to death.

Desperate, the men searched for Mr Barr. They went through the crowded rooming-houses, and everywhere else where a man might hide, even through the hay in the livery barns, and as they hunted they said he ought to be lynched.

'Surely they wouldn't have gone that far?' Mother said when Bill Banks, who was in Lloydminster at the time, told us of the goings-on.

'I don't know.' Bill shook his head. 'They were sure mad, though. I wouldn't have wanted to be in his shoes if they'd caught him. Some said he wasn't ever there, but I think he saw what was coming and slipped away in the night.'

Mr Lloyd, however, didn't try to leave. He had preached to us when we seemed lost in the fog, and now when the colony was in much greater danger he found a way to help. He stood on the steps of the land office and talked to the crowd. At first the men booed and shouted at him, and asked where old Barr was, but they were not naturally unruly people, and in a little while, when they realized he was as worried as they were, they listened to what he had to say. He assured them they would neither freeze nor starve. He had already negotiated for tents, and they would be pitched immediately.

Some of the men said what good would tents be in such cold, but Mr Lloyd pointed out that the Indians lived in teepees all winter and didn't freeze, so it was only reasonable to think that the Barr colonists could also survive. Space was allotted to all who needed it, about enough room for a bed, and as soon as the tents were pitched the colonists prepared for winter. They banked the tents with snow to keep out as much cold as possible, and the men took turns sawing wood.

The old-timers shook their heads when they heard of the tents. 'What on earth is Mr Lloyd thinking of?' they asked. 'White men, and greenhorns at that, are not used to cold the way the Indians are. They'll freeze solid just as sure as fate.' Even when Sidney Claxton was born, and survived sub-zero weather, they only shook their heads and said it was a miracle that wouldn't happen again.

Mr Lloyd, of course, must have known that the tents were poor shelter, but they were all he could find. Sod houses were out of the question by then. The prairie had frozen and the sod couldn't be turned. Log shacks, even if they could have been built in time, were too draughty unless they were mudded, and mudding in such bitter cold was impossible. Taking everybody to Battleford wouldn't have helped, either. There were no extra houses there.

The colonists grumbled about the cold and the crowding, but most of them were young and they got used to the inconveniences. They had plenty of company, which helped a great deal, and the heavy canvas kept the worst of the wind out. Fortunately, no one realized how cold fifty below zero really was. They did not know how marrow-chilling it was, and how it pushed from every side like a dead weight, squeezing every bit of warmth out of you until only a spot in your chest felt alive.

Perhaps Mr Lloyd knew how flesh-shrinking the cold could be, but he said nothing about it. He visited the tents every day, a tall, serious man, unafraid and friendly. He told the settlers there was enough food, though it might be a bit monotonous since it consisted mostly of beans, but they wouldn't starve. They had all the wood they could burn, and everyone knew that Eskimoes lived in snow houses all winter, so they wouldn't freeze.

To inspire confidence Mrs Lloyd also remained in Lloydminster that first winter. She was a wisp of a woman with brown eyes and a gentle face, and no matter how cold it was she visited the tents regularly. She encouraged the women, made soup for those who were ill, and did what she could when babies were born.

'Now aren't you glad we didn't go to Lloydminster?'

Dad asked when Bill Banks finished telling his tale. 'You wouldn't have liked being cooped up in one of them tents. It's as I've allus said, Sarah, you'll allus be all right as long as you have me to look after you.'

'I don't know about that.' Mother brushed a speck of ash off the stove. 'The winter isn't over yet, and Lloydminster may be a bit crowded, but I could do with some company now and then.'

'The Metherells aren't far away,' Dad pointed out, 'and Willie Gardiner's practically next door. We'll have that much company we won't know what to do.'

Mother sniffed a little at that. She was used to relatives at the end of the street, and neighbours only a step from the door. People half a mile away would have been strangers in England, but if Mrs Metherell and Mrs Johnson could put up with a winter on the prairie so could she.

Everyone was surprised when the Johnsons decided to spend the winter on their homestead. Mrs Johnson enjoyed people, and everybody had thought she would be the first to leave. Mr Johnson, however, had heard about the tents while he was working, and they decided to stay in the little house he had built during the summer.

Bill Banks also surprised everyone by electing to stay on the homestead while his partner, Mr Forest, went away to work in the lumber camps. Bill hated to be alone, but he also hated to work steadily day after day, so loneliness won.

CHAPTER TWENTY-SIX

THE cold that had driven many of the Barr colonists to Lloydminster was bad enough, we thought, but it wasn't long before it got much worse. The thermometer went down to fifteen below zero, and more snow fell.

'The snow will warm things up a bit,' Dad said hopefully, but for once he was wrong. The cold became so severe that Lily and I were content to huddle by the little stove, and no longer coaxed to go out and play.

Dad sawed wood for a long time every day in order to satisfy the hungry little stove, but the corners of the house were always cold, and at night when the fire went out everything froze, including the bread dough.

The potatoes were another casualty. The hole under the packing-box wasn't deep enough and they froze solid. We tried thawing them in both hot and cold water, baking them, and boiling them in their skins, but no matter how we treated them they tasted horrible, like sweet potatoes gone sour. Mashed they were gum, whole they were leather, and fried they were sticky. 'I guess we might as well throw them out,' Mother said at last. 'And to think I dug them and carried them half a mile so that they wouldn't freeze in the ground. This is a terrible country.'

Dad's ears almost went the way of the potatoes during that first bit of winter. When he went to Battleford for the winter supplies he brought us moccasins and mitts, but he didn't get himself a winter cap. He said the caps in the stores weren't much better than the cap he had. The ear tabs, though fur-lined, covered only half the ears, and what good would that be? He might as well have no ear tabs at all. But when the wind got really cold Dad's ears almost froze. He tried tying Mother's shawl over his head when he went out to saw wood, but it kept slipping off, and the ends got in his way. At last Dad decided to solve the problem by making himself a cap.

He had a fair idea of what he wanted, but he didn't know how to go about making it, and neither did Mother.

'It has to have a top,' Dad said. 'We'll start there.'

'How big a top?' Mother asked.

Dad didn't know, so he put a plate on his head and asked how it looked.

'Crazy,' Mother told him, and laughed.

'I mean for size,' Dad explained.

Mother said she was sure the plate was too big, so Dad put Jack's porridge plate on his head. Mother thought that looked better, and Dad cut a circle of cloth the size of the plate. The cloth, of course, flopped where the plate didn't, and Dad was about to cut another circle when Mother warned him to be careful, if he wasn't the old coat he was using for material would soon be gone. Dad cut the circle a little smaller, then he cut a straight piece about two inches wide and sewed it around the circle like a cuff.

When Dad tried on the result the cuff came down to his eyebrows, and Mother said it looked queer, but Dad said it felt warm, and added a sort of curtain to the cuff to protect his cheeks, the back of his head, and his neck. He left tabs in front to go under his chin, and sewed strings to them. An interlining came next. Just before freeze-up Dad had killed a musk-rat and dried the skin; he used this for the interlining. A red flannel lining completed the cap. It looked very gay, but it was the only soft material Mother had, and Dad said since it wouldn't show it didn't matter. Dad did all the sewing himself. It took him two days, and he pricked his fingers often, and tangled the thread, but he did a good job, and he was proud of it. 'How does it look?' he asked when the cap was finished.

Mother said it looked queer, unlike any cap she had ever seen, and she thought Dad ought to put it away and send to Battleford for a store cap at the first opportunity. Dad, however, said the cap was warmer than anything that could be bought, and he was going to wear it. Looks weren't everything.

'You'll be laughed at,' Mother warned, and sure enough when Mr Metherell saw Dad wearing the cap he said it made Dad's head look like a football, and Bill, who always followed Mr Metherell's lead, said it made Dad look almost like a side-show freak. Mr Gardiner was the only one who had a good word for the cap. 'It looks all right,' he said in his slow, quiet voice. 'I wish I had one like it.'

As soon as we were more or less accustomed to the cold Dad and Mr Gardiner began going to the Big Gully every day to cut logs. It was hard, cold work. They had to walk about two miles each way, and the snow was deep, but they said they couldn't sit around the stove all day, they had to be doing something, and anyway, if they didn't get the logs now somebody else soon would.

Mother told Dad to go ahead and wear himself out if he wanted to, but as far as she could see cutting logs was a waste of time. She was quite sure one winter in Canada would be more than enough for Dad, once he saw how lonely it was. He had never liked being alone. At Castle Hill George Henry or Uncle Arthur had always been somewhere about, and at night Dad had either gone to his club for a game of billiards, or spent the evening talking to men who lived near by. Here there was no club, and no billiards, and except for Mr Gardiner very little company. The Metherells came now and then, but they never stayed long. They had to melt snow so that their two oxen and one cow would have something to drink, and it kept them busy.

Dad, however, showed no signs of being lonely, and when he got a little used to the cold he almost seemed to enjoy it. We didn't get up early because daylight came late, but as soon as we had eaten our oatmeal and finished our tea Dad hurried off to look at his rabbit snares, then he filled the pails with snow and put them on the back of the stove to melt. Snow was our only source of water, and melting it was a steady job, because a pailful of snow made only about a quarter of a pail of water. Having no animals to care for helped, but water for washing was a problem.

As soon as the chores were done Dad went to cut logs. At first he took bread for lunch, but it froze in his pocket and was unappetizing, so he had some tea before he left and nothing more until he got back at night. After supper, usually stewed rabbit, bread, stewed prunes, and tea, we three children went to bed, and Dad and Mother sat by the little stove and talked.

I was supposed to go to sleep, of course, but those evenings were so pleasant I couldn't bear to miss them. I crept down to the foot of the bed and huddled there enjoying the yellow lamplight, the fire in the stove (Dad had taken out the front grate), and the cheerful sound of Dad's and Mother's voices.

Usually at that time they had a last cup of tea, and while they sipped they talked of England, and their relatives and friends there. They discussed who had married whom and why, and wondered how they were getting on, then they talked of things that had happened before they were married when Mother was going with Edmond Bastow, and Dad wasn't going with anybody in particular. They reminded each other of Huddersfield Fair, the bob-dolly show, and the merry-go-round, and sometimes they argued in a friendly way, and usually they laughed.

Often, of course, they talked of Grandfather Gomersall, and of Grandmother Pinder, and Aunt Jane, and the little shop by the Spen, and wondered how they were getting on, and how the farm at Castle Hill was doing, and if Bob, our old dog, still liked chasing cats. Their voices always got a little lonely when they talked of Castle Hill, and Dad leaned forward and poked the fire, and Mother poured more tea.

Sometimes they wondered how the people living in tents in Lloydminster were getting on, and if the Metherells' thin old cow would live through the winter. Often Dad brought the talk around to the future, and once he suggested that perhaps Uncle Sam might like to come to Canada in a year or two if we did well. There would be plenty of opportunity for a man with his building ability when the railway came, and Battleford and Lloydminster began to grow. Mother said well, he might, you never could tell, but it was plain she didn't think much of the idea.

Often, of course, they looked up from the fire and told me to get back into bed where I belonged before I caught my death of cold, and always I said all right, but I never moved until Dad got up to take a last look at the night, and Mother emptied the teapot. I couldn't bear to miss a moment of those happy evenings. They gave me a sense of security even the wind and the howl of the coyotes couldn't take away.

The wind blew often that winter. It was like a lost person wandering over the snow. Sometimes it went one way, sometimes another, but always it called, and its voice was lonely even when it was loud. When the wind was really angry it scooped up the snow and tossed it high into the air, then it whirled it around and piled it against the groves and the house in huge drifts. Sometimes we couldn't even see the sun, the air was so full of flying snow; then Dad said a blizzard was blowing.

Mother was always afraid a blizzard would begin to blow when Dad was away cutting logs. 'Be sure to listen to the wind now and then,' she told him. 'And come home if it doesn't sound right.' For the wind always gave warning before it flew into a whirling tantrum. It coughed as if clearing its throat, and when it went around the corner of the house it snarled a little.

There was a harsh cough in the wind all day before the first big blizzard. Dad came home in the middle of the afternoon, and cut some extra wood, and brought the axe into the house. The old-timers had warned us never to leave the axe outside even in the day-time if the wind was blowing. The snow might cover it, and we could easily freeze to death before we found it. 'I don't think it will amount to much,' Dad said as he shut the door on the snow, that was still only playing ring-around-the-rosy, 'but you never know. Them old fellows tell such tales.'

Mother agreed that the blows we had had before were nothing to be afraid of, she'd seen a lot of fog that was thicker, but this wind had a growl in it, and the sky was darkening early.

As darkness came on the growl in the wind increased to a roar, and after supper, when Dad went out for more wood, tall snow women with long veils streaming behind them went flying past the door. 'Gosh, but it's getting cold!' Dad said. 'And that wind! It seems to be coming from every direction at once. I never saw anything like it.' He shut the door and put a sack against the crack at the bottom to keep out the wind and the snow.

'It's neither fit for man nor beast outside.' Mother put the kettle on.

The wind threw snow against the window, then it roared off across the prairie, making a strange whoosh as it went through the bare branches of the frozen trees. 'I never heard anything like it,' Mother said.

Dad opened the door a crack and looked out. 'You can't see a thing,' he reported, 'not even the woodpile, the air's that full of snow.'

Mother told him to shut the door, the house was cold enough. Dad closed it and replaced the sack, but the wind came in through the cracks around the door and the window, and it brought snow with it and piled it in little drifts.

Mother and Dad put their coats over their shoulders. The wind seemed to blow all the heat out of the little house, and though they sat close to the stove their backs were cold. The house, however, was cosy compared to the turmoil outside. The fire burned crisply, the lamp cast a pleasant yellow glow over the packing-box table, the wagon bench, and the pile of white flour sacks in the corner. 'I wonder how them poor folks in Lloydminster are getting on,' Mother said.

'Probably blown away.' Dad looked at the little window that was white with flying snow. 'Aren't you glad you have a house to live in instead of one of them tents?'

'I'd rather be in England where they don't have blizzards,' Mother said, and poured boiling water into the blue teapot.

'It's a humdinger, all right.' Dad sweetened his tea and stirred it slowly. 'Just hearken to that,' he said as a gust shook the little house, and dashed snow against the partly frosted window.

'It's a night you wouldn't turn a dog out into.' Mother sipped her tea, then she looked at me huddled at the foot of the bed. 'Mary, aren't you asleep yet?' she asked as if she were surprised.

'No,' I shivered. 'The wind's too loud.'

Mother said the wind wouldn't hurt me, but I didn't trust it. I had never heard it scream so loud before.

Dad got out a book and began to read aloud to Mother, but the storm was so bad they lost interest in the story, and just sat there listening to the wind. 'I think we might as well go to bed,' Dad said at last and went to take a last look at the storm. When he opened the door a gust of wind heavy with snow almost knocked him off his feet. 'I'm glad I'm not out in that,' he said as he slammed the door in the face of another blast.

'So am I.' Mother set the teapot on the back of the stove and bent to unlace her moccasins. Suddenly she sat up and looked at the little window. 'What's that?' she asked and leaned forward, her eyes round and her face listening.

Dad listened, too, his moccasin laces in his hand. 'It's nowt but wind,' he said at last.

'No, it isn't the wind.' Mother stared at the white window. 'There's somebody out there.'

'There can't be.' Dad, flipped off his moccasin. 'Nobody would be silly enough to go out on a night like this.'

'There it is again,' Mother said. 'Can't you hear it? Somebody's lost.'

We listened as hard as we could with our faces turned to the window, and in the next lull the voice came to us, thin and frightened. It was only a shred of sound torn by the wind, but there was no mistaking it. 'Lost, lost,' it called.

'You're right.' Dad pulled on his moccasin. 'There is somebody out there.'

'What are you going to do?' Mother sounded frightened.

'See if I can find him.' Dad knotted the moccasin laces.

'You'll never find him in that.' Mother looked at the window just as the wind gave a terrible roar, and threw snow rattling at the glass. 'You'll get lost as well, then what will become of the bairns and me?'

'We can't let him freeze to death without trying to do summat.' Dad put on his big, home-made cap, and his thin coat that wasn't meant for a blizzard. It was of cloth and not interlined, and the wind could easily whistle through it. Dad's other clothing wasn't warm enough, either. His shirt was of good cotton, and his trousers of wool, but he had no long underwear, and Dad had thought the old-timers were trying to make game of him when they told him to buy some.

'You'll freeze in them thin things.' Mother opened the blue box and brought out another pair of trousers. 'Here, put these on if you insist on going out,' she said.

Dad pulled the extra trousers over the ones he already wore, and turned up his meagre coat collar. 'Do be careful, and don't go far,' Mother said anxiously. 'You won't do anybody any good if you get lost.'

'I'll be back in a bit. Hold the lamp in the window, will you?' Dad said, then he smiled at Mother and turned and went out into the darkness.

Mother shut the door and turned the wooden button that kept it closed, then she picked up the little lamp, turned it as high as it would go without smoking, and held it close to the frosted glass.

'Hallo, hallo.' Dad's voice came to us on the wind. We listened hard, but there was no answer. In a few minutes Dad called again. His voice was much fainter than it had been, and the wind blurred it until the words were not plain. We heard Dad's voice once more, faint and far away like an echo, then there was only the rushing roar of the wind and the swish of the flying snow.

Mother stood by the window, her face anxious in the lamplight. 'He'll never find him,' she said in a low voice. 'It was silly of him to try.' She leaned forward a little and listened intently, her eyes wide and her lips parted. 'Can you hear anything, Mary?' she asked at last.

I shook my head.

'Try as hard as you can,' Mother urged.

I listened until my ears bent forward, but there was only the cry of the wind, and the queer rushing sound made by the flying snow.

The fire burned low and the little house got cold, but Mother remained by the window. 'Nolan warned him not to go out in a blizzard,' she said at last, and tears shone on her cheeks. 'I'll never see him again.' Her red lips trembled. 'Walter,' she shouted suddenly at the top of her voice. 'Walter, Walter.' There was no answer.

We waited for what seemed to me a long time. Tiny crystals of snow came through the window cracks and shimmered in the lamplight, and the shadows that always lurked in the corners turned darker and crept closer.

Mother didn't seem to notice that the fire was almost out, and that the cold was coming in. She didn't even notice the shadows. She stood by the window and looked at the flying snow, and tears ran down her young cheeks, but she did not notice the tears, either. I spoke in a low voice, but she did not answer, she simply stood there holding the light, and after a little while I became afraid. I seemed to be alone in the storm.

I crouched at the foot of the bed scarcely daring to breathe, and Mother stood with her face to the window, and so we waited while the storm thundered around us. At last, when we no longer hoped to hear it, the door rattled.

I thought it was only the wind, but Mother turned and in one swift movement she wiped her eyes, crossed the room, and opened the door. Two figures, white from head to foot, stumbled in. One crumpled to the floor, but the other wiped the snow from his face and smiled. 'He's about done in,' Dad said.

'It took you long enough,' Mother said in a completely normal voice.

'I thought for a bit I wasn't going to find him.' Dad shook off some of the snow and turned to the white shape he had pulled out of the storm.

Mother and Dad dragged the snow-covered figure to the wagon bench and pulled off his cap. 'Why, it's Bill,' Mother said. 'Whatever was he doing out on such a night?'

Dad took off his snow-covered coat and cap and built up the fire, and Mother put the kettle on, then they loosened Bill's coat and brushed off the snow, and Mother rubbed his cold hands. After a minute or two Bill stirred and opened his eyes. At first he didn't seem to know where he was, then Dad spoke to him and asked how he felt. Bill didn't answer. He sat up and looked at Dad and Mother, then he began to cry.

'There, there,' Mother said and patted his shaking shoulder, 'you're all right now, don't take on so. You'll feel better as soon as you've had some tea.'

Bill, however, continued to sob. He was only about eighteen and he'd had quite a scare. 'I thought I was a goner,' he said at last. 'All that wind and snow!'

'Here, have some tea.' Mother gave him a steaming mug.

Bill took the mug, but he was shaking so much that some of the tea spilled on the earth floor. 'I'd have been a goner if you hadn't found me,' he said, looking at Dad.

'It was nowt,' Dad smiled. 'Anybody would have done the same.'

Bill shook his head. 'No, they wouldn't,' he protested. 'They wouldn't have kept looking when they might get lost themselves. They'd have gone back before they lost the light.'

'It was me cap that saved thee,' Dad said. 'If it hadn't been for that I couldn't have kept on. It kept the wind out of me face.'

'And I laughed at it.' A sob caught in Bill's throat.

After a while Mother persuaded Bill to drink his tea, and when the worst of his fright had passed he told us what had happened. He had spent the afternoon and evening at Mr Gardiner's, then at about nine o'clock he had decided to go home.

'In that wind?' Dad asked.

Bill said he realized now he'd been awfully foolish. He knew the wind was blowing, but he thought the Metherells would worry if he didn't go home, also he thought the old-timers overrated blizzards. He thought he knew how to use his watch as a compass, and set a course by the stars. He was also sure the wind would help him. All he had to do was note its direction, and he couldn't fail to get home. On top of all that he was sure he knew every bush and grove between Gardiner's and the Metherells', and could find his way by instinct even if he couldn't see. 'I guess I thought I knew too much,' he said dismally.

'I can't understand Willie letting thee go,' Dad said.

Bill admitted that Mr Gardiner had tried to persuade him to stay and sleep in Mr Maule's bunk, but he had refused. He'd even told Mr Gardiner not to put a light in the window. He wouldn't need it.

'The wind wasn't bad till I got away from the house,' Bill said, beginning to tremble all over again. 'Then it was terrible.' It blew from every direction at once and sometimes seemed to go in a circle. He tried to walk towards the Metherells', but the wind pushed him, and he couldn't see either the stars or his watch. He tried to strike a match, but the wind blew it away. The whirling snow filled his eyes and his nose, and when he tried to breathe through his mouth it went down his throat and almost choked him. He tried to keep going in the right direction, but in a short time he stumbled into a grove that shouldn't have been there. He paused for a moment and tried to get his bearings, then he went on and became entangled in some willows he didn't remember. Confused and a little frightened he decided to go back to Mr Gardiner's. He looked for his footprints. All but one or two near his feet had been obliterated by the wind and snow.

He was still sure, however, that he could find his way back. He lowered his head against the wind and began walking. A grove loomed up in front of him, and he stumbled and fell. When he got up he was completely confused. The wind pushed from first one side then the other, and the snow hissed as it whirled like a shroud around him. He stumbled on, but he had no idea where he was going. He was lost, and the cold dark arms of the blizzard were closing around him. He fell and got up and fell again. His feet were numb and his hands like ice, and even his body in his too-thin coat felt stiff and half frozen. Soon he knew he would fall and not get up again. It was then that he began to shout. Not because he thought anyone would hear him, he was sure he was miles from both our house and Mr Gardiner's, but because shouting was a last resort, a final effort before the wind and snow smothered him. 'If you hadn't heard me...' He looked at Dad and shivered.

'Sarah heard you,' Dad said. 'It's a good thing for you she has sharp ears.'

'But you went out and looked for me.' Bill glanced at the snow ghosts flying past the dark little window. 'How did you ever find me?' he asked.

'It was luck, mostly,' Dad said. 'I heard you shout once after I got outside, and I shouted at you, but you didn't seem to hear, so I kept going, and after a bit I caught up with you.'

'And you knew the way back, even though you couldn't see the light.' There was wonder in Bill's brown eyes.

'That was a bit of luck, too,' Dad said gravely.

'You saved my life,' Bill said. 'And you might have been frozen to death yourself.'

'It was me cap that saved us both,' Dad insisted. 'If it hadn't kept the wind out of me eyes neither of us would be here.'

Mother told Bill to drink some more tea and eat something, then when he had got over the worst of his shakes she began to wonder where he was going to sleep. Our bed was already crowded, and we had no extra blankets.

Bill was willing to sit in the chair the rest of the night and keep the fire going, but Dad thought he ought to have some real rest after his ordeal. Besides, if he fell asleep and let the fire go out he could very easily freeze without proper covering even in the house. Dad and Mother discussed the matter for some time, and finally decided that Bill had better go to Mr Gardiner's.

'No,' Bill said and started trembling all over again. 'I'd never make it. I'd get lost. I can't face that wind and snow any more.'

'Sure you can,' Dad said. 'It's only a bit of a way, and I'll go with you.'

Bill protested, and said he'd be quite all right on the wagon bench until morning, but after a while Dad persuaded him to put on his coat and cap, and they went out into the storm.

Mother held the lamp in the window until Dad came back. 'I had to take him all the way,' Dad said as he took off his coat. 'He wouldn't let go of me until Willie opened the door.'

'He might have had a little thought for you.' Mother poured herself and Dad a last cup of tea. 'Why he ever set off in such a storm is more than I'll ever know.'

'He's only a lad.' Dad yawned and began unlacing his moccasins. 'Like most lads his age he thought he knew everything. He'll have a bit more sense after this.'

'When it was very nearly too late,' Mother said. 'What would I have done if you'd been lost?'

'You'd have been all right.' Dad smiled slyly at Mother. 'You'd have gone back to England and married Edmond Bastow.'

'Well, what a thing to think of,' Mother said. 'It would serve you right if I did.' Her tone was sharp, but her eyes were smiling, then both she and Dad laughed.

The blizzard lasted three days. When the wind finally died down the drifts were as high as the eaves, and packed so hard Dad could walk on them. 'I never saw anything like it,' he said when he came in out of the sparkling, frozen outdoors. 'That snow is as hard as a board. The wind must have been awful to pack it that way. No wonder Bill got lost.'

'He's just lucky he isn't under that snow,' Mother said. 'And so are you.'

A few days after the blizzard subsided Bill Banks dropped in for a visit. As usual we were glad to see him, for besides being a pleasant person Bill, who visited a lot, always knew what was going on in the colony.

Bill Banks was good-natured, and everybody liked him. He had a round pink face, a turned-up nose, sandy hair and eyebrows, and pale blue, trusting eyes. And his ways were as trusting as his eyes.

'Everybody seems to be doing all right,' Bill said as he sipped his second mug of tea. 'The tents didn't blow down.' Bill sounded a little disappointed. 'And nobody froze to death, not even the little kids, but one man came close.' He paused and his blue eyes brightened. 'But they think he'll lose both legs,' he added, and took a deep, satisfying drink of tea.

'Poor man,' Mother said. 'What happened?'

'He was out cutting wood or something, and didn't pay enough attention to the wind,' Bill said. 'He walked as long as he could, then he came to a grove and tried to make a fire, but the wind blew the matches out as fast as he lit them. When the last match was gone he thought sure he was a goner, but he didn't give up. He started to walk again, and kept going for quite a while, then he got so tired he had to stop and rest. He very nearly fell asleep, but he'd heard somewhere that if you went to sleep in the cold you'd freeze as stiff as a poker, so he got up and went on again. After a while his feet got numb and he couldn't walk, so he crawled. He crawled round and round the grove all night. When he got sleepy he rubbed his face with snow until he got too tired even for that, then he concentrated on moving. He moved first one hand then the other, then he moved his knees. When the Mounted Police found him next morning he was almost unconscious, but he was still crawling; but his feet and legs were frozen to the knees.'

'How awful!' Mother shuddered.

'Yes.' Bill Banks smiled. 'And what do you think them old-timers said? They said they wouldn't have believed it if they hadn't seen it. They didn't think a greenhorn had sense enough to keep moving, and it just seemed as if you couldn't kill those goddamned English.'

'What an awful way to talk!' Mother puckered her pretty mouth. 'But I still think this country is fit for nobody but the Indians, and it's hardly fit for them, either, but they seem to like it.'

'It isn't the country,' Dad said. 'It's folks that haven't sense enough to stay inside when it's blowing that are to blame. But they'll learn.'

'Learn enough to leave it if it isn't too late,' Mother said.

Besides bringing the news, Bill Banks also brought the mail. There were letters that Dad and Mother read and re-read, and discussed by the fire at night, and papers that were read carefully, then passed on, but the most exciting mail of all as far as Lily and I were concerned was the square box containing the Christmas cake.

We had known for some time that the cake was on the way. A previous letter had told us about it, and we had been looking forward to it for some time. We hadn't had any real cake since we left England. Sometimes Mother put sugar in baking-powder bread and we pretended it was cake, but a real cake with currants and raisins in it, and perhaps nuts on top, was something we had almost forgotten. Lily couldn't remember ever seeing such a cake, so I told her all about it in great detail. I described the big fat raisins, the nuts that crunched, the lemon peel, the juicy currants, the smell of the spice, and the way it looked. I told her it was big and round and brown, and thick, a regular marvel of a cake, and we licked our lips and looked forward to it.

Now at long last it was here, but Mother and Dad were in no hurry to open the enticing box. They listened to Bill Banks, and had tea, and paid no attention to the cake.

At last, however, after Bill Banks had gone to see how Mr Gardiner was getting on, and Mother and Dad had read the letters, they turned to the cake. 'It seems light for a Christmas cake,' Mother said, lifting the box.

'Maybe it's a small one,' Dad said.

'Shall we save it for Christmas, or do you think we ought to open it now?' Mother asked.

Dad rubbed his ear and thought the matter over while Lily and I waited, our eyes round and our lips wet. Christmas was two or three weeks away. 'Maybe we'd better take a look at it,' Dad said at last.

Mother agreed with him. Judging from the weight of the parcel the cake must be rather dry already; it would be a shame to let it spoil completely. Besides, Bill Banks had brought the cake and ought to have a slice of it. So Mother put the kettle on, you couldn't have cake without tea, and Dad found the scissors and cut the string that bound the package. He unfolded the brown paper carefully, revealing a bright tin box.

'It's well wrapped,' Mother said.

'It sure is.' Dad shook the box, but there was no sound. He cut the string around the tin and pulled off the bright lid.

Lily and I almost fell forward in our eagerness to see the cake, but it still wasn't uncovered. There was a wad of tissue-paper under the lid. Dad pulled the paper out carefully. There were several layers. In fact paper was all the box contained.

Even Mother couldn't believe it. She unfolded the paper and shook it carefully, but there wasn't even a crumb. One lonely currant, dark and dry, was all she could find. Somebody else must have been hungry for cake,' she said at last. 'But why did they re-wrap the tin and send it on?' Nobody answered. We were too disappointed.

The kettle, however, was boiling merrily, and Mother said we might as well have some tea even if we couldn't have cake. She brewed a teapotful, and Mr Gardiner and Bill Banks came over and helped drink it. Lily and I had no appetite for tea. We shook out the paper all over again, and looked at the tin both inside and out. There was a faint smell of cake but that was all.

Our cake wasn't the only thing that didn't arrive that Christmas. Packages from Grandmother and Aunt Jane didn't arrive, and a box sent by Grandfather Gomersall and Uncle Sam also got lost, but the cake was our bitterest disappointment. Even when Bill Banks invited us to his shack for Christmas dinner Lily and I were not comforted.

Dad and Mother, however, were delighted at the invitation. Christmas in England had always been a happy time, but here, away from all our relatives and friends, a lonely, quiet day seemed all we could expect. Even the traditions would be missing. There would be no church bells, no carol singers, no cake and wine, no glad handshakes and good wishes. Bill Banks's invitation, however, changed everything, and Dad and Mother thanked him warmly.

'That's fine,' Bill said grandly. 'I'm glad you can come. I've invited everybody: the Metherells, the Johnsons, and Willie Gardiner. I have a good team, so I'll pick you all up early Christmas morning and bring you back at night.'

Mother said that was wonderful of him, and offered to make something with sugar in it for dessert. But Bill Banks wouldn't hear of it. This was his party, and nobody else had a thing to worry about. A friend of his, another bachelor, was going to do the cooking. This party was to be a change for the women as well as the men.

Mother said that was very thoughtful of him, and very generous, and she knew everyone would appreciate it.

Lily and I immediately began to wonder if there would be cake at Bill Banks's party. I asked Mother, and she said maybe, but she couldn't be sure. One thing, however: there would be something good to eat, and there would be the Johnson children to play with.

The Johnson children! We had never seen them, but we had heard of them often, and the prospect of really meeting them and playing with them was a treat as far as I was concerned. According to their mother, Mrs Johnson, they were the most wonderful children in the world, and she never tired of bragging about them. Dora, the eldest, could do practically everything, and Bertie, the baby, was perfect. He never got into mischief the way Jack did, and he never cried. Mrs Johnson seldom mentioned Elsie, the middle one, but we assumed she was as perfect as the other two. Now at last I was going to meet these wonders, and the prospect was so pleasing I almost forgot about the lost cake.

What did the Johnson children look like, I wondered, as I played by the stove with what was left of my doll. Had they long or short hair? How old were they?

Mother couldn't answer these questions, because she hadn't seen the wonder children either, but she found out from Mrs Metherell (who knew everything, I thought) that Dora was about eight, Elsie close to six, and Bertie, the baby, just Jack's age, a little over a year. 'I do hope you'll play nicely with them at the party,' Mother said.

I promised to be perfect, but I speculated endlessly, and asked so many questions that Mother said she wished Bill Banks had waited until I was asleep to mention his party. She was tired of hearing about it already, and if Christmas didn't come soon she'd lose her wits. She'd never seen anybody in such a twitter as I was. I counted the days every morning, and ticked off the nights before I went to bed. The time seemed never-ending, but at long last Christmas Eve came.

I had been warned not to expect much from Santa Claus that year. He had a long way to come, and couldn't carry as much as usual, but even though I expected very little I was as excited as ever about hanging my stocking.

Where to hang the stocking was a problem. In England they had been hung on the mantel, but here there was no mantel, nor even a real chimney. This lack worried me terribly, even though I strongly suspected there wasn't a real Santa Claus.

Nobody had told me there was no such person. Even the cousins in England, Gladstone and Walter Walker Pinder, who loved to tease me, had never gone that far. But I had caught words here and there and painstakingly put them together. I didn't want to believe the answer, so I said nothing about it and worried a great deal, mostly out loud, in order to convince Mother, Dad, and myself that Santa really did exist.

How could a big fat man like Santa get down our little stove-pipe, I wanted to know? And if he managed to squeeze down the pipe how would he get out of the stove, especially if there was a fire in it? Did he know we had moved, and would he be able to find us?

Mother told me to stop fretting. Santa was smart and knew how to manage stove-pipes. He might not bring much, apples and oranges would freeze in this cold, but he would bring something. 'Just shut your eyes, and everything will be all right,' Mother told me. 'Santa will find the stockings even though they are at the foot of the bed instead of hanging from the mantel.'

I did as I was told, and the next thing I knew it was Christmas morning.

Sure enough Santa had found us, and left nuts and candy in our stockings, and books on the floor. Lily and I were delighted, and counted every candy two or three times, or at least I did: Lily couldn't count.

As soon as we had eaten our oatmeal Mother began dressing us for the party. We hadn't worn our best clothes since we left England, and putting them on again was an event.

My dress was red, the yoke trimmed with ruching that ended in streamers with gold-coloured spikes at the ends. The spikes were about two inches long, and had a pattern of tiny raised flowers in them. For some reason I called the spikes spells, and I never tired of playing with them. Aunt Jane had bought the dress for me mostly because I liked the spikes. As I put the dress on I wondered if Dora Johnson had spells on her dress. If she hadn't I decided to let her play with mine.

When Mother looked at my dress, however, she said: 'My goodness, you can't wear it. You've grown so much it's too short.'

Not wear my spells! I began to cry, and after a while Mother decided to let me keep the dress on even though it barely covered my knees.

Lily had also grown, but not as much as I had, and her dress, too big to begin with, just fitted. It was a soft blue with white lace around the neck and at the edges of the puffed sleeves. Under the full skirt she wore a white embroidered petticoat that showed a little when she moved. A matching blue ribbon around her soft, light brown curls completed her costume. She looked like a serious, round-faced doll.

Jack, the hardest to keep clean, was dressed last. In those days little boys, no matter how boyish they looked, were dressed exactly like little girls. Jack's everyday dress was plain and dark, but his Sunday best was something to behold. It was white, and the full, gathered skirt was heavily embroidered. It had a close-fitting yoke, and puffed and lace-trimmed sleeves. Lily and I had both worn the dress, and no one saw any reason why Jack shouldn't wear it. If he had been a soft-eyed little boy with silky hair he might have looked passable in the dress, but there was nothing soft about Jack. His blue eyes sparkled with fun and mischief, and his smile, very much like Dad's, was lively and boyish. His fair hair curled a little, but it was crisp, and he had a cowlick at one side. Even his arms and legs, though plump, were firm and sturdy. In the lace-trimmed dress he looked as if he were going to some juvenile masquerade.

'He doesn't look right, does he?' Mother asked anxiously, and tried to brush Jack's hair into a curl on top of his head, a fashion for boys at that time, but the curl wasn't a success. The minute Mother got it to stand up, Jack put up his hand to feel it and knocked it down.

In desperation Mother tied a wide pink sash around Jack's middle, but it didn't help, Jack looked more boyish than ever. The sash gave him a swashbuckling look. If Mother had added a black patch to one eye he would have been a pirate. 'It's no use,' Mother sighed, and took off the sash, and parted Jack's hair on the side. 'I don't know why the dress looks so queer now,' she said. 'It looked so pretty when Lily wore it.'

'It looks all right.' Dad smiled proudly. 'He's a lad, and you can't make him look like a lass, that's all.'

While Mother was putting on her red waist with the big sleeves and high neck, and the skirt that was at least four yards round at the hem, I kept an eye on Lily and Jack. Lily sat primly on the wagon bench, but Jack was determined to explore the dark place under the bed where Dad kept his tools, and I had difficulty keeping him clean.

Mother hurried with her dressing, she was afraid Bill Banks might come before we were ready, but nine-thirty came, then ten, and still no Bill. 'Maybe he forgot all about the party,' Mother said bleakly. 'He looked as if he might have had a drop too much when he invited us.'

'He'll be here,' Dad said. 'Bill never looks at a clock.'

I wore a path between the window and the door watching for him. Not that I cared about Bill Banks, or the party either. It was Dora Johnson I was anxious to see. I had been looking forward to playing with her ever since Bill asked us to the party. I imagined her as another Katie Daw, good-natured and agreeable, and willing to play with me even though I was a little younger than. she was. And I was going to be just as agreeable as Dora. My Christmas candy was in Mother's one and only glass dish waiting for her, and I held my new books in my arms, so that I wouldn't forget to show them to her. I even intended to let her borrow them if she wanted to. Mrs Metherell had said that Dora could read.

Half past ten came and still no sign of Bill Banks and his sleigh. 'He must have forgotten,' Mother said, and gave Lily and Jack a piece of bread. She gave me a piece, too, but I couldn't eat it. Disappointment was beginning to nibble at my stomach.

'I think I might as well get Jack out of that dress,' Mother said after a while. 'He can't keep still much longer.' She began to unbutton the white dress, and tears of disappointment began to burn my eyes, and buzz around in my head. Another moment and I would have been weeping loudly, but just as my mouth went square there was a jingle of bells, and shouts, and the sleigh, full of people, was at the door.

Mother and Dad hurried outside, and there was much handshaking, back-slapping, and good wishes. I grabbed my candy and books and ran to offer them to Dora. She looked down her thin nose at my candy, sniffed, and said: 'I've had all the candy I want, thank you.'

I was so surprised I very nearly dropped the dish. I'd never heard of anybody having enough candy before, and it took me a few seconds to get over the shock, and offer the candy to Elsie. She looked at the red-and-white candy with hungry eyes, but Dora said Elsie didn't care for any, either, and neither did Bertie. It would make him sticky.

Crestfallen, but not discouraged, I took some candy myself and offered the books. 'They have lots of pictures in them,' I said eagerly, 'and you can look at them if you want to.'

'Those old things,' Dora said scornfully, glancing at the titles. 'I read them long ago.'

I took the books into the house and put them tenderly away. Dora might scorn them, but they were still dear to me.

The frosty air was still ringing with good wishes when I went outside again, and Mother and Dad were urging everyone to come in and get warm. Bill Banks was in favour of resting a while, but everyone else said they had rested too long already, we had a long drive ahead of us, and it was almost half past eleven. The dinner would be ruined if we didn't hurry. Overruled, Bill found a chair for Mother, and the rest of us squeezed into the sleigh as best we could, and all went well until I discovered that Dora had provided herself with a box to sit on. If Dora could have a seat so could I, and I immediately demanded one.

Mother said Dora had to have a box to sit on because she was holding Bertie. Why couldn't I be a good little girl and sit on the hay like the other children? I replied that I was as big as Dora and had as much right to a box. Mother said there wasn't a box for me, but that was no argument as far as I was concerned. I refused to sit on the hay. At last Dad found a piece of wood that resembled a stool, and I finally condescended to sit on it.

The sleigh ride was fun for a while. The bells jingled gaily, and the runners squealed happily as they slipped over the frozen snow. The sky was a clear hard blue, and millions of cold diamonds glittered on the snow and on the twigs that poked above it. The frost diamonds were so bright they dazzled my eyes, and I had to close them now and then against the glare.

One thing that entranced Lily and me was the way our breath turned to smoke as soon as it left our noses, and for a while we puffed as hard as we could and tried to out-smoke each other. Dora wouldn't join in the contest. She said it was silly. She wouldn't let Elsie make smoke either. Our breath, of course, settled as frost on our bonnets., and in a short time we all had halos around our faces.

After a while the cold made our fingers and toes tingle, then it crept under our thin coats and made us feel stiff and cross. The piece of wood on which I was sitting got frightfully hard, and only pride kept me perched on it. To keep warm the men, who had to ride standing, got out of the sleigh and walked or ran behind for a while. They bent their heads against the keen wind, and put first one hand then the other over their noses and ears. Often they glanced enviously at Dad's big warm cap. He never had to protect his ears. But he had to walk often to keep warm, and I was constantly afraid he would be left behind. Mother told me to stop worrying, Dad was all right, but I always watched closely until he was safe on the sleigh again.

After a while Mother said she thought we children looked cold, and Bill Banks told us to put the horse-blankets around us. We did, and they helped a lot, but they smelled terrible, like old barn and horses combined.

With a big load and very little trail the horses, white with frost, couldn't make much time, and we were two hours going from our house to Bill Banks's shack. When we finally arrived we were almost too stiff to move, and I at least hated to unbend my legs and get out of the sleigh. I was congealed by the cold and half asleep.

We stumbled out of the sleigh and into the warm shack. Like most log houses it was small, and furnished with the bare necessities: a stove, and a double bunk, and a table made of two trestles and four boards. The man who was supposed to be doing the cooking had gone to help with the team, but the food he had prepared smelled delicious.

The fire was low, but Mother and Mrs Metherell soon got it burning brightly, then, while the men tended the team, the three women and we six children crowded around the stove and took off our coats.

For Mother this was a very simple business. She was never one to fuss much about her appearance. She pinned her hair securely, made sure her waist and skirt met properly, and expected them to stay that way, and usually they did. Now she simply untied the shawl she had worn over her head, smoothed her hair and her skirt, and turned to care for Jack.

Mrs Metherell fussed a little more than Mother. She took the side combs out of her hair, fluffed it a little and put them in again, then she smoothed her brown skirt and gave her waist a tweak or two, and said she supposed she'd have to do.

Mother told Mrs Metherell she looked fine, and she did. Her brown hair was soft about her face, and her dress went well with her green eyes and pale skin. She was pregnant, but her figure was still trim and stately, though a trifle round. 'I really think I ought to have stayed at home,' she said as she turned from the tiny mirror near the stove, 'but Frank wouldn't come without me. Are you sure it doesn't show?'

'You did right to come,' Mother told her. 'It doesn't show at all yet.'

I asked what 'it' was, but Mother told me to be quiet, and Dora curled her lip, and told me I was silly.

While Mother and Mrs Metherell were smoothing their hair and skirts Mrs Johnson was busy with her children. She smoothed Elsie's honey-coloured braids none too carefully, and gently combed Dora's mouse-coloured locks. Bertie's hair came next. It was soft and blond, and he didn't push his big curl down the way Jack did.

Bertie hardly ever moved. He was a lovely child, pink and white and plump, with big serious blue eyes, a soft unsmiling mouth, and dark eyelashes that almost touched his eyebrows. In his white dress, daintily trimmed with blue ribbon, he looked like one of the least expressionless of the cherubs. He was content to sit on Dora's lap and be admired, and even I knew he was prettier than Jack.

When her children were neat Mrs Johnson told them to sit still, then she began doing her own hair. She took out the curlers that had been hidden by her scarf and fluffed her hair carefully, taking great pains with every brown wisp, then she bit her lips carefully and smoothed her face with her handkerchief. She gave her black skirt a pull or two, and smoothed it over her ample hips, and turned from the mirror and began looking into the steaming pans, apparently quite pleased with herself. She didn't ask how she looked, and Mother and Mrs Metherell didn't say anything, but they did glance out of their eye corners now and then as if they didn't quite know what to make of the shabby, loose-hanging black jacket Mrs Johnson wore.

Mrs Johnson must have noticed their darting glances, but she paid no attention. She kept looking at the little window, then all at once she slipped in front of the little mirror and fluffed her hair once more and wiped her face, and turned towards the door, giving her well-rounded hips a little shake. 'Here they come,' she announced, and tossed her head, and took off the shabby jacket, revealing a thin, lace-trimmed, white blouse.

The men poured into the little room, laughing and talking. They crowded around the stove, sniffed the steam, and held out their hands to the heat. Mrs Johnson fluttered around them, her lips smiling, her brown eyes sparkling, helping them with caps and mitts and coat buttons. 'As if they aren't old enough to help themselves,' Mrs Metherell muttered.

The men stamped the cold out of their feet and laughed and talked and chaffed one another, but at last all the caps and coats were off, and either hung on nails or stowed behind the stove, and there was a moment of comparative quiet, when everyone sighed a little, and licked their lips, and perhaps wondered how much longer dinner would be.

Bill Banks, who had by now found enough enamel mugs and tin cups to go round, said he thought the women as well as the men ought to have a little something to drive out the cold. Mrs Johnson said she thought it a good idea, but Mother said she didn't think she wanted anything, and Mrs Metherell said she didn't care for any, either. Bill, however, argued that Christmas didn't come often, and they had just had a cold drive. It was only sensible to take a little just as a precaution against cold.

Mother said in that case she'd have just a sip with plenty of water, and Mrs Metherell also decided to try a taste well diluted.

'Don't put any water in mine,' Mrs Johnson said sweetly. 'I like mine straight.'

There was a shocked silence, then Bill Banks, who had been pouring, handed mother a mug. 'My word!' she said to no one in particular.

Bill Banks's bottle was only small, but the grown-ups got a lot of pleasure out of it. They sipped the contents slowly, and laughed and talked, and for a while they were carefree again, and the snow and cold were forgotten.

While our elders were driving out the cold and feeling pleasantly wicked, for they were sober people and seldom tasted liquor, Lily and I tried to make friends with Dora and Elsie. Elsie smiled shyly, and looked as if she would like to play with us, but Dora refused to let her. Dora sat on a box and held Bertie on her lap, and made Elsie sit in silence beside her. She wouldn't say a word to us, or even look at the cat's-cradle I made with a piece of string. After a while Lily and I turned our backs on her, and began to amuse ourselves by trying to decide where we were going to sit when dinner was ready.

We had all brought our own knives and forks, and Mother and Mrs Metherell had set the table while Mrs Johnson was combing her hair. Bill Banks hadn't a table-cloth, and no one had thought to bring one, so the boards were bare. The plates were an odd assortment, some enamel and some tin, more or less dented and chipped. I had hoped for some glass dishes with jam in them, but there was no such luxury. Two of the tin plates, however, were new and very bright, and Lily and I discovered we could see our faces in them.

We hadn't seen our faces for a long time. Mother took good care of her little two-inch mirror, so the plates were a novelty. They distorted our images a little, and we found that by making faces we could produce something quite startling. It was a lot of fun. We looked at the plates and made a face, then we looked at each other. I was sure I could make a worse face than Lily could, and ended with my eyes pulled down and my tongue out. It was such a horrible face that Lily began to cry, and Mother looked our way. 'Mary, stop that,' she said firmly, and took the plate away from me.

The cold was about driven out by that time, and the whisky gone, and Bill Banks said he thought the roast must be about ready. He opened the oven door, pulled out the pan containing the brown, juicy joint, and carried it triumphantly to the table.

There were cries of admiration, and everybody surged around the table looking for a place to sit. Mrs Johnson, who had been almost forgotten, suddenly announced that she thought husbands and wives ought not to sit together, and to cement her argument planted herself beside Mr Metherell. A lot of moving and seat-changing took place, and as a result somebody asked me to move over.

Give up my bright plate! Never! I resisted fiercely and clung to it with both hands. I had found my place and meant to keep it. When somebody tried to move me by force I kicked and screamed.

'What's up?' Dad asked, and frowned.

'I thought she could just as well sit there,' the mover said, indicating a place with a battered plate in front of it.

'It's my plate. I got it first,' I cried.

'Why can't she keep her plate?' Dad asked, his eyelids low. 'She's only a bairn.'

The mover stammered and turned red, and the plates were changed. I moved nearer the roast, but I took my bright plate with me.

There was nothing fancy about that Christmas dinner: no cranberries, no salad, no pickles, no trimmings at all. We had thick slabs of roast beef, mounds of mashed potatoes, white and soft, that Bill somehow had kept from freezing, yellow turnips, also mashed, pie made with dried apples, and lots of hot brown tea.

There was also a lot of fun and good fellowship. Bill Banks carved the roast, pausing often to wave the knife and tell a story that didn't seem a bit funny to me, but the grown-ups seemed to enjoy it. One story led to another, and soon everyone was laughing and talking. Mrs Metherell stopped frowning at Mrs Johnson, and the person who had wanted my place offered me a piece of pie. The voices of the men were deep and hearty, and the laughter of the women was light and gay as yarn after yarn went around the board table. The walls of the little shack almost bulged with the noise, and yet in spite of all the fun loneliness was very close. We could not see it, but it was there, a grey shadow hovering over the little cabin, ready to slip in and surround us the moment the laughter ceased.

The laughter, however, lasted for a long time. When most of the roast beef and all of the pie had been eaten, everyone still sat at the table drinking mug after mug of tea, and telling one story after another. They seemed unwilling, even a little afraid, to let the dinner end. We all lived only a few miles from each other, and yet this seemed like a farewell gathering that nobody wanted to bring to a close.

After a while, of course, the fire burned low and the waiting cold came in, and somebody remembered that it was time to feed and water the horses once more. The men went out to do the chores, and Mother and Mrs Metherell began to clear the table.

Lily and I tried once more to be friends with Dora, but she would have nothing to do with us. She took Bertie on her lap, soothed him to sleep, and made Elsie sit quietly beside her.'

Mother and Mrs Metherell said Dora was wonderful with Bertie, almost as careful as an old woman, and perhaps that's what she was, a child born old.

When I saw that Dora was being admired I tried to imitate her. I pulled Jack on to my small lap and tried to rock him to sleep. Jack, however, had other ideas. He had slept in the sleigh, eaten a good dinner, and was full of ginger and ambition. Instead of co-operating so that I could be a good girl like Dora, he wriggled and squirmed until Mother told me to leave him alone, then, smiling happily, he trotted off to explore the wood box and the space under the table. His white dress was soon soiled, and when the men came in, blinking and half blind from the snow glare, they stumbled over him. Jack didn't mind in the least. He smiled cheerfully, and showed them the log he was dragging, and fell over their feet. The men laughed at him, and said he was a real boy, and Dad's eyes smiled and his face looked proud. But Mrs Johnson sniffed and said she was glad Bertie wasn't a dirty child. Mr Johnson didn't say anything. He looked at Bertie's soft sleeping face, then looked quickly away.

The men, a little sleepy after their hearty dinner, settled down close to the stove. They sat on the floor and the wood box with their knees drawn up and either dozed or talked in low voices. Mrs Johnson fluttered about like a restless moth. Mother and Mrs Metherell sat on the edge of the lower bunk not quite asleep and not quite awake, but too drowsy to talk. It was a comfortable, dreamy time, full of soft sleepy sounds, but it didn't last long.

The sun, low even at midday at that time of year, was now about to slip out of sight between the pale sky and the white snow. Before it disappeared, however, it paused a moment on the rim of the prairie and sent long shafts of pale golden light across the cold snow. One such shaft found the little window on the west side of the shack. It touched the frosted glass gently, then it came in and made a pool of golden light on the rough wood floor.

Mother looked at the ray of light and rubbed her eyes, then she got up and went over to the window. I followed. The place where the snow and sky met was already shadowed by a thin grey haze. In a very short time night, dark and cold, would rise from the snow and stalk across the prairie. 'I think it's about time to go home,' Mother said, and shivered a little.

'Home!' Bill Banks got up from his place behind the stove. 'Oh, no,' he said in a loud voice. 'You can't go home to-night. Just listen to that wind! It sounds like the start of a blizzard.'

Mother said she couldn't hear any wind, everything seemed very still to her.

'Well, maybe it isn't blowing much right now,' Bill admitted. 'But look at the sun.' He waved his arm. 'Practically bright red, a sure sign of wind. And that thickness at the edge of the prairie, a sure sign of snow. Everybody simply has to stay all night.'

There was a general stir and buzz. The men looked out of the little window and agreed with Bill Banks. You never could tell when a blizzard would start, especially in the afternoon, and if we started home and got caught in one we would most likely freeze to death.

The only safe and sensible thing to do was to stay where we were until morning.

The women objected a little. The shack was crowded, and they hadn't come prepared to spend the night, but the trip home would be long and cold, and at the end there was only a bare, cold little house, and the home-sickness they had been avoiding all day. They looked at the long sweep of snow already turning grey, then at the warm stove. 'The kids can sleep on the bunks,' Bill Banks said cheerfully. 'The rest of us can stay up. It's a lot better than freezing.'

'Well…' Mother said uncertainly.

'Sure, it's the only sensible thing,' Bill said, and all the men agreed with him.

I thought it was a good idea, too. I'd never stayed up all night, but I'd often wanted to. I sidled up to Dora and asked what she thought about it. Surely such a fascinating prospect would interest even her. Dora looked up from the book she was reading and told me to leave her alone.

'We're going to stay up all night,' I told her, thinking she hadn't heard the good news.

'Not you, silly,' she said.

'Yes, I am,' I insisted.

'Go away. I want to read.' Dora turned a page.

'Read out loud,' I invited, and sat down beside her.

Dora paid no attention to me, so I began teasing her to read to me. She pushed me off the edge of the bunk and told me to leave her alone.

I was not easily put off, however; I sat down beside her once more and began to coax. I offered every inducement I could think of, even the bright plate at the next meal, for I loved to be read to, but Dora shook her head. 'I don't believe you can read at all,' I said at last. 'You're only turning the pages and pretending.'

'Yes, I can,' Dora said, and read a few lines out loud, then she turned her back and refused to even speak. I sat still for a few minutes puzzled by such apparent meanness. Katie Daw had never acted that way.

After a while Mother found a box of old dominoes, and Lily and I began to play with them. We built castles and houses, and made tunnels and trains, and in a short time Elsie, who had been sitting quietly by

Dora, sidled over and joined us. She slipped silently into our make-
believe without causing a ripple, and after a while she began to talk.
Not out loud the way Lily and I talked, but softly and under her
breath as if she was afraid someone would hear. 'Why do you whisper
like that?' I asked after a while. 'Can't you talk out loud?'

'Hush,' Elsie cautioned under her breath. 'Dora will hear.'

We played quietly after that, whispering softly to each other, and
taking care not to rattle the dominoes. Elsie, we discovered, could
turn dominoes into engines and houses just as easily as we could, and
enjoyed doing it. The pleading smile left her pale face, and pleasure
replaced the vacant stare in her blue eyes.

Dora, of course, got to the end of her book eventually and looked
up. 'Elsie, you come here,' she ordered sharply. Elsie merely smiled
and sat down by Dora.

'Come and play,' I urged. 'Dora isn't your mother. You don't have
to do as she tells you.'

'Yes, she does,' Dora said. 'Elsie has to sit there if I tell her.'

Tears filled Elsie's round blue eyes and rolled down her cheeks,
but she did not make a sound.

'Elsie, behave yourself,' Mrs Johnson said sharply.

Mother and Mrs Metherell exchanged glances, but they said
nothing, and after a moment the grown folk began to talk again. Dora
found another book and began to read, and I sidled around and sat by
Elsie. She did not look at me, but after a while her fingers began to
move, and I saw that she had two or three dominoes in her left hand.
'What are you doing?' I whispered.

Elsie smiled and shook her head ever so slightly, and looked at the
far corner of the bunk. I knew she wanted me to go and sit over there,
and I did, but I was fascinated by her fingers. They moved quickly
and quietly building little castles and bridges, and taking them down
and building them over again. Elsie never looked at her work, but a
happy little smile hovered on her pink lips.

While we children were playing the men were doing the chores:
they fed and watered the team and bedded them down for the night,
brought in a barrel of snow to melt for water, and sawed a huge pile of
wood for the greedy stove. They laughed as they worked, and being

young, all in their twenties, they tossed snow at one another, and pushed each other into the drifts. The work, however, was finished at last, and the men came into the little shack bringing a white cloud of cold air with them. They were red and breathless, and they stamped the snow off their moccasins, rubbed the frost from their eyebrows, and took off their coats and mitts. Bill Banks came in last. He stamped his feet and shut the door, and put a sack at the bottom to keep the cold out, then he hung the barn lantern on a nail. 'Well, I guess that's it,' he said cheerfully. 'We won't go home till morning.'

'Hurrah for Bill,' somebody said, then everybody began to sing:

> 'We won't go home till morning,
> We won't go home till morning,
> We won't go home till morning,
> Till daylight doth appear.'

They sang the verse over and over, changing the last line and clapping their hands. Everybody seemed gay and happy, and the waiting loneliness was for a time forgotten. They sang one song after another: 'Clementine,' 'Little brown jug,' ' Good night, ladies,' and many others, ending with 'Here we come a-wassailing,' which made everybody hungry, and Bill Banks said it was time we had something to eat.

We had the last of the roast beef, bread, and tea, and a small Christmas cake that Bill Banks had saved for a surprise. Everybody talked and ate, and now and then somebody laughed, but the loneliness that was outside on the wide prairie was coming closer.

As soon as the meal was over Bill said everybody had to sing, recite, or tell a story, and to get things going he sang first. His voice had a squeak in it, but when he finished everybody shouted 'Ray, Bill' and clapped like mad.

Mrs Johnson offered to sing next. She slipped off the bunk, stood in the middle of the small floor, swayed her hips, and started. She had a clear voice, and they clapped even louder than they had clapped for Bill Banks, and insisted that she sing again.

Mother wouldn't stand in the middle of the floor when it was her turn to sing. She stayed where she was on the edge of the bunk and sang 'Genevieve' in a clear, sweet voice. She looked very pretty, I thought. Her cheeks were pink, and her blue eyes bright and smiling. Everybody helped with the chorus, and clapped very loud when the song ended. Dad, who was sitting behind the stove, didn't clap much, but his thin face, clean-shaven and young, glowed with pride.

While all this was going on I was on tenterhooks waiting for my turn. I couldn't sing, but I could recite, and I had 'Little Bo-peep' all ready. But Bill Banks, who was master of ceremonies, overlooked me completely, much to my disappointment.

When all the turns were over Mrs Johnson sang several extra numbers, then Bill produced a mouth-organ. He played a waltz, and Mrs Johnson danced a turn or two with him.

About that time some thoughtless person looked at the clock ticking on the shelf behind the stove and asked if it wasn't time the children went to bed.

Jack and Bertie were already asleep, and Lily and Elsie were tired and settled down without a struggle. Even Dora consented to get up on the top bunk, but I insisted I wasn't tired.

I had always been a little owl, and I knew from experience that parties got better as time went on. When Aunt Jane, who had been a spiritualist at one time, had friends in to help coax the spirits to knock, the best knocking always occurred late at night. I had always enjoyed the spirits, and one night, in order to get a better look at them, I hid under the table. I didn't see any spirits, but I did get a good hard kick from Aunt Emma, also a spiritualist. Aunt Emma, however, was more upset than I was. She screamed and had hysterics, and was sure she had kicked a ghost.

No spirits were being invoked that night, but that made no difference to me. The party was getting better all the time, and I was a big girl, and not a bit sleepy.

Mother tried to coax me to at least sit on the bunk. Dora, she pointed out, wasn't being a naughty girl. Why couldn't I be like her?

Unfortunately I no longer thought much of Dora. If she missed the best of the party it was her own fault and served her right. I insisted I wasn't a bit sleepy, that I could play ring-on-a-string as well as anybody, and promised not to cry if I got caught.

'Let her play for a bit, anyway,' Dad said at last. 'She'll soon be tired.'

So Mother stopped coaxing, and I joined the circle passing the ring. I sang at the top of my voice, and passed like mad, and was thrilled pink when Dad caught me with the ring, and I got a turn in the middle of the circle.

After ring-on-a-string we played musical chairs, spin the plate, and There-was-a-farmer-had-a-dog, and I was terribly proud because I could spell Rover.

When the hands of the little clock behind the stove pointed straight up I was still awake. 'Midnight,' somebody said, and everybody seemed to hold his breath for a moment, then everybody stood up, crossed arms, joined hands, and sang 'Auld Lang Syne.'

The voices filled the little cabin to the corners, and perhaps drifted out over the snow. They made a brave try to be hearty and cheerful, but every now and then there was a catch and a stumble, and before the second verse was over there were tears in Mother's eyes.

The song ended and there was silence for a moment, then the thought that must have been at the back of everyone's mind all evening found words. 'I wonder what they are doing in England to-night?' young Bill who lived with the Metherells said.

Again there was a little silence. Everyone sat still as if waiting for something. The door did not open, but suddenly there was another presence in the little room. The loneliness that had waited patiently out in the cold suddenly came in and sat with us. And strangely enough it was not unwelcome, everyone seemed relieved to at last be able to talk of what was uppermost in his thoughts. They talked more to themselves than to each other, as with voices soft and home-sick they recalled places long loved, and people who were dear.

They talked of the Yorkshire rain and the London fog, of the mighty Thames and the little Spen; of Trafalgar Square and the Church Fields, of the Strand, the Embankment, Piccadilly, and Big Ben. Dad and Mother talked of Grandmother Pinder's little house and Grandfather Gomersall's shop, and of Aunt Jane and Castle Hill. They talked of the Christmas carols and the singers who went from house to house with lanterns in their gloved hands, of the church bells and the tunes they played, 'Hark, the herald angels sing' and 'Nowell.' They recalled the handclasps and the greetings, the holly and the mistletoe, and the warmth and happiness in the homes of fathers and mothers. Now and then a voice faltered and a tear hovered, but the talk went on; and some time during that quiet, lonely time England became the Old Country, a place associated with happiness and tender memories, a place for ever dear.

'It won't be long before we're going back,' Mr Metherell said at last. 'Another year or two…'

'If we can stick it that long.' Mr Johnson looked at the cold window.

'Once the railroad comes through we'll be in clover,' Dad said.

'But will it come?' Mr Gardiner asked. 'If them folks in the tents freeze…'

Everybody was silent for a moment. So much depended on the people in the tents. If they froze to death, and the old-timers were sure they would, the rest of the colonists might easily lose heart. 'They must be awfully cold this weather,' young Bill said, and shivered.

'They've done all right so far,' Dad said cheerfully, 'and the worst of the winter's about over. By this time next year we'll all have houses, and be doing so well even Sarah won't want to leave.'

'Oh, yes, I shall,' Mother said. 'I shall always want to go home.' But there was a little smile in her eyes.

The talk turned to the future then, and became more cheerful, for they were all young and full of hope, and not even home-sickness could depress them for long. If they got through this first winter, and of course they would, they would all be on easy street, and have nothing more to worry about. Canada was a great country in lots of ways, even though it was a bit cold. Once they got the land tilled and wheat growing they would soon have money enough to go home for Christmas every year. One or two doubted this, but Dad said it was not only possible, but probable. 'There's no limit to what a fellow can do in this country,' Dad said, his eyes shining. 'That's what I like about it. There's a big future, allus something to look for'ard to.'

I don't know when I fell asleep, but all of a sudden it was morning, and I was cold. The cabin also was cold, and the light that came in through the little window was hard and bright, and as unfriendly as a block of ice. The voices that had been warm and friendly the night before were also chill, and cross, and irritable. I was cross, too. I didn't want to get up, and I didn't want any breakfast, and I didn't want to watch Jack, either.

Mother said if I'd gone to bed when I should I wouldn't be so tired, but Dora had gone to bed, and she was just as cross as I was. Lily was also irritable. She couldn't get her feet into her shoes, but she wouldn't let me help her, and when she finally did permit me to put her shoes on I got them on the wrong feet, and Dora laughed at me and told me I was stupid.

The grown-ups were almost as out of sorts as the children. Mrs Metherell, having no children to worry about, took her time over her tea, and dozed a little, but Mrs Johnson scolded her husband sharply. All the lilt had gone out of her voice, just as all the starch had gone out of her blouse.

Mother had smoothed her hair first thing, and though her blue eyes were tired, her dark red waist and her black skirt were as neat as ever.

The men were almost as tired as the women. They stumbled out to feed the horses, and came back yawning and rubbing their eyes. Only Dad had a smile.

In all the crowd Jack was the only one unaffected by the long night. He had slept well, and his good humour and energy were almost annoying. While Mother was getting breakfast he got into the wood box and strewed wood all over the floor. Mrs Metherell, half asleep, almost tripped over a piece, and Mrs Johnson said it was a wonder she didn't have an accident. Everybody was relieved when breakfast was finally over and the sleigh came to take us home.

The trip home wasn't anywhere near as pleasant as the drive the day before had been. There was no cheerful talk, and when the men walked to get warm their feet dragged. The sleigh runners whined dismally as they slid over the cold snow, and the sleigh box creaked wearily.

Even the day seemed dull and tired. There was a white fog in the air, a sort of ghostly thickness that hid the horizon and made the trees look like lonely, dark shadows, but there was no moisture in the fog, only strange icy particles suspended in the air. When we breathed the tiny fragments stung our noses, and a few went down and chilled our chests. The sun, obscured by the mist, looked like a ball of hard, cold ice, and its harsh light woke no glitter on the snow. There was no glitter anywhere, only the queer, unearthly whiteness that covered the earth and filled the sky. It intensified the silence so much that the noise made by the sleigh runners was like a sound from another world.

After we had travelled through the icy mist for a while we felt as if we had somehow taken the wrong turn and stumbled into a strange and unfriendly world. The sleigh and the team looked small in the vast whiteness, and when Mother asked if we were lost she put everyone's thoughts into words. Bill Banks, who was driving, said we were going in the right direction, but he sounded uncertain, and it was a relief when we finally rounded a ghostly grove and saw our house huddled low on the snow.

Mother and Dad asked everyone to come in and have tea and get warm. They said they would like to warm up, but it seemed to be getting dark, and they still had quite a way to go. So Dad and Mother thanked Bill Banks for a wonderful Christmas, then the sleigh and the little crowd in it went off into the frosty mist.

Our house was ice-cold, but Dad soon had a fire going and the kettle on. 'Well, we had a fine Christmas,' he said as he stood by the stove warming his thin hands. 'It will be something to remember.'

'Yes.' Mother put tea into the blue teapot. 'It will be something to tell them about when we go home.' She smiled a little and looked through her eyelashes at Dad, but he didn't seem to have heard. There was a happy look on his lean young face, and contentment in his eyes as he watched Jack, already busy investigating the tool box.

CHAPTER TWENTY-EIGHT

FTER Christmas the winter, that we thought was at least half over, really began. During December the thermometer had dropped to thirty degrees below zero once or twice, but soon after the new year, which was my birthday, it dropped to fifty below, and hovered there for at least a month.

In the day-time the air was clear, and so crisp it almost crackled. The smoke from the stove-pipe went straight up in a thick white column, and sun-dogs, small false suns that looked like small round rainbows, shimmered frostily on either side of the real sun from its late rising to its early setting. The sky was a dome of pale ice, and the snow was a sheet of white that glared in the cold sunlight. Against the snow the frozen trees looked like etchings, dark, still, and dead. It was in many ways a beautiful world, but much too cold to enjoy.

At night when the moon was bright the prairie was a little more friendly, at least in appearance. The snow still glittered, and the trees were stark and dead, but the world seemed unreal. It was a sort of cold fairyland full of enchantment. The white owls that skimmed silently over the snow were fairy birds, the dark blue sky arched high overhead became a meadow, and the far-away stars were crocuses on the fields of heaven. Everything seemed a little more friendly than it was in the day-time, at least until the coyotes began to howl.

The howl of the coyotes was the one and only sound in the vast silence, but it did not dispel the silence, it made it much worse. The howl was the embodiment of all loneliness, all hunger, all cold, all pain, and all the misery of death. It was a terrible icicle of sound jabbing desperately at the frozen sky.

I put my fingers in my ears when the coyotes howled, and asked Mother to tell me when they stopped. Mother said the coyotes wouldn't hurt me, they were a long way off, and they didn't like houses or people. Maybe they didn't, but I thought they sounded hungry enough to eat anything even though they didn't like it.

Sometimes when Dad walked home alone from the woods two or three coyotes sometimes appeared as if out of the snow and trotted along with him. They always kept a short distance away, and they never tried to attack, but Dad said he always took care not to stumble and fall when those quick, grey shapes were about.

Mother thought Dad ought to stop cutting logs now that the cold was so bitter. Dad, however, said he had to have some exercise, he couldn't sit around the stove all day. But the glare of the sun on the snow soon made it necessary for him to stay at home. His eyes swelled shut, and became red and painful.

Mother put cold cloths on his eyes, and in about three days they were well again, but after a day in the woods they swelled all over again, and Mother was sure Dad was going blind. 'It's all the fault of this awful country,' Mother said as she bathed Dad's eyes in cold water. 'I wish we'd never heard of it.'

Mr Gardiner came over while Dad's eyes were still swollen. His eyes were red, too, and he said he had been unable to see for two days, and he'd had to stay inside and cover the window, the light hurt his eyes so.

'Then it must be something catching,' Mother said, and was more worried than ever. We could all get the strange disease, and all go blind before anything could be done for us. The nearest doctor was in Lloydminster, twenty long, cold miles away, and we had no team.

Dad said nothing would happen to the rest of us if we were careful, and kept our towels away from his, so Mother hung Dad's towel on a nail all by itself, and told Lily and me not to go near it.

Knowing the rest of us were reasonably safe from swollen eyes didn't help Dad. He could barely see, and the glare of the sun on the snow was painful. Mother tried to chop wood, but the axe was too heavy for her. Mr Gardiner tried to help, but his eyes were as bad as Dad's; finally Dad tied Mother's little green shawl over his face to protect him from the glare, turned his back to the sun, and sawed enough wood for a day or two.

We struggled along that way for about a week. Mother brought in the snow to melt for water, and helped with the wood, and Dad spent most of his time sitting in the darkened house with a cold cloth over his red and swollen eyes. Then Mr Metherell came to see us.

'You're snow-blind,' Mr Metherell said when he saw Dad's eyes.

That frightened Mother until Mr Metherell said it wasn't permanent. He'd been blind for a while, too, and didn't know what to do until Mr Pike, who freighted between Battleford and Lloydminster, told him to wear green mosquito-netting over his eyes when he went out. 'It's the glare of the sun on the snow that causes the swelling,' Mr Metherell told us. 'The green netting takes the glare away.'

We were relieved to know that Dad's illness wasn't serious, and glad to know there was a way to prevent it. Dad sat in the dark until he was able to see again, then he tied several thicknesses of green netting over his eyes every time he went out.

We had been so worried about Dad's eyes that we hadn't had time to think of anything else, but now that they were better we began to notice the cold, that by then was really terrible. Everything in the little house froze. A pail of water left near the stove overnight froze solid and the pail split. The coal oil in the little lamp froze and cracked the glass, and we had to use the barn lantern for light. The clock behind the stove stopped, and we had to guess at the time until Mr Gardiner came over. The bread, even though set in the morning, wouldn't rise: the house was too cold. 'I don't know what we're going to do,' Mother said as she mixed bannock. 'This country seems bent on getting rid of us.'

'It's bad, all right,' Dad agreed. 'Willie Gardiner's thermometer was down to sixty below this morning.'

'I wonder how them folks in the tents stand it.' Mother looked at the frost ferns on the window and shivered.

Dad said the last he heard they were doing fine, but he looked and sounded uneasy. So much depended on the people in the tents. If they froze to death the remainder of the colonists might easily lose their nerve and return to England as soon as the trails were passable. A few of the single men might stay, but most of the married ones would leave. Canada would clearly be no place for women and children. 'How are they doing in Lloydminster?' became a stock and anxious question whenever we saw anyone who might have any news.

The tent-dwellers so far had managed very well. The man who was lost all night in that first big blizzard lost both legs, but he recovered, and everyone else seemed in good health. There were a few frozen toes, fingers, and ears, but nothing serious. Even Sidney Claxton, the baby, was thriving. The old-timers shook their heads and said they couldn't understand it. By rights all the tent-dwellers ought to have been icicles long ago. Mr Lloyd was certainly doing a good job, but winter wasn't over yet by a long way. It would certainly be a miracle if anyone was still alive when spring came.

Now it seemed as if the tent-dwellers were not the only ones in danger of freezing. Dad spent long hours sawing wood, and Mother said she spent half her time feeding the little stove, but we were always cold. Lily and I put our coats on when we got up and kept them on until we went to bed, but if we strayed a yard or two from the stove we were cold. There was frost all around the door, and on the nails that held the boards together, there was even frost on the strands of hay that hung down between the poles of the roof.

Dad and Mr Gardiner no longer went to the Big Gully to cut logs. The cold was too bitter, and sawing wood for the stoves took most of their time and energy. Jack seemed to be the only one who didn't mind the cold. His fingers were often blue, and his little nose red, but he wouldn't stay by the stove. He loved the dark space under the bed, and the tools Dad kept there. The chisels were like ice, but Jack played with them until the day he put one in his mouth. The cold steel stuck to his tongue, and Dad and Mother were frantic. They were afraid Jack might lose his tongue. They finally got the chisel off by putting the free end in hot water, but Jack had a sore and swollen tongue for days.

Mr Gardiner, who came over every day, said his house was as cold as ours, and he was almost afraid to go to bed, everything seemed to freeze so quickly. His nose had frozen while he was walking the short distance between his house and ours.

Mother looked anxiously at the thickly frosted window, and said she was afraid, too. It would be so easy to freeze while you were asleep.

Dad didn't say anything, but his thin young face was troubled, and his usually smiling eyes were bleak and tired.

'If this awful—' Mother began, then she caught sight of Dad's anxious face and stopped. 'I think some tea might warm us up a bit,' she said, and reached for the teapot.

The tea did warm us for a while, but the cold still filled the little house, and that night Dad stayed up to keep the fire going.

The house was warmer in the morning, but staying up all night was hard on Dad, and after about a week he began to look ill. If he could have slept in the day-time he might have got along all right, but we three children couldn't help making noise, and there was wood to saw, and snow to bring in for water. Finally Mother persuaded Dad to go to bed and let the fire go out. 'If we freeze we'll at least be together,' she said. 'What would we do if something happened to you?'

'You'd probably marry somebody else in a hurry,' Dad said, and smiled.

'Not me!' Mother pursed her lips. 'Once is enough.' So Dad went to bed, and the stove went out, but not before Dad and Mr Gardiner agreed to keep an eye on each other's smoke.

First thing in the morning, as soon as the fire was going, they stepped outside to see if the other's stove-pipe was smoking. If our stove-pipe was smokeless Mr Gardiner agreed to come and thaw us out, if his was Dad promised to do the same. There was, of course, the possibility that we might all freeze stiff the same night, but it was a chance we had to take.

We got along that way for quite a while, then Mr Pike, an Englishman who had been in Canada a year or two, came and spent the night. He stabled his horses in our little barn, bedding them and feeding them with the hay Dad had put up in the fall, then he came into the house.

'How are them in the tents getting on?' Dad asked as he and Mr Pike warmed their hands at the stove.

'Not bad.' Mr Pike pulled the icicles off his thick black moustache. 'They're cold, but they take turns keeping the fires going. You aren't any too warm here, are you?'

'No.' Dad looked at the stove to hide the worry in his eyes. 'To tell the truth,' he said in a low voice, 'I'm scared to go to sleep at night, and scared to wake up in the morning. It's that cold I don't hardly dare look at the bairns until they stir. I'm that frightened of finding them frozen.'

'It happens now and then.' Mr Pike looked around the little house, then he went close to the wall and looked at the clay, and put his hand against it. 'No wonder you're cold,' he said slowly. 'There's so much space between your logs and your mud you might as well be living outside. Just hold your hand here, or almost anywhere, and you can feel the wind blowing in.'

Dad held his hand against a crack, and consternation covered his thin face. 'I can't understand it,' he said. 'We mudded that careful.'

'But the logs were green then,' Mr Pike explained. 'When they dried they shrank. The mud shrank too, and left these cracks. First thing to-morrow dig some mud from under that box in the middle of the floor, and mud up the whole house, and you'll be twenty degrees warmer.'

'I will that,' Dad said. 'And I'll tell Willie Gardiner what's wrong, too.' His voice suddenly sounded cheerful again, his face became once more young and happy, and the twinkle returned to his deep emerald-flecked eyes.

As soon as Mr Pike left next morning Dad moved the big packing-box and tried to dig some clay, but the ground was frozen solid, and it looked as if the job would take the rest of the winter, and probably part of next summer. Dad tried building a fire in the hole, but it made too much smoke and he had to put it out. 'We might as well freeze to death as smother,' Mother said as she wiped her stinging eyes. 'Canada's bound and determined to be rid of us, and there's no use trying to outwit it.'

'There's more than one way of doing things,' Dad said, and filled the iron kettle and put it on the stove. When the kettle boiled Dad poured the water into the hole. The hot water helped a little, and Dad brought in snow for more water, then he tried again to dig.

It was hard work, but Dad didn't seem to mind. He chipped at the frozen dirt until he had a little, then he kneaded it until it was the right consistency for spreading. His hands were soon red and chapped, but the smile never left his young face. 'We'll beat this cold yet, Sally,' he said gaily as he pushed mud in to the cracks. 'I allus told you you'd be all right as long as you stayed with me.'

'The winter isn't over yet,' Mother said darkly. 'Don't crow too soon.'

Although the little house was much warmer after the cracks were filled we still had to stay near the stove if we wanted to be warm. Lily and I played near it, and Mother did most of her work close beside it, and at night she and Dad sat beside it while they sipped their last cup of tea. It was the centre of our lives, and was such a comfort we forgot how dangerous it could be.

Our first accident with the stove wasn't bad. Mother, usually very neat and tidy, put the comb on the little shelf in front of the firebox instead of on the high shelf on the wall. The stove, of course, was hot all over, and the celluloid comb burst into flames, and was gone in a few seconds.

'Oh, my comb!' Mother cried, but there was nothing left of it, not even a decent cinder.

I was rather glad the comb was gone. My hair was curly, and the daily combing wasn't pleasant, but Mother liked to comb her yard-long hair, and was much upset. 'What am I going to do now?' she asked, and looked helplessly at the soft baby-brush, the only hair tool we had left. 'And the bairns! Their hair will be nothing but wads.'

'We can cut their hair,' Dad said, and got the scissors.

I didn't mind my short hair at all, but Mother cried, and said I didn't look like a little girl any more. As for Lily, her looks were completely ruined, and it was certainly a terrible country that demanded even children's hair. Mother never thought of cutting her hair. Somehow, with the help of the little brush, she managed to keep it smooth and neat, but it was a job, and she lamented the loss of the comb almost every day.

Soon after the comb burned we had a much more serious accident. It was partly due to the cold, and our habit of living close to the stove, but it could have happened even if the weather had been warm.

When Mother made tea she usually put the teapot on the little shelf in front of the stove where she put the comb. The tea stayed warm there while it brewed, and the teapot could be reached from both the wagon bench and the box table. The back of the stove would have been a safer place, but it was usually crowded with pails and bowls of melting snow. In any case Mother had put the teapot on the little shelf every day for months, and nothing had happened; that morning, however, was different.

Mother poured the boiling water into the blue teapot and put it on the shelf, then turned to cut bread. The minute she turned Jack ran to the stove, put his mouth to the teapot spout, and drank the boiling tea.

He was so quick I couldn't stop him even though I was sitting close by on the wagon bench. I grabbed the handle of the teapot as soon as I could, and added my screams to Jack's, but the damage was done. Jack's lips and mouth were terribly scalded.

We had no salve of any kind, only bacon fat. Dad thought it might help and smeared some on Jack's lips, and tried to get a little on his tongue.

After a while Jack stopped crying, but he had no desire to get off Mother's lap. He lay limp in her arms, his face pale and his legs dangling. In a little while his blue eyes closed part way, and his head sagged. 'He's asleep,' Dad said hopefully. 'When he wakes up he'll be better.'

'If he just got the tea in his mouth and didn't swallow any he'll be all right,' Mother said. 'That calf in England...' She choked and stopped, her eyes full of tears. I didn't say anything, but I remembered the calf. It had died because a hot lump in its food had scalded its stomach.

Dad looked in the teapot, and asked Mother if she could remember how full it had been. She couldn't, of course. It was a fat, round teapot, and there was still a lot of tea in it. There was no way of knowing how much Jack had swallowed. 'Maybe he stopped drinking when he felt the heat,' Dad said hopefully. 'Anyway, he's having a good sleep, and that ought to help.'

Mother didn't say anything. She looked at Jack's pale face, and rocked him gently in her arms.

Mr Gardiner came over later in the day. He was shocked when Dad told him what had happened, and sawed and brought in some wood so that Dad could stay with Mother.

Much to Dad's disappointment Jack did not wake up that night, or the next day, either. He lay limp in Mother's arms, his eyes half closed and his swollen mouth half open. 'Don't you think we ought to take him to Lloydminster and see a doctor?' Mother asked.

Dad, who usually had some plan, for once didn't know what to do. We had no team, and Lloydminster was twenty drifted miles away. 'Let's see what Willie Gardiner thinks,' Dad said.

Mr Gardiner had stayed late the night before, but he came over first thing that morning. He looked at Jack's pale face, but he didn't say whether he thought Jack looked better or not. Dad asked what he thought about going to Lloydminster.

'Well,' Mr Gardiner said slowly, 'it's awfully cold, and with the drifts the way they are it might take two days to make the trip.'

'And then they might not be able to do anything.' There were tears in Mother's blue eyes.

'I don't believe he's as bad as you think, Mrs Pinder.' Mr Gardiner's voice was deep and steady. 'With such a swollen mouth anybody would feel ill, but he doesn't look too bad to me. And he's sure to be a little better in the morning.'

'You don't think he swallowed any tea?' Mother asked hopefully.

'Well, very little. If he had I think he'd look much worse. Besides, a youngster would naturally spit out anything as unpleasant as boiling tea.'

Mother and Dad were cheered by Mr Gardiner's optimism, and tried to believe he was right, and Jack was not seriously ill; but when the day dwindled and Jack showed no signs of improving their courage faded. 'If only we hadn't come to this country,' Mother said in a low voice.

'If anything happens to him we won't stay,' Dad said wearily. 'There'd be nothing to stay for.' His voice was low and heavy, and his thin face, turned towards the frosted window, was drawn and lined. He looked almost as Grandmother Pinder had looked when she said good-bye to us.

Mother and Dad had stayed up most of the previous night, and they both looked tired, but they were so worried they could neither sleep nor rest. Dad kept the fire going so that Jack wouldn't get cold, and every little while Mother bathed Jack's swollen lips with weak tea, and tried to get him to take a sip. Jack, however, refused to swallow.

He simply lay pale and still in Mother's arms, but he wasn't really asleep. His blue eyes were half open, and too much of the whites showed beneath his pale lids. And so the second night passed, and finally the sun, cold and pale, shone on the frosted window, and Mr Gardiner knocked on the door.

'How is he?' Mr Gardiner asked.

Mother and Dad looked at him out of red-rimmed eyes and shook their heads.

Mr Gardiner came over to the stove and looked down at Jack's pale face, then he took off his mitts and sat down.

'Maybe we ought to have taken him to Lloydminster at first,' Dad said.

'I don't think it would have helped,' Mr Gardiner said quietly. 'It's a long, cold trip, and there's nothing much there. I doubt if the doctor could have done more than you have.'

'There might have been something,' Mother said wearily. 'Some oil that we know nothing about. At least we would have been trying. But just to sit here and do nothing...' Mother blinked her tired eyes.

'I'll walk over to Bill Banks's any time,' Mr Gardiner offered. 'He'll be glad to take you to Lloydminster.'

'Well...' Mother said, and bit her lip.

'It's hard to know what to do.' Dad walked over to the little window and stared at the frost.

'Let's wait a bit and see how he is this afternoon,' Mr Gardiner suggested. 'If he's worse I'll go and get Bill, and you can start first thing in the morning.'

Mother thought this over for a while. 'Well, all right,' she said at last. 'He doesn't look any worse than he did yesterday, does he?' she asked.

'No,' Mr Gardiner said quietly.

Even the prospect of doing something cheered Mother and Dad a little. 'The doctor may know of something,' Mother said, and smoothed her hair a little. She had not brushed it since Jack's accident, which was to me a sure sign that the world was about to end. Mother had never had an unkept head for as long as I could remember.

'He might know of a lot of things,' Dad agreed, and made some porridge for breakfast. We had lived on bannock and tea for two days and both Lily and I were getting tired of it. Mother and Dad had eaten practically nothing since Jack scalded his mouth. Mugs of strong tea seemed all they could swallow. They didn't eat much that morning, either. Mother said the porridge was fine, but she wasn't hungry, and Dad gave up after a spoonful or two. They bathed Jack's mouth, and tried to persuade him to sip a little weak tea, but he made a queer noise, half whimper, half gurgle, and they gave up. Dad, however, was sure Jack had swallowed a little tea, and was quite cheered.

Mr Gardiner came over early in the afternoon as he had promised. 'How is he?' he asked, the moment he was inside the house.

Mother looked down at Jack's quiet face. His mouth wasn't quite as swollen as it had been, but his skin was the colour of a candle, and only the whites of his eyes showed. 'I don't know,' she said in a low voice.

Dad, who had been walking slowly back and forth between the bed and the stove, went over to the window and looked out between a frost fern and a miniature snow bank. The sun was bright, but frost particles glistened in the cold air, and the sun-dogs glared like malignant eyes. 'It's that pneumonia that bothers me,' Dad said. 'If he gets that on top of what he has now he'll be a goner.'

'We could wrap him in blankets,' Mother said.

'But he'd have to breathe, and that cold air...' Dad turned from the window. 'What do you think, Willie?' he asked.

'It's a chance, all right,' Mr Gardiner said.

Mother put her small hand on Jack's forehead. 'He doesn't seem any warmer than usual.' she said. 'Maybe if we wait a bit...'

They finally decided to wait until to-morrow morning, then if there was no change Mr Gardiner would go and get Bill Banks first thing.

'If he would only drink something,' Mother said over and over, but Jack refused to swallow anything.

That afternoon seemed never-ending. Lily and I played quietly. Mother sat in the hard wooden chair with a pillow at her back and cradled Jack in her arms. Dad walked from the window to the stove and back again.

After a while the cold sun went down and Dad lit the lantern. In the yellow light Jack looked worse than ever. He had lost weight, and his little face looked drawn and old, and there were blue shadows under his half-closed eyes. When Mr Gardiner came after supper he didn't try to be cheerful. He looked at Mother's tired face, and there was pity in his brown eyes. 'You know, Mrs Pinder, you've done everything you could,' he said in a low voice.

'We'll take him to Lloydminster no matter what, to-morrow,' Dad said.

Mr Gardiner didn't say anything. He just sat and looked at the stove for a while, then he went home.

Dad put Lily and me to bed, then he and Mother prepared for another night of waiting. They dimmed the light so that it wouldn't disturb Jack, and Dad put his top-coat on for extra warmth and wrapped a blanket around Mother.

I huddled down in the big bed beside Lily, but the worry that filled our little house kept me from sleeping, and I was still awake when the coyotes began to howl. They seemed to be all around us, and first one then another sent its high, thin voice up to the stars. 'I do wish those things would stop making that noise,' Mother said after a while.

Dad looked at the little window that was silver-white in the moonlight. 'It isn't as if they were dogs,' he said after a moment. 'Coyotes are different.' He put more wood on the fire.

'I still wish they'd stop,' Mother said uneasily.

'It's the moon that makes them howl,' Dad said. 'And maybe they're hungry. It doesn't mean anything.'

'No,' Mother said, and stared wide-eyed at the window. I put my fingers in my ears. I knew that in Yorkshire when a dog gave voice to a low, mournful wail it was considered a sure sign of approaching death.

After a while the coyotes quieted, and Mother told Dad he ought to get some sleep. 'I can keep the fire going if you leave some wood near me,' she said. 'We may have a long trip to-morrow.'

'What about you?' Dad asked.

'I can't sleep knowing them things are out there.' Mother nodded at the window.

'Neither can I,' Dad admitted, but after a while he put his arms on the table and let his head rest on them.

I pulled the blankets over my head, and the next thing I knew it was morning, and Dad was making tea. As soon as it was cool Mother bathed Jack's lips, then she picked up a spoon and offered him a sip. His lips moved a little, and so did his throat. 'Walter, Walter!' Mother cried in a glad voice. 'He tried to swallow, he tried to swallow! My bairn's better. He's going to live!' Then she began to cry.

Dad took the spoon and offered Jack another sip, and again Jack swallowed a little. 'He's better. Thank God!' Dad said, and wiped his shining eyes.

Mother and Dad were both smiling when Mr Gardiner came a few minutes later. Weariness had completely left their faces, and they were young and happy again. 'He's better,' Mother said the minute the door opened. 'He drank a drop of tea. I'm sure he's better.'

Mr Gardiner looked at Jack's pale face, and Dad and Mother watched anxiously. They were terribly afraid even yet. 'He has improved a bit, hasn't he?' Dad asked.

'Yes.' A slow smile warmed Mr Gardiner's usually serious face, and his dark eyes beamed. 'Yes,' he said again. 'He looks a lot better.'

'See, he can swallow,' Mother said, and gave Jack more tea.

Once he was around the turn Jack recovered surprisingly fast. He drank quantities of weak tea and cold water, and, although still thin and pale, in about a week he was his cheerful self again.

'I never saw anything like it,' Dad said proudly when Jack rummaged under the bed and found the little axe Dad had hidden behind the tool box. 'Half dead one day and swinging the axe the next. He's going to be a hard one to beat.'

'He'll kill himself if you don't put those tools out of his reach,' Mother said.

'Not him!' Dad's eyes were bright as stars, and the smile on his thin young face warmed the whole room. 'He's a real pioneer, that one.'

CHAPTER TWENTY-NINE

AFTER Jack got well happiness filled our little house for a long time. Mother sang as she stirred the bannock, and Dad's eyes smiled every time he looked at Jack. Even when the cold dragged on and on Mother said we had a lot to be thankful for. We were all in good health. But when February was half gone, and Mr Gardiner's thermometer still registered forty below zero, both she and Dad began to get a little uneasy.

'There will be snowdrops in bloom in England now,' Mother said one day, 'and maybe even a few early daffodils.'

'There'll be flowers here soon,' Dad replied. 'This snow will go fast once it starts.'

'Then I wish it would start,' Mother said. 'The baking-powder is almost gone.'

The snow, however, showed no signs of going, and the cold continued. The smoke from our stove-pipe still went straight up, and when Dad chopped wood the cold axe rang like a bell in the crisp air. One of the drifts touched the eaves of our little house, and even the snow on the level was deep.

To make matters worse our food was getting low. Not the flour, we had plenty of that, but the bacon, the prunes, and the dried apple rings had all disappeared. We still had a small supply of white beans, oatmeal, and jam, but our tea was very low. There were plenty of rabbits for the catching, and Dad's snares were seldom empty, but the meat tasted of bark, and we were very tired of it. The candles also were getting low, and we had to be careful of them, so we did not light one until it was quite dark.

Mr Gardiner's food was as low as ours, and he and Dad discussed walking to Bill Banks's asking him to take them to Battleford. The cold, however, was intense, and they finally decided to wait a while. Spring, they were sure, couldn't be far away.

I suppose the other settlers spending the winter on the prairie were no better off than we were. The Mounted Police visited some of them and took them supplies, but they completely missed us and Mr Gardiner.

Even though the weather was cold, and the food poor, there were still many happy moments that winter. On Sunday afternoons, and sometimes in the evenings, Mother read aloud to us. We hadn't many books, but that didn't matter, I never tired of a story. Mother read the fairy-tales Santa brought until she said she knew them backwards, but I still urged her to read them just once more. I always cried when the three bears almost ate Goldilocks, and when Beauty gave herself to the Beast, and at last Mother said she thought the stories upset me too much, and it was time for a change. I hastily explained that I enjoyed the stories more when I cried, but Mother said I was getting too emotional, and began reading the Bible to us. I enjoyed David and Goliath just as much as I enjoyed 'Jack and the Beanstalk,' and I had a good cry when poor old Goliath got killed. I knew he got only what he deserved, but I was sorry for him.

Often in the evenings when it was too dark to read and too early to light the candle Mother sang to us. Sometimes she sang old favourites such as 'Sweet and low' and 'Genevieve,' and sometimes the old familiar hymns: 'There is a green hill far away,' 'Abide with me,' and 'Onward, Christian soldiers.' She had a sweet voice, and I never tired of listening.

After supper, when Lily, Jack, and I were in bed, and the little house was dark except for the glow from the stove and the yellow light of the one candle, Dad often read aloud while Mother worked at her knitting.

Some of the books were rather dull, but one of them, *White Company*, I think, was terribly exciting. There was a great deal of fighting in it, and a fierce and wonderful man who was always saying: 'By these ten finger bones.'

I used to huddle at the foot of the bed and shiver with fright. Mother, of course, often told me to get under the covers and go to sleep. I did pull the blanket around me, but sleep was out of the question while Ten Finger Bones was fighting the whole French army.

Sometimes, to save the candle, Dad and Mother sat by the stove light and talked. Usually they relived things that had happened before I was born, but one night they named our farm.

They had discussed giving our quarter section a name several times, but Mother had always managed to put the naming off. She thought a name for our land would be one more link in the chain that was binding us to Canada. Dad, however, said we ought to decide on a name before the best were gone.

'What difference does it make what we call it?' Mother asked. 'We might not even stay here.'

'It won't do any harm to give the place a name,' Dad pointed out. 'What do you think about Gully Farm?'

Mother didn't care for the name. She said we were a long way from the Big Gully. If the farm had to have a name why couldn't it be named after a place in England?

Dad said that was fine with him. What name did she want?

Mother suggested Skipton, Millbridge, and several other names, and Dad said any one of them was all right, but he was plainly disappointed, and refused to say which name he really wanted, and at last Mother told him to name the farm anything he liked.

Dad didn't want to displease Mother, but he didn't want her to be constantly reminded of England. He still hoped she would change her mind about going back, but the long cold winter, its hardships, and Jack's accident had been no help. Mother now had a strong case against Canada.

Dad, however, wasn't one to give up without a struggle. He admitted Canada wasn't exactly a picnic spot right now, it was colder than Billy-be-danmed, but he still insisted it was a wonderful place with plenty of possibilities, and so he caught at every straw that might turn Mother's mind away from home. Naming the farm was one such straw. It made the hundred and sixty acres of prairie we had homestead more intimately ours.

'Let's see how the names look written,' Dad suggested, and found a stub of pencil and wrote 'Gully Farm, North-West Territory, Canada.' 'How does that look?' he asked.

Mother said it looked all right, but she preferred 'Littletown, Liversedge, Yorkshire, England' for her address. Dad said he would, too, if everything was equal, but it wasn't. There were far more opportunities here than in England. 'In two years you won't know this country,' Dad said. 'It will have changed that much, and by the time Jack's grown it will be something wonderful.'

'A cold country is always a cold country,' Mother said.

'No, it isn't,' Dad insisted. 'When this country is ploughed the climate will change. It will be ten or twenty degrees warmer.'

Mother said she'd never heard of such nonsense, or met a more pig-headed man, and to go on and name the farm anything he liked. It would still be the place God forgot as far as she was concerned.

Nothing more was said about the name, but after a while Gully Farm became part of our address, and Mother seemed to like it.

We did not spend all those long cold evenings alone. Mr Gardiner often came over and sat in the stove light with us. His coal oil and most of his candles had gone just as ours had, and the hours of darkness were lonely. He was almost as enthusiastic about Canada as Dad was, and they discussed its advantages and drawbacks by the hour.

The cold, they both decided, was a real obstacle, and the shortage of marriageable women was another. Single men had a tendency to drift about. You had to have families for any real stability, and where were the women coming from? Madeline Edwards in Lloydminster was almost the only single girl, and she was only about eleven.

'There's plenty of girls in England who'd be more than willing to come out if they were asked,' Dad said.

'They won't if they've any sense,' Mother said.

Mr Gardiner was inclined to agree with Mother. He also thought it would be unfair to ask a girl to come to Canada unless she knew something of hardship. 'When we get going it might be all right,' he said thoughtfully. 'But it will take a while for that, and then all the girls we knew when we left England will be married.'

'Forget about them girls in England,' Dad said with a twinkle in his eyes and a chuckle in his voice. 'I know of some a lot better. Next summer when you go to Battleford go and see them Dukhohors. There's some fine lasses there. They're strong and used to work. Ploughing's nothing to them. They aren't bad looking either. One of them, about seventeen, was fair bonny. A man could do a lot worse than marry her.'

'Well!' Mother exclaimed, and drew her small figure up to its full height. 'What a shame you can't get rid of the bairns and me if that's what you think.'

'I didn't say I wanted her.' Dad chuckled again. 'I was only telling Willie she was a good prospect.'

'You certainly sound as if you have your eye on her,' Mother snapped. 'Just remember, there's a law here as well as in England, and if you try to get rid of me—'

'I never said anything about getting rid of you.' Dad was still smiling. 'I only said if I happened to be single—'

'Which you're not, and don't you forget it.' Mother's blue eyes sparkled. 'And anyway, that girl wasn't so much. In a year or two she'll be fat and out of shape.'

'She isn't bad now,' Dad said.

'So you've been thinking of her all this time!' Mother got up and slammed wood into the stove. 'Well, Walter Pinder, you married me, and there's nowt you can do about it.'

'I never said I wanted to, did I?' Dad asked mildly.

'It sounded a bit that way to me.' Mother put the kettle on, and flounced across the room to empty the teapot.

'You have a rare imagination,' Dad chuckled.

After a while the kettle boiled and Mother made tea, and the Dukhobors were forgotten for a while, but every time Mother was irked with Dad she remembered them.

A matter much more serious than the Dukhobors, however, began to haunt us. We were almost out of food.

Dad was sure that spring was almost here, and any day the chinook would start to blow, but the cold sky glared at us day after day without any sign of softening. Flour and water gruel for breakfast and rabbit and bannock for dinner and supper was all the food we had left, and when our small supply of baking-powder was gone we wouldn't even have bannock to eat. 'We'll have to get food someway soon,' Mother said. 'The bairns can't live on air.'

Mr Gardiner was as short of food as we were, and after talking things over he and Dad decided to walk to Bill Banks's and get Bill to take them to Battleford. Lloydminster was much closer, but we had heard there wasn't much food there, either.

Mother thought Mr Gardiner might do our shopping as well as his own, and save Dad the trip, but Mr Gardiner wasn't sure about coming back, at least for a while. Bill Banks, of course, could have brought our food. But though Bill was a nice fellow time meant nothing to him, and if there was no one to remind him he might forget we were hungry.

Before Dad left he sawed a huge pile of firewood, enough to last for ever, I thought, then he and Mother made a list of things we needed, and early one morning Dad and Mr Gardiner started off.

As usual the house seemed a little colder and darker when Dad was away. Mother tried to be cheerful and read to us in the afternoons, and told us bedtime stories, but her voice seemed lonely, and I realized for the first time that when Dad left a little of Mother went with him. The part that went wasn't anything I could see, like a lock of her fair hair, or even the silver brooch she wore at her throat. It was something invisible, but still real. Mother smiled, but it was only her lips that bent, and when she spoke there was no lilt in her voice. Her feet lost their lightness, and her blue eyes seemed a little dim. It was as if the lamp of her spirit had been turned low.

During the day Mother worked hard. She brought in snow and wood, and kept a bright fire in the little stove. At night she lit the candle as soon as the sun went down and the shadows began to gather in the corners. 'We'll have more candles soon,' she said, 'so we don't have to be so careful.'

In spite of not having to be careful of the candles, however, we went to bed early. There seemed nothing to stay up for.

Without Dad to replenish it our wood dwindled surprisingly fast. Mother didn't worry about it for a while. 'Dad will be home in a day or two,' she said when five days had passed. 'We have enough to last.' But seven days passed, and there was still no sign of Dad.

The weather turned colder, and an icy haze hung over the prairie. Some of the frost settled on the stiff branches of willows and poplars, and turned them into ghost trees. The haze hid the sun and greyed the sky, and the whole world looked as if it was wrapped in a winding-sheet.

Mother took the big cross-cut saw and tried to saw some wood. The cold, however, soon numbed her hands and feet, and the frost in the atmosphere made breathing difficult. She came in to rest often, and even I knew the sawing wasn't going well.

'I think I might do better with the axe,' Mother said at last, and picked it up and went back to the woodpile. She chopped for a while, but she wasn't used to such work, and only a few sticks resulted from her effort, and they burned in no time.

Mother looked at the fire that was eating up the last of the wood, and her face went pinched and pale. 'We'll have to saw some wood in the house,' she said at last. 'I can't stand it outside any more, but it will be warmer in here.' She went out and dragged several long pieces of wood into the little house. A lot of cold came in along with the wood, and we had to put our coats on, we were so cold.

Mother shut the door as soon as she could, then she and I sat on the floor with the saw and a piece of wood between us, and tried to cut off a few stove lengths. We pulled and we pushed, but all we managed was a little dent. The big saw jumped from side to side, and bent in the middle, and did everything but saw straight. It was our fault, of course, but Mother knew nothing about handling a saw, and I was only a little over seven, and small for my age.

At last we managed to persuade the big teeth to go back and forth in approximately the same place long enough to cut half-way through a six-inch stick of wood, and we were beginning to think our troubles were about over, but at that point the saw stuck in the cut. It bent and buckled, and refused to go either one way or the other. We pulled and pushed, but the big blade with the inch-long teeth refused to move.

'You aren't half trying.' Mother's eyes were bright with fear.

'Yes, I am.' I pulled extra hard, and the saw jumped and I fell over.

'You don't have to jerk like that.' Worry made Mother's voice sharp. 'It's either all or nothing with you. First thing you know you'll hurt yourself. Now try again, and be more careful.'

I took the cold saw handle in both hands and tried to pull when it was my turn, but my knees on the cold earth floor were soon numb, and so were my hands and feet. My fall, and Mother's sharp tone, had also frightened me, and I was clumsy and not much help. The gathering shadows also added to my confusion and fear. They crouched in the corners and frowned at us, and as the little room got colder they crept closer. I was sure they were only waiting until night came to devour us completely. Already I could feel the big one behind me touching my coat, and my little shoulder-blades began to tremble, and the saw stuck.

'We shall never have any firewood at this rate,' Mother said in despair. She crouched on the floor as if she too was afraid of the shadows.

We crouched in silence for a few minutes, then Lily, who was sitting on the wagon bench, suddenly said: 'I'se told.'

There was no complaint in her voice. She was merely stating a fact, and even as she spoke she seemed to accept the fact that Mother could do nothing about the cold. Instead of crying, as she usually did when she was uncomfortable, she huddled in a corner of the wagon bench, a completely helpless little figure waiting stoically for whatever came next.

Lily's quiet acceptance of the gathering darkness and the increasing cold upset Mother far more than any tears would have done. She looked at Lily's little figure and her lips began to tremble. 'This awful country,' she said in a despairing voice. 'I allus knew it was only biding its time. My bairns will freeze.' She looked hopelessly at the little window, now almost dark, and slow tears ran down her pale cheeks.

I huddled on the cold dirt floor beside the unfriendly saw. My knees were soon stiff, and my toes tingled with cold, but I was afraid to move. Somehow I felt that if I kept still night would not come, and this creeping cold would go away.

Jack, however, was too little to be troubled by fear. While Mother and I had tried to saw some wood he had played happily in the empty wood box, but when quiet settled over the little house he lost interest in the chips and bits of bark, and came over to the saw to investigate. Mother was still sitting beside the stubborn saw. She had stopped crying, but her eyes were wide and empty, and she didn't seem to see Jack at all. Jack stood and looked at Mother for a moment, then he sat down on her bent knee and huddled close to her. Mother put her arms around him, and her tears fell on his fair hair.

They sat there on the cold floor for a little while, then Mother wiped her eyes and looked around the dark little house. 'We have to have a fire someway,' she said, and got up.

There was a spark or two left in the firebox, and we coaxed them to burn again with a few bits of bark, then Mother shoved the ends of the uncut pieces of wood into the stove. The long ends hung down and pushed the lids on top of the stove up, and the stove smoked, but Mother put the little chair under the sagging ends and the stove lids settled into place. 'There, we'll have enough heat to keep us from freezing,' Mother said, then she began getting supper.

When the wood in the firebox burned Mother pushed another section of pole into the stove, and so kept the fire going. It wasn't a completely satisfactory system. The open door of the firebox created a draught, and a lot of heat went up the stove-pipe, and quite often a log burned and fell on the floor before we noticed it. The flames didn't hurt the dirt floor, but the smoke made our eyes sting, and Mother was worried in case a burning end fell on one of us and set fire to our clothing. 'Stay away from that side of the stove,' she warned. 'We have enough to bother about without burns.'

A fire wasn't our only problem by any means. Our food was almost gone. Mother had been careful with the tea, but the tin was now empty. Coyotes had stolen the rabbits Dad had left hanging frozen outside, and Mother hadn't been able to catch any more. She set snares, but the rabbits avoided them. We still had a little baking-powder, and to make it last as long as possible we ate flour gruel twice a day instead of bannock. Lily and I hated the gruel even when there was sugar in it. We called it skilly because it was the most unpleasant name we could think of.

Mother said gruel was good for us and we had to eat it whether we liked it or not. 'This country is doing its best to be rid of us,' she said, 'but I'm not going to be bested by it. I'm bound and determined to get away from here alive. Walter Pinder can do as he likes, but when spring comes I'm going, and not in a box, either. Flour gruel will keep us going for a long time.' So we had skilly for breakfast and supper, and bannock for our midday meal.

The cold days passed slowly, one very much like another. Mother brought in snow to melt for water, pulled pieces of wood out of the dwindling woodpile to keep the fire going, and cooked what little food we had left. The cold was still bitter, about thirty degrees below zero, and the work outside was hard. When Mother came in her nose and cheeks were red, and there was frost on the shawl she wore over her head, and on her eyebrows and eyelashes. Once she thought an ear was frozen, and we rubbed it with snow until the feeling returned to it.

Always when she went outside Mother looked for Dad first thing. Once she tried to walk to the corner of the grove that hid the trail, or at least the place where the trail ought to be, but the deep snow and the cold wind soon drove her back to the shelter of the house.

Harsh as our lives were at that time, however, there were still pleasant hours. In the evenings when the dark was gathering at the little window, and the wind was fretting at the corner of the house, Mother took Jack on her knee and sang to as. Her sweet voice sometimes trembled a little as she sang 'Genevieve' or 'Sweet and low,' but Lily and I always urged her to go on. We never tired of hearing her sing. When our favourite songs were finished we asked for hymns: 'Till we meet again,' 'Peace, perfect peace,' Dad's favourite, 'Abide with me,' and Mother's favourite, 'Lead, kindly light.' We listened to them over and over until Mother was tired, then we asked her to tell us about England. She told us about going to church on Sunday mornings, and walking across the church fields in the afternoon, and of how Grandfather Gomersall loved to play his piano. 'I wonder if I shall ever see him again?' she said softly, her blue eyes full of mist.

Sometimes while it was still daylight Mother read to us. Lily and I stood one on each side of her while Jack, who was not interested in stories, played near by. We knew the fairy-tales in the Christmas books almost word for word, but we loved to hear the sound of Mother's voice. Somehow it hushed the wail of the seeking wind that for ever prowled over the prairie, and when the coyotes howled, as they sometimes did in the late afternoons, its sweet cadence made us feel secure.

When Mother wearied of the fairy-tales she read the Bible to us. One afternoon she read to us from the Book of Ruth. Her voice flowed evenly until she came to the place where Ruth elected to go with Naomi. "'And Ruth said: Intreat me not to leave thee,'" Mother read slowly, "'or to return from following after thee: for whither thou goest, I will go; and where thou lodgest, I will lodge: thy people shall be my people, and thy God my God: Where thou diest, will I die, and there will I be buried: the Lord do so to me, and more also, if ought but death part thee and me.'"

Mother's low voice faltered as she read, and when she came to the end of the verse she stopped reading altogether and looked at the little window for a long time, then softly and as if speaking to herself she said: 'It ought to have been written about marriage.' And slowly and thoughtfully she closed her small gilt-edged Bible that held on its first leaf the date of her marriage to Dad, and the dates of our births. She fastened the clasp that held the black leather covers together, then she sat there in the fading light holding the little book tenderly between her hands: her thumbs, one long and thin like her mother's, the other short and stubby like her father's, making a cross over the book. And after a little while she lifted her hands and held the Bible close to her chest, and a tear rolled down her cheek and fell on it. 'What shall I do if you don't come back?' she murmured softly.

As the days went by it was plain even to me that Mother was worried about something even more important than food and fire. She tried to hide her anxiety, but she was young, and very much alone, and it was hard for her to keep fear at a distance every waking minute. She said very little about her fear, but there were times when her eyes looked far beyond the walls of our little house, and sometimes as she did the routine work she moved as if she was only partly awake. Sometimes when I spoke to her she did not answer. It was as if she was listening so intently for some distant sound she could not hear the voices around her. At such times Mother did not seem to be with us at all, and I at least felt very lonely.

Mother's voice also changed during that time. It became as flat and expressionless as the voice of a deaf person, and when she read to us she sometimes stopped in the middle of a story and stared at the window.

When we said our prayers at night Lily and I had prayed that Dad would come back soon; now Mother told us to pray that he would come back soon and safe.

Although Lily and I were too young to actually share Mother's fear, it did begin to press upon us. We played quietly in our nook behind the stove, stopped snatching cards from each other, gave up arguing over names for our future dolls, and tried harder than ever to eat our skilly.

At night when we went to bed I always pulled the blankets over my head, and refused to have them removed even though Mother said I might smother. I insisted I wasn't cold, and not the least bit frightened, but fear seemed everywhere, and the little dark cave the blankets made gave me a feeling of security. The wind and the cold could never find me there., I was sure; and neither could the hungry, hunting coyotes.

Mother, of course, soon noticed our unusual good behaviour, and asked if we didn't feel well, but she wasn't really disturbed until Jack lost some of his energy and sparkle. He still rummaged in the tool box, but he was listless about it, and seemed to regard it more as a duty than a pleasure. Mother's lap became his favourite spot, and he was content to nestle there for half an hour at a time, something very unusual for him. 'I do hope he isn't coming down with something,' Mother said. 'I don't know what I'd do if he got ill.'

Jack's malaise lasted three or four days, then one morning he woke up bright and cheerful as ever. 'Dad, Dad,' he said happily, and began trying to pull the long pieces of wood out of the stove.

'No, no,' Mother cried, and ran to push the blazing wood back into the firebox.

'Dad, Dad,' Jack said cheerfully, and bent over the empty wood box.

'I wonder if he's feverish?' Mother felt Jack's forehead, and tried to hold him on her knee for a while, but Jack wriggled down and began exploring the dark place under the bed.

Mother made breakfast, the hated skilly, then she brought in snow and wood, made the bed, swept the dirt floor, and put the kettle on for the noon tea, now only hot water. Her face was pale and tired, and when she sat down to rest for a moment the listening look came into her eyes. 'This awful cold,' she murmured softly to herself. 'I wonder where he is?'

'Dad, Dad,' Jack said, and came out from under the bed dragging a scarf belonging to Dad that he had pulled out of the blue box.

'I don't think calling will do a bit of good,' Mother said, and took the scarf and folded it tenderly. 'This country was bound and determined to do for one of us,' she said, and wiped her eyes.

'What are you crying for?' I asked.

'I'm not crying. It's the sun in my eyes, that's all.' Mother tried to smile, then she picked up a knife and began slicing stale bannock for our lunch. Suddenly, with the knife lifted, she paused and leaned forward listening, a queer look on her face.

'What's the matter?' I asked, a little frightened.

'There's bells somewhere.' Mother stared at the wall. 'Can't you hear them?'

I listened as hard as I could, but all I could hear was the wood burning in the stove, and the little wind fretting the house. 'I can't hear a thing,' I said at last.

'Listen again.' Mother's blue eyes were fixed on space, and her whole body seemed to listen. 'There,' she said after a moment, 'can't you hear that?'

'No.' I shook my head and sat down on the wagon bench.

'It can't be just me.' Mother's voice was low and a little frightened. 'What will become of my bairns if— Can't you hear them now?' she asked.

'No.' I moved to the far corner of the wagon bench. Mother's staring eyes frightened me.

There was a long silence in the little house. Lily came and sat beside me, and after a moment Jack squeezed in between us. We were all so still we could hear the fire holding its breath.

'There they are again,' Mother said suddenly. 'Mary, you must be deaf if you can't hear them now.' She looked beseechingly at me.

I leaned forward and held my breath and listened as hard as I could, and at last I heard them: sleigh-bells faint and far away as a dream. 'It sounds like bells,' I said uncertainly.

'It is.' The stare left Mother's eyes, and all at once she seemed to glow all over. 'It's him!' she said joyously. 'It must be him!' She opened the door and ran outside without even putting her shawl on.

Lily, Jack, and I ran after her. There was nothing to be seen, only the snow and the bare trees, but we could hear the sleigh-bells faint and far away, and after a while a team and a sleigh came around the corner of the grove.

We all held our breath for a moment, for somehow the frosted horses, half hidden in the white cloud made by their own breathing, seemed unreal: a sort of vision that the sun and the snow and our own desire had caused to appear. We could hear the clear tinkle of the sleigh-bells, of course, but they also seemed part of the dream, that would vanish if we so much as blinked. And so we stood there in the snow, our lips parted and our eyes wide, until a man jumped out of the sleigh and came running towards us.

'Walter!' Mother cried, and ran to meet the approaching figure without even pausing to lift her long skirts out of the snow. But after she had gone a few yards she stopped, and her little figure stiffened, and her small chin went up. 'Well, it took you long enough,' she said as soon as Dad was within hearing distance.

What a happy day that was! Dad and Mother talked and laughed a great deal, but somehow they managed to cook a meal. We had all the bacon we could eat, and as much jam as our bannock would hold, and quantities of strong brown tea with condensed milk in it. While he fried the bacon and told us scraps of news, Dad paused often and looked around the little house as if he could hardly believe he was home again. And when he looked at Jack his eyes and his face were so bright that even the far corners of the small room seemed to glow.

After we had eaten, and Bill Banks had gone on to the Metherells', Dad told us about his trip.

Bill had been glad enough to go to Battleford, but once started he had dawdled at every opportunity: the horses needed a rest, he thought he was coming down with something, it was too cold to travel. They were twice as long on the trail as they should have been, and Dad thought they were never going to get to Battleford. But getting Bill out of Battleford was even harder than getting him there. He had a number of cronies, and he insisted on seeing everybody. What was there to hurry for, anyway, he asked? It had taken them a long time to get there. Why not stay a while?

Progress was slow even after Dad finally managed to get Bill started towards home. The stopping-places were warm, and there was company. He saw no reason to hurry back to his lonely little shack.

Before they were half-way home Dad was so worried he couldn't sleep, and when Mr Chisholm shook his head and said: 'Man! I doubt if you'll have any family left by now. They'll all be frozen' he was frantic. He harnessed the team while it was still dark, then he hauled Bill out of bed and told him to get a move on.

Bill said he wasn't going anywhere at that hour, and certainly not without breakfast, and got back into bed again.

Dad almost took Bill's team then, but Mr Chisholm advised him against it. Horse-stealing was a serious offence. Dad, however, was determined to get home. He hauled Bill out of bed again, and told him he could eat if he hurried, but he was leaving in ten minutes, and if he hadn't got his pants on by then he would leave without them.

Dad said Bill sulked for an hour or two, but he wasn't really mean, only thoughtless, and when he finally realized how worried Dad was he hurried the team as much as possible.

Getting home, however, was an ordeal for Dad. 'When we got near that grove I was that scared I couldn't look,' he said. 'I sat down in the bottom of the sleigh and asked Bill to look for smoke. I could hardly believe it when he said you were outside waiting.'

'We very nearly froze,' Mother said, and told him of the difficulty with the fire.

'Why didn't you go to the Metherells'?' Dad asked. 'Frank would have come and cut some wood.'

'I thought about it,' Mother said slowly. 'But it was that cold I thought I might not get there, then what would have happened to the bairns?'

'Yes.' Dad looked at the frosted window and his eyelids went low over his ocean-flecked grey eyes, then suddenly he smiled at Mother. 'You did what was best, all right,' he said. 'Sally, you may deny it, but you're a real pioneer.'

'You needn't try to soft soap me,' Mother said, and smiled a little. 'I don't want to be a pioneer, and you know it.'

⌣ · CHAPTER THIRTY · ⌣

WITH Dad home again, and plenty of food and supplies, including a new all-metal comb that wouldn't burn, we thought we had nothing to worry about until spring, and happiness filled our little house from morning to night. Spring, however, was late that year. In March the bitter cold relented a little, but the thermometer still registered far below zero, the wind still blew, the coyotes howled, and now and then more snow fell.

Dad said every new snowfall was the last, but in a day or two the wind would shake the clouds and more snow-like feathers would fall. Mother looked at the big drifts and said all that snow would never melt, and we might as well leave Canada before the really bitter weather came again. There would be daffodils in England by now, and the hawthorn would be in bloom at Castle Hill. 'I can just see those hedges all white in the sun,' Mother said wistfully. 'And that big oak breaking into leaf. The larks will be singing, too, and the sparrows will be starting to nest.'

'I bet it's raining cats and dogs,' Dad said.

Mother said she much preferred rain to snow, and Dad said he wouldn't mind a little rain, either. It would take the snow away in a hurry, then he could get about a little better, and get a team and haul some wood.

'Wood!' Mother looked surprised. 'What do we need more wood for?' she asked.

'Our wood's about gone,' Dad said quietly.

The snow, however, showed no signs of going. It was thick and heavy on the prairie: a white blanket smothering the earth. Above the sullen snow the dark poplars looked old and weary, and when the wind blew their branches creaked like tired, rheumatic joints, and now and then a frozen branch snapped off and fell like a bone to the snow.

Day by day our woodpile, that had looked as if it would last for ever, dwindled until there were only a few sticks left. 'What are we going to do?' Mother asked.

'I'll drag some wood out of the bush,' Dad said. 'Spring's bound to come in a day or two.'

Winter, however, dragged on. Dad hauled firewood on his back, and staggered under the heavy loads.

'We are no better than slaves,' Mother said one day when she saw Dad's young body bent double under the load. 'Even horses aren't strong enough to work like that.' She put the kettle on so that Dad could have some tea before he started sawing the wood he had hauled into stove lengths.

'You'll kill yourself working so hard,' Mother said when Dad came in for the tea. 'This country's far too hard for little folk like you and me. Even a big man couldn't stand the work you're doing for long.'

'Sometimes I think you're right,' Dad said wearily. 'Winters seem to be a lot longer and a lot colder than old Barr said. If there was only some way of getting a bit out of this land I think I'd leave, but we've put in close on a year now, and I hate to get nothing for it.'

'It's better to leave and get nothing than it is to kill yourself,' Mother pointed out.

'We'll see.' Dad held out his mug for more tea. 'I hate to give up, but if it's allus going to be as bad as this…' He stared at the cold little window, and for once he looked tired and discouraged, and there was no light in his eyes.

'You've done your best,' Mother said. 'Hauling wood on your back the way you do is too much for anybody.'

'Maybe Frank Metherell would lend me an ox for a day,' Dad said, 'but I don't like to ask him.'

'He could only refuse,' Mother said. 'With the help of an ox you could haul enough wood in a day to last a week or more.'

Dad thought the matter over for a while. The Metherells had two oxen, Billy and Curly, but Billy had lost a leg during the winter. A rope had got tangled around it, and the leg had frozen and fallen off. Curly, however, was still in good condition. 'Even half a day would be a big help,' Dad said at last. He put on his big cap with the green mosquito-netting around it, and his thin coat, and started off through the snow.

About an hour later Dad came back. He walked slowly, and looked more tired than ever. No ox followed him.

'Didn't they lend him to you?' Mother asked incredulously.

'No.' Dad took off his coat and cap and sat down. 'They say they have to haul wood, too.'

'But for only half a day…' Mother's blue eyes were bleak.

Dad didn't say anything. His lips were thin, and there was a shadow on his face.

Fortunately for us Mr Pike came by in a day or two, and helped Dad haul a supply of wood. 'You'll kill yourself,' he said when he heard Dad had been hauling it on his back. 'Even the folks in tents don't have it that hard.'

Mother asked how the tent-dwellers were getting on, and Mr Pike said many of them had scurvy, but otherwise they were doing fairly well. When Mother asked if they were going to leave when spring came, he shrugged his shoulders and said he wouldn't be surprised if they did. They'd had a hard winter, but you never could tell what a warm spring might do.

Winter, however, lingered on, and at last April was not far away. 'It looks as if we aren't going to have any spring at all this year,' Mother said. 'The sun will never be hot enough to melt such big drifts.'

'It's the wind that melts the snow, not the sun,' Dad said. 'When the chinook begins to blow them drifts will be gone in no time.'

'I'll believe it when I see it,' Mother said. 'No wind that I ever knew melted anything.'

'This wind will,' Dad insisted, 'and it will start blowing any day now.' Dad tried to sound convincing, but he looked uneasily at the snow outside the little window. Last fall, when the musk-rats were building their extra big houses, the old-timers had said something about a year without any summer to speak of. The drifts had been so high they had barely melted before the fall snows fell. The trees didn't leaf that year, and even the geese didn't return. Nobody, of course, had believed such a yarn. It was just another tall tale invented to frighten the settlers away. Now, however, it began to look as if there might be some truth in it, and this was going to be another such year.

Mother was quite sure that this was going to be a year without a spring, and in a way she held Dad responsible. When Jack was ill he had half promised to leave when spring came, but if it didn't come his promise wouldn't hold water.

'I don't see why we have to wait for ever to leave,' Mother said one day. 'Anyone can see this cold is going to last. The tulips will be in bloom in England now. We could be back before the roses come out. Why don't you get Bill Banks to take us to Saskatoon?'

'We'll see,' Dad said, and put on his coat and went out to saw wood.

Mother looked around the little house. 'I think we can get everything into the packing-case and the blue box,' she said thoughtfully. 'The mattress and the blankets can go in the bottom of the sleigh for you three to sit on.'

'Yes,' I said, and wondered if the little house would be lonely after we were gone. Somehow I was sure it would be, for every time Mother mentioned leaving it looked gloomy and miserable.

I couldn't help feeling a little miserable, too. I still missed Grandmother and Aunt Jane, and the house by the Spen, but this little house on the prairie with its crooked log walls and sod roof seemed part of me. I had helped to build it. I had watched Dad chop down the trees for it, helped put one log on top of another, pushed mud into the cracks, carried sods for the roof. My legs had been scratched by the logs, and my fingers bruised. I had seen fire threaten it, and had rejoiced when the danger passed. All winter long the house had sheltered us. It hadn't kept all the cold out, but it had done its best. It didn't seem right, somehow, to go away and leave the house to the loneliness and the coyotes. 'Are we going to take the shelf with us?' I asked. It was the only part of the house that was movable.

'No, of course not.' Mother opened the blue box and began packing our stockings and petticoats. 'You can wear your red dress on the trip,' she told me. 'It's short, but it will do. And Lily can wear her blue. We'll all have to have new things when we get home.'

The prospect of wearing my red dress every day was very pleasant, but it didn't quite make up for leaving the little house.

Dad didn't want to leave the log house, either. Every time Mother asked when he was going to get Bill Banks to take us away he looked wistfully at the brown walls and suggested that we wait a bit. 'The chinook will blow any time now,' he said, 'and when it does this snow will go like wildfire.'

'A likely tale,' Mother said, and tossed her little head. 'This cold is going to last for ever.'

'Maybe,' Dad admitted, 'but let's give it a bit longer.' Dad put on his coat and went to look at the rabbit snares. I went to the little window and watched him through the clear space in the glass. Somehow Dad no longer looked young. His feet were heavy, and they dragged a little, leaving scoop marks in the snow, and his shoulders in his thin coat hung downward and forward as if he was very tired. Suddenly I realized why the little house seemed unhappy. Dad's eyes hadn't smiled for a long time.

⌇·CHAPTER THIRTY-ONE·⌇

ND SO we drifted from day to day: Mother pleased because she was at last going home, Dad depressed because Canada had failed him, and all the bright days beyond to-morrow would never be realized. They would remain only dreams fading gradually with the years until they were nothing but half-remembered shadows. 'If spring had only come a bit sooner,' Dad said one day when he and I were looking at rabbit traps. 'But it didn't, and there's nowt I can do about it.' His thin face looked empty. Then suddenly, and without warning, the weather changed.

When we went to bed the harsh, withering wind of winter still stalked the prairie, making the trees shudder, and driving small snow ghosts before it until they ran among the willows to escape its whip. But some time during the night the wind changed. Instead of stalking stealthily along the hollows it bounced from one drift to another, shaking life into the poplars and the willows, and wiping the frozen whiteness out of the sky. It was a hoyden of a wind: not warm, but crisp and refreshing—a dancing wind that shouted and stamped its feet as it whirled over the snow. Dad went out for wood, and came in, his face one big smile. 'Spring's come, Sally,' he called in a voice full of hope. 'The chinook's blowing.'

Mother put on her coat and went outside. 'That's not the chinook,' she said disgustedly. 'That wind's as cold as it ever was. There'll be a blizzard by night.'

'The snow will be half gone by night,' Dad crowed, and gave Jack a toss, something he hadn't done for a long time.

Mother said she didn't know where Dad got his queer ideas, and began mixing bannock for breakfast. The wind, however, was much warmer and more powerful than Mother thought. It took winter by the scruff of the neck and shook it until it relaxed its icy grip, then it honeycombed the drifts, and loosened the thick ice on the mighty Saskatchewan River, and we heard the thunder the ice made when it went out.

In no time at all there was water everywhere. The sloughs were brimful, and every little depression was either a lake or a torrent. We couldn't start for Saskatoon now; the trails were far too soft.

Sticky buds appeared on the branches of the poplars, and shy silver pussies clung to the wands of the willows. As if they had been waiting somewhere on the edge of winter the birds came back. Crows black and shining cawed in the poplars, meadow-larks trilled in the grass, prairie chickens cooed and mated on the little hills, blackbirds, trim and beady-eyed, bubbled in the willows. The gophers came out of their holes, sat on their haunches, and stared at us as if to say: 'Well, for goodness' sake, are you still here?'

Flowers appeared almost on the edge of the snow. Crocuses sent up silver buds that opened into five-petalled mauve stars with golden throats. Tiny yellow buttercups carpeted the low spots as soon as the water disappeared. Slim green spears of grass thrust up from the burned-over roots. The heart-shaped leaves of the blue and white violets began to unfold, ferns like lace shook out their tight-curled heads, and leaves appeared on the trees as by magic.

In the sloughs the frogs began to sing, and soon the ducks floated quietly on the blue water. The geese also began to fly overhead. Day and night they crossed the sky in long wide V's. They never visited us as the ducks did, but as they came out of the south and disappeared into the north they called to us. 'Glad to see you,' they seemed to say. 'Glad to see you.'

'Hi, hi,' Lily and I called, and waved our arms in welcome.

Dad walked all over his hundred and sixty acres as soon as he could cross the many streams. 'Just look at that!' he said, his face glowing, as he pointed to a clump of grass. 'This is a fair wonderful country. Snow only yesterday, and now look at it! Covered with grass and flowers. And just smell that air.' He paused and breathed deeply of the perfume of rising sap, warming earth, unfolding leaves, and opening flowers. 'It's worth a bit of cold to breathe such air. There isn't a trace of soot in it.'

The other men in the colony also seemed to feel the need to move around. Bill Banks visited everybody, and Gordon Watson came riding on his big brown horse. He still wore his riding-breeches and leather leggings, and while he talked he slapped his thigh with his riding-crop, and laughed louder than ever.

Mr Maule and Mr Gardiner also came home. 'Well, by God, Pinder, it's good to see you again,' Mr Maule cried, and walloped Dad's shoulder.

'You're just the man I'm looking for,' Dad said, returning the wallop. 'You used to be a pretty fair barber, didn't you? How about cutting my hair?'

'I'll be damned!' Mr Maule cried. 'I come all the way to Canada to get away from them blasted scissors, and now you want your hair cutting. Sit down.' He did a very good job, but he complained loudly at every snip.

One haircut led to another. Men seemed to come from everywhere. Mother and Dad asked them to come and sit in the little house, but they preferred to sit outside on the saw-horse or on the ground: anywhere where they could enjoy the clean, stimulating air and feel the energy of the awakening earth. Somehow the earth seemed to impart its energy to all who touched it. The men's eager faces glowed with it, and it throbbed in their voices, and gave buoyancy to their feet. It caused them to hold their heads higher, and gave warmth and firmness to their handclasps. They were as full of surging hope as the sun and the wind, and they talked of the future as if it was already with us. Canada wasn't going to be great, it was great. They talked as if the railroad was already complete, and of fields of wheat waving in the sun, and of pastures full of fat cattle, barns full of hay, and homes bursting with food and warmth.

Even as the men talked, however, there was a slight uncertainty in their voices, as if there was something somewhere that they were not quite sure about. They did not actually speak of whatever was troubling them, but the discord was there like a flat note in an otherwise perfect symphony.

It was Mother who put the small undercurrent of uncertainty into words. 'What are the women in Lloydminster going to do?' she asked one evening.

The men stopped talking and glanced at one another, then one or two coughed. 'How do you mean?' someone asked at last.

'I thought they were all going home when spring came!' Mother said. 'I thought Mr Lloyd was going to arrange it?'

'Where did you hear that?' Dad asked.

'I heard.' Mother smiled mysteriously. 'Things get around even on the prairie.'

'There was talk of a petition,' Mr Watson said uneasily.

An awkward silence followed, then someone said: 'Nobody seemed to want to be the one to start it, and anyway the weather's warm now.'

'It will be cold again next winter,' Mother said.

'But not like it was last winter,' an eager voice said. 'Even the Indians say that was the worst winter in memory, and we may never have another like it. And look at the way things grow. Wheat will grow just as fast.'

'Yes, and there aren't any weeds here.' Another voice took up the happy refrain, and the men went on talking of the wonderful life just ahead. Air castles, Mother called their hopes.

The men went away after a while, and Dad went to look at his land. Mother said he counted every blade of grass every day, which was an exaggeration, but he never tired of walking across his acres. He was terribly proud of this new farm, and he inspected it as a king inspects his kingdom. When he returned from a walk his face was always bright, and his voice hopeful.

'I never saw owt to compare with this place,' he said when he came home that afternoon. 'It's fair surprising the way it warms up. No fog, no drizzle, just sunshine. If you stand still you can see the grass growing. Another week and the trails will be passable, then work on the railroad will start. Once that's finished, Sally, we'll be rich in no time.' He took off his cap, the one he had brought from England, hung it on a peg, pulled his home-made chair close to the packing-box table, and waited for Mother to pour him some tea.

Mother paused with her hand on the handle of the little blue teapot and looked sharply at Dad. 'I thought you said we were going home as soon as the trails were passable?' she said.

'Well . . .' Dad looked uneasily at the brown log walls, and the green trees not far from the open door. 'I thought maybe we might try it a bit longer now that the weather's warm,' he said.

'It won't be warm for ever.' Mother filled Dad's mug with steaming brown tea and handed it to him. 'And there'll be other winters.'

'But not as bad as the last, and when we get some breaking done—'

'The prairie doesn't plough easy.' Mother put sugar in her tea. 'And it won't be ploughed in a day, either. It will take years, and a lot of things might happen. Have you forgotten how we nearly lost Jack last winter? Next time we might not be so lucky.'

'I was thinking on buying a farm for him, and for the lasses as well, one of these days.' Dad stirred his tea, though he hadn't put any sugar in it.

'They may not want a farm.' Mother stirred her tea carefully. 'Farming's a hard life for a woman.'

'You don't think you could stick it another year?' Dad stopped stirring, lifted the spoon out of the brown tea, and watched the drops fall off the tip of the spoon back into the mug. They made soft little plinks in the silence.

'It's that lonely. All winter and hardly a word to another woman.' Mother picked up her mug of tea, but her hand trembled and she put it down again.

'We might go to Lloydminster next winter.' The warm glow was going from Dad's voice.

'And live in a tent, and have scurvy?'

'There might be houses by then.'

'But it's more likely there won't'. Mother's blue eyes were beginning to look angry.

'It's a shame to lose the farm after we've lived on it a whole year.'

'It isn't as if it was one of the bairns.' Mother glanced at Jack, busy in the wood box.

'If we go,' Dad said slowly, looking at his spoon, 'the rest of the colony might go, too. I wouldn't want to start something like that.'

'You're making excuses, that's all.' Mother's voice trembled.

'No, I'm not. You heard what Watson said; nobody wants to be the first to go. They'll say we're running away.'

'I don't care what they say.' Mother flounced across the room and shut the door as if she couldn't bear the sight of Canada. 'I've had enough of this place,' she said.

'It's a shame to give up now,' Dad said. 'In another year the farm will be worth a thousand dollars, and when Jack grows up—'

'If we stay here he may not live to grow up,' Mother said.

'He has more chance of growing up here than he would have in England,' Dad said. 'All that soot. And if he did live, what then? He'd never be independent there the way he will be here. If we go back he'll allus have to work for somebody else.'

'It isn't Jack you're thinking of,' Mother said. 'It's you that doesn't like to work for somebody else.'

'No, I don't.' Dad frowned. 'And Jack won't, either, or the lasses. It's better to live on crusts and be independent than to live on beef and have to knuckle down to somebody for it. Not that we'll live on crusts if we stay here. This country's going to amount to something some day, and them that stays will be a lot better off than anybody in England ever thought of being. But if you want to go back that's what we'll do.'

'You might be able to get a farm.' Mother sounded uncertain.

'I could if we had a bit of money,' Dad said thoughtfully. 'So I'll tell you what I think would be a good plan. You and the bairns go back now, and I'll stay a while. I'll work in summer and live here in winter till I prove up, then I'll sell out and come back. I can make more money here than I can at home, and I'll send you plenty to live on. You can get one of them cottages on Ramsden Street near Sam. Happen in a year or two you'll be tired of England. If you are you can come back here, and Sam might come with you. There's going to be a lot of building when the railroad gets to Lloydminster, and that's in Sam's line. He allus wanted to get out of England. It might be a rare opportunity for him, and he'd be company for you. What do you think of it?'

A gurgling sound came from Mother's throat. Later she said Dad's wild idea fairly took her breath away, and for a minute she did look queer. Her face turned red and then white, and her blue eyes looked like glass, then all at once she exploded.

'Well!' she cried, and jumped out of her chair, her eyes full of sparks, her small fists clenched, her figure stiff, and her little chin lifted. 'So you're trying to get rid of me, are you? Let me tell you something, Walter Pinder, you aren't going to. Not that way or so easy. They're your children, and you're going to look after them.'

'I'll be danmed,' Dad said. 'I told you I'd send plenty of—'

'Don't think you can push your bairns off on me,' Mother interrupted, 'or on Sam, either.'

'I'm not. I—'

'Yes, you are.' Mother glared at Dad. 'You want to be rid of us, and you know it. Well, your little scheme won't work.'

'I said I'd come home in two years.' Dad's voice was getting loud.

'And in two years you'll have another excuse.' Mother's voice was loud, also.

'You're never satisfied.' Dad jumped up.

'And you never say what you mean.'

'You can go home if you want to,' Dad stormed.

'So you're turning me out.' Mother's round chin quivered.

'Good God! I thought you said you wanted to go?'

'I do. I wish I'd never seen Canada, but they're your bairns, and you're going to look after them.'

'I allus intended to look after them.' Dad's eyebrows were low over his eyes, and his mouth was thin.

'So it's me you don't want.' Mother's voice trembled, and tears stood in her eyes. 'And after all I've gone through coming to this country with you.'

'Oh, for God's sake!' Dad grabbed his cap, crammed it on his head, and strode out, slamming the door after him.

'And that's all the thanks I get.' Mother sat down and looked unhappily at the door for some time. Her eyes were open, but she didn't seem to see or hear anything that went on in the little house. Lily and I fought over a piece of wood that looked like a doll, and Jack hit his finger with the hammer and said 'Damm't,' but Mother paid no attention. She seemed to be turning something over in her mind, first one way then another. 'I wonder if it's that Dukhobor?' she murmured at last, and her whole face frowned.

Still frowning, Mother got up and went outside and brought in a prairie chicken Dad had shot the day before, and began to skin it. Lily and I watched her, and asked what she was going to make. We rarely had meat for supper.

'Run and play,' Mother said absently, and rolled the dark red meat in flour, and put it in the frying-pan. Then she set the packing-box table, a job usually mine, and cut some slices of fresh bread, another treat. Mother said fresh bread wasn't good for us.

The kettle was singing cheerfully and the prairie chicken was sizzling merrily and filling the house with its rich meat smell when Dad finally opened the door. He had a few sticks of stove wood on his arm, and he came in slowly, and glanced around as if sizing up the situation before he spoke. 'Looks like supper's about ready,' he said at last, and dropped the wood into the box by the stove. 'Smells good, too. I won't be getting such meals when you go.'

Mother straightened her trim shoulders and tossed her little head, topped by its neat coil of hair. 'I'm not going,' she said primly. 'If you think you're going to bring that Dukhobor into my house you're mistaken.'

Dad looked as if the roof had fallen on him, then his eyes began to twinkle. 'I never thought of such a thing,' he said.

'You'd better not.' Mother poured boiling water from the black kettle into the blue teapot.

'Well, I'm glad you changed your mind.' Dad sat down at the packing-box table. He looked perfectly happy.

'It's for the sake of the bairns that I'm staying.' Mother served Dad a large piece of chicken. 'Out of sight is out of mind.'

Dad put a slice of bread in the chicken gravy, and a little smile curved his lips. 'It wasn't because of the bairns that you gave Edmond Bastow the slip that day at Cleckheaton,' he said. 'We hadn't any bairns then.'

'Me give him the slip!' Mother stared at Dad. 'I never did any such thing. He went to look for Emma—'

'You asked him to go and look for Emma, and then you asked me to go and look at the bob-dollies,' Dad said, and his grey, ocean-flecked eyes sparkled.

'Tell the truth if you can,' Mother said. 'It was you that asked me to go and look at the bob-dollies.'

'Well, anyway, you went,' Dad said contentedly.

'And look where it got me.' Mother shook her pretty little head, but her voice sounded pleased, and her eyes and her lips were smiling.

Chapter Thirty-Two

S o, with the rest of the Barr Colony, we stayed in Canada. Prosperity, however, did not come as quickly as Dad and most of the colonists expected. The new country, long untamed and wild, was not easily subdued. Unexpected difficulties appeared one after another.

The railroad did not come as quickly as Mr Barr had promised. The bitter winters brought work to a standstill, and the rivers and hills slowed progress in the warm weather. Even if we had been able to turn the stubborn sod and grow a crop there was no way to get it to market.

In spite of there being no incentive to plough, however, our second summer in Canada was not nearly as carefree as the first summer had been. The prairie was as lovely as ever: crocuses and buffalo beans spread their mauve and yellow carpets, the wild roses were pink drifts around the groves, the chook-cherry blossoms were white lace on the hillsides, and clouds of butterflies were everywhere; but the spirit of the settlers, especially those with families, had changed. The harsh winter just past had awakened them to the stern realities with which they had to deal. They realized now that if they were to survive in this wild new country no more time could be lost visiting, enjoying their new freedom, and waiting for the railroad. They had to earn money now when the weather was warm for the food and clothing they would need the following winter. Even loneliness and home-sickness had to be thrust aside and made the best of. The moment the trails were dry enough to be passable most of the men hauled wood, renewed the fire-guards around their little homes, then hurried away to where the construction camps on the railroad were opening up again.

A few of the bachelors who were said to have independent incomes stayed on in their log shacks and tried to revive the picnic spirit of the previous summer, but they were not very successful. They visited one another, and now and then they paused at our house, ostensibly to see how we were getting on, but actually hoping for a cup of tea and a slice of real bread. They still talked a great deal of what they were going to do one of these days, but the gay spirit of adventure that had been everywhere the summer before was missing: responsibility had taken its place, and those who did not pick up their share seemed lonely, out of the stream of life, and a little uncertain of themselves and where they were going.

Dad was among the first to go looking for work. He left early one morning before we three children were awake so that he would not see us cry. The little house as usual seemed very quiet without him, and Lily and I talked in low voices for a long time.

Mother, who always insisted she was never lonely, soon found the days and nights long and quiet. She carried water from the slough and washed all our clothes, including the blankets, then, in the interminable afternoons, she took us for walks to look for flowers. At night we went early to bed to save the precious candles.

Now and then new settlers looking for land passed our house, and one day a man asked Mother to sell him some bread. 'The children haven't had a thing but porridge for a week,' he said. Mother gladly sold him a whole batch of bread, and that gave her an idea.

We still had several sacks of flour stacked in the corner, and Mother was afraid they would spoil. Every time it rained water seeped through our sod roof, and though we set pans to catch the drip there was no telling when a new drip would start when we were not looking. But if the flour was made into bread and sold the danger would be over, and there would be a tidy profit to boot. Mother immediately baked a huge batch of bread. Sure enough a bannock-weary bachelor dropped by that afternoon to bring us some mail. Through the open door he eyed the bread standing brown and fragrant on the packing-box table. 'Will you sell me a loaf or two?' he asked, licking his lips. Mother disposed of most of our flour that way. She could have sold it all and much more besides, but she had to keep enough to last us until fall.

In spite of the washing and the baking Mother found the quiet days and nights very long and lonely. She had not visited with another woman for a long time. Mrs Metherell had gone to Lloydminster early in the spring, and Mrs Johnson lived several miles away. Someone coming for bread had told us that Mrs Claxton was living alone about two miles to the south, and from time to time Mother talked of her, and wondered if we could find her if we went looking in her direction. Two miles across the prairie in those days was a long way. There was no trail, at least part of the way, and the groves, unless you knew them well, had a trick of all looking alike. 'I'd like to go and see her,' Mother said. 'But what would we do if we got lost?'

Loneliness, however, finally overcame the fear of getting lost. 'We can at least go part way,' Mother said. 'If we don't find the Claxtons' we can come home. Be sure and look carefully at the groves and bushes, Mary,' Mother warned as she dressed me, 'then getting home will be easy.'

I promised eagerly, and the four of us started walking in what we hoped was the right direction. The sun was warm, and the grass thick under our feet. Butterflies fluttered over the rose-bushes, and grasshoppers, big and green, went whirring past. We did not hurry. Jack was only about eighteen months old, and though his legs were brown and sturdy they were quite short. How Mother found the way I don't know, but she lined up the groves and kept the sun on our left, and after a while we came to a faint trail. 'This ought to go somewhere,' Mother said and decided to follow it, but first we noted carefully the place where we would have to leave the friendly little trail on our way home.

The trail wandered casually around hills and between groves, not seeming to care much where it went, and Mother began to think we were going in the wrong direction after all. Jack was getting tired, Lily was beginning to lag, and even my legs were beginning to ache. 'If we don't see a house soon we'll go home,' Mother said, her voice flat with disappointment.

We crept along, around another grove and over a little rise, and suddenly there it was, a tiny house nestling between two big groves of poplars. 'Maybe there's nobody at home,' Mother said, not able to trust her good fortune. Another step or two and Mrs Claxton, a tall, eager woman with warm brown eyes, came running to meet us. She was a complete stranger to us, but she seized Mother's hands and shook them warmly. 'How did you ever find the way, dear?' she asked.

Mrs Claxton, we soon found, was not living alone; Mrs Johnson and her three children were with her. Mrs Johnson didn't feel well, but the three women had a wonderful time exchanging experiences, and asking about people who had come up the trail. Mrs Claxton told in detail about the winter in the tents, and of how wonderful Mr and

Mrs Lloyd had been. The nicest part of the visit as far as I was concerned was the bread and jam and cake we had for tea.

About four in the afternoon Mother suddenly noticed how long the shadows were getting, and said it was high time we were going home. Dora Johnson and I were playing house, and getting along well for once, and I did not want to leave such a friendly place. Mother didn't really want to leave, either, and some of her loneliness must have crept into her voice when she said we would be caught in the dark if we didn't hurry. 'Why don't you stay, dear?' Mrs Claxton asked. 'There's plenty of room if you don't mind sleeping on the floor.'

Mother looked around the one little room, already crowded. 'It will be putting you out,' she said, but there was longing in her voice.

Mrs Claxton insisted she would be delighted to have us. 'It isn't safe for you to live alone, dear,' she said.

Mother, however, could see there was no extra bed, and decided that we had to go home at least for a day or two until we could find someone to move our things. 'Then I'll walk a bit with you,' Mrs Claxton said. All the children decided to come, too, but they did not walk far.

How we found our way home I don't know, but by some magic we finally arrived at our small log house just as the mosquitoes were starting out to look for their evening meal.

A passing team took us to the Claxtons' a few days later. Three adults and eight children filled the little house to overflowing, but a hen and her ten chickens decided there was room for a few more, and, eager for company, they popped in every time we opened the door. We had to shoo them out constantly, and at meal times they were a real hazard. Grasshoppers, which they had to catch themselves, were almost their only food, and they were constantly hungry. Often they flew on to the table, and they snatched bread and cake right out of our hands. Meals were a real contest, especially for Jack who was still little. 'Sometimes I'm tempted to fry those chickens right now,' Mrs Claxton said once, 'but they'll be so good roasted in the fall.'

One day the chickens very nearly were roasted. We had gone for a short walk leaving the little house to a moment of peace and quiet. When we came back the wind had blown the door open, and there were the chickens, their feet and legs deep in a batch of bread dough Mother had set. They were flapping their wings and squeaking, and the old hen was running around on the floor scolding her head off. 'What are we going to do?' Mother cried when she saw the chickens. 'And all that dough! It will be ruined.'

'And the chickens: they'll die with all that dough clinging to them,' Mrs Claxton said.

'Maybe we ought to eat them while we can,' Mother suggested.

'Can you...?' Mrs Claxton, very pale, looked at Mother.

'No,' Mother said, and shook her little head.

'Maybe Mrs Johnson...?' Mrs Claxton looked hopefully at the pretty, plump little woman who often saw bears, and wasn't scared a bit, and so ought to be able to behead a chicken.

'I don't feel a bit well,' Mrs Johnson said, and laid down on the bed and turned her back.

'Perhaps if we wash them!' Mrs Claxton got a pan of warm water, and she and Mother washed chickens all afternoon. 'They'll be delicious in the fall,' Mrs Claxton said as the last chicken, clean but subdued, scuttled into the brush after the old hen.

'They certainly will,' Mother agreed.

I licked my lips, wondering how far away fall was. But as far as the chickens were concerned fall never came. One by one they disappeared, and at last even the old hen vanished.

We had been living at the Claxtons' about three weeks when Mrs Johnson decided to go to Battleford. Their going was a great relief to me. Dora and I had avoided a slapping fight, but we had argued constantly, and Mrs Johnson, who still wasn't well, scolded Elsie a great deal.

The little house seemed quite empty after the Johnsons left, but I for one did not miss them. Our bed was put on the now vacant bedstead, and there was room enough for all of us to eat at the same time.

Bachelors going back and forth still stopped by now and then, and some of them asked Mother and Mrs Claxton to do washing. They said it would be a great favour. They hated to wash their own clothes, and they hated to go dirty. Neither Mother nor Mrs Claxton had ever done such a thing, but they had plenty of time, and finally agreed to do just one wash. One wash, of course, led to another, and they took in washing all the rest of the summer. The money was very useful. It bought jam for our bread, condensed milk for our tea, coconut to enrich cake short of eggs and butter, and even a can of cocoa.

We saw Dad only twice that summer, but when freeze-up came he returned for the winter. Mr Claxton, who had not been home all summer, found work for the winter, and wrote and told Mrs Claxton to go to Lloydminster and get a small house. For a while Dad and Mother discussed going with her, but they were sure houses would be scarce and rent high, so they decided to go to our own little house and spend the winter there. Mrs Claxton began to pack, but it was plain she didn't care much for the idea of spending the winter alone even in town. A house, if she could find one, would be unheated, and wood was hard to cut. 'Why don't you come and spend the winter with us?' Mother asked. 'Then you won't have to worry about wood.'

Our house was quite crowded, but the second winter was not nearly as cold as the first had been, and we children got out to play almost every day; and yet the time seemed long. We were almost the only ones left on the prairie that year. Mr Gardiner's little house stood empty, and all the other bachelors' shacks were cold, their owners either in the lumber camps or the towns. Even Bill Banks had gone. When Christmas came Santa left candy and nuts in our stockings, but there was no party. The snow fell and the wind blew, and we saw almost no one until spring, which came very early.

'What did I tell you, Sarah?' Dad exulted when the snow went. 'All the winters in Canada aren't cold. The first was a humdinger all right, but we may never have another like it. This isn't much colder than England. When the railroad comes, and we get some breaking done, we'll be on our feet in no time.'

'If you think Canada is going to give up so easy you're mistaken,' Mother warned. 'It's been wild too long to turn soft in a hurry.'

Dad, however, was sure that the worst was over, and he went gaily to work on the railroad as soon as the roads were dry. Mother and Mrs Claxton stayed in our house, and began once more to take in washing, and bake bread for the bachelors who had returned to put in the required time on their land. I was now big enough to help with a little of the housework, but I spent most of my time playing with the other children under the big tree at the corner of the grove near the house.

We did not expect Dad to come home until late in the fall, but one morning towards the end of summer he came around the grove, and with him were two cows and a team of oxen. At first Mother thought something must have happened, but Dad said everything was fine. He got the cows at a good price, and since the railroad was getting close he thought it about time we did some breaking, and got ready to grow a crop.

Mother thought Dad was in too much of a hurry, but the idea sounded wonderful to me. I helped clean the plough, and when Dad actually started ploughing I went along to help keep the slow-moving oxen going. For about two days I felt big and important, and very proud of myself, then I became weary of walking up one long furrow and down another, and decided to stop ploughing and go back to playing again.

To my surprise I found that going back was not easy. Dad said that after all I was a big girl now, and a great help to him, but I could rest for a day if I wanted to. I returned to the group under the big cottonwood expecting my old place as head of the little gang to be waiting for me. Lily, however, had taken charge. She assigned the roles when they played Indians and told everyone what to do. I felt lonely and left out, and somehow all the shouting about nothing did seem a little foolish. I returned willingly to the ploughing, but sometimes when my bare feet were raw from the rocks and rose-bushes I couldn't help wishing that I was little and young again like Lily.

Rose Ellen was born that fall. She was a small baby, but cute as a doll, with big blue eyes and fair hair. By then I was old enough to do real work, and the new baby was Lily's special charge. Lily was still only a little girl, but she took good care of Rose. She spent hours playing with her, and when Rose was sleepy Lily would sit down on a five-pound lard pail, pull Rose on to her small lap, and rock back and forth on the tin and sing the baby to sleep.

Our crop the following year didn't amount to much, and it was obvious that Mr Barr had been wrong when he said all we had to do was plough and plant, and sit back and wait for a bumper crop. The new-turned sod, well laced with the roots of grass and rose-bushes, had to be well disked and harrowed for a season before it was really ready to grow anything. 'We'll do better next year,' Dad said as we harvested the spindly grain he had sown by hand. 'What we need is a seeder and a binder.'

Dad bought a seeder the following spring, and when the grain, now tall and thick, was big in the ear he bought a binder. Before the grain ripened, however, a sharp frost damaged it. We threshed, hauled the grain to Lashburn, a little town that had sprung up since the railroad came, loaded it into a freight car, and sent it on its way to the big elevators in the east. 'Unless it grades very low we ought to have enough money for a payment on the seeder and binder,' Dad said, 'and maybe enough over for tea and sugar, but there won't be anything for new clothes this year.'

Mother thought the implement company ought to be willing to wait a bit for their money. After all, what were a few dollars to them one way or the other? Surely they didn't need them? Their underwear wasn't patched as ours was, and they hadn't holes in their shoes, either.

Dad said we would see what the grain brought, and walked the nine miles to Lashburn, hoping for good news. When he came home his thin face was drawn and old, and his mouth tight. 'They took it all,' he said, and slumped into his chair by the stove without even taking off his coat, or the home-made cap he still wore.

'What do you mean?' Mother asked.

'The implement people,' Dad said bitterly. 'They garnered the grain, and took everything to pay for the seeder and binder.'

'Didn't they even leave us enough for flour?' Mother sounded frightened.

'They didn't leave us a cent. I don't know what we're going to do.' There were tears in Dad's eyes.

Mother was silent for a few minutes. She looked as if she was going to cry, and her mouth trembled a little, then she gave her head a quick shake, blinked a time or two, and picked up the poker and stirred the fire. 'Don't you fret,' she said as she filled the kettle and put it on to boil for tea. 'You've done your best. We'll manage someway.'

Fortunately for us and many others the store-keepers, Watson and Gillingham, had more faith in us than the implement company. They let us have flour on credit, half a sack at a time, and Dad bought some unrendered suet at the butcher's. That was all we had to eat all winter: bread with a smear of fat on it, potatoes, and oatmeal without either milk or sugar. Sometimes we had weak tea, but mostly we drank hot water. 'This is the worst winter yet,' Mother said.

It was a hard winter for almost everyone else. Work on the railroad had stopped, the lumber camps were crowded, the bachelors even did their own washing. Dad tried to sell one of the cows, but nobody had any money to buy anything. It was a gala day for us when the cows freshened, and spring came.

Dad bought a small ox on time, one of the others had died, and we managed to put in another crop that by some miracle didn't freeze, but it was not by any means the end of hard times.

Some years we had a fair crop, but set-backs seemed to be the rule. There was the dry summer when no rain fell and the crops withered before our eyes. We had to cut the little that did mature with the mowing-machine, it was too short to cut with the binder, and most of it we raked by hand; then we picked up the last of the precious stalks one by one in order to save enough for seed. Another year wind and rain flattened most of the grain just before harvest. Once snow fell while the wheat was still in stooks, and we had to shake the sheaves and restook them.

Little by little, however, we progressed. New warm underwear replaced the old, patched garments. I became the proud possessor of a sheepskin-lined coat, and Dad bought a real winter cap, though he insisted it wasn't half as warm as the one he had made himself.

The men got together and built a small church on a hill donated by Mr and Mrs Metherell. A school district was formed, and a one-room school-house was built about half a mile from our house. As I watched the building grow I dreamed of going to school again, and of some day being a teacher.

By that time, however, I was a fair farmer. I could milk cows, handle the oxen as well as anyone, and plough and plant and stook and stack, and haul the grain to town as well as any boy. Now and then, of course, I got in a tight spot. Once I miscalculated a turn and got stuck on the railroad crossing. The train from the east was about due, but the wagon, loaded with oats, wouldn't budge an inch either one way or the other. Finally I unhooked the oxen, drove them to a safe place, and waited for the worst. Fortunately Dad arrived before the train and got the wagon off the track just in time.

So the years passed. Better seed was developed, and the well-tilled land produced bigger crops. Prices improved, and even the climate seemed to change. The winters were still cold, but they did not seem quite as long as they had been at first, and at last Dad decided it was time to build the long-dreamed-of house and barn.

There were seven of us by that time: Dad and Mother, Lily, Jack, Rose, Marguerite, the baby, and myself. There would have been eight, but Richard, the longed-for second son, born between Rose and Marguerite, had lived only four days. A house for such a family had to be fairly large, but, like the first house, when Dad staked the new home out it looked very small. There were three bedrooms, a large living-dining-room, and a good-sized farm kitchen. Mr Hickson, a neighbour, built the house for us, and I was very proud of it. But the little house that Dad, Mother, and I had built was always a special place for me. We had put it together log by log, and a little blood from my scratched knees had gone into it. When I was a nurse and went home for vacations I always visited it, and enjoyed once more the deep feeling of security it gave me.

The new house, however, was exciting. It had plastered walls and ceilings, a veranda all the way across the front, and windows that would open and close easily. Dad looked at our old furniture and decided we had to have new.

We thumbed the catalogues for weeks deciding on first one bedroom set, then another, and finally decided on one with a big mirror. The little stove that had served us faithfully ever since we came to Canada was worn out, and Dad decided it was time we had an up-to-date range. He ordered a handsome kitchen queen with six lids, a warming oven, and a boiler for heating water. He also bought new dishes; white with garlands of blue flowers, and a china cabinet with a bowed glass front to keep them in. Nicest of all, we had a kitchen sink. We hadn't any plumbing; Saskatchewan was too cold for that, but the sink had a drainpipe that went through the kitchen wall, a long pipe was attached to the drain, and in summer we were able to pour all our wash-water and dish-water down the sink.

We moved into the new house just before harvest. The new hayloft was full of sweet-smelling hay, and everything was ready for the new grain. The granaries were clean and the binder well oiled, and both its big white canvases mended, so that it was ready to go to work the moment the last green shadows in the wheat turned to gold. It was a lovely time of year: warm and drowsy in the afternoons, but crisp and cool in the mornings and evenings. Pleasant as the days were, however, there was still a breathlessness about them; so much could happen to the crop even now, frost could damage it and rain flatten it. Dad walked around his fields every day, and scanned the sky often, fearing last-minute hail.

Nothing disastrous, however, happened that year. The green-tinged yellow wheat that had replaced the wild roses and the prairie grass waved gently in the warm wind, that now smelled faintly of bread instead of flowers. Bees hummed sleepily as they hovered over the last of the marigolds, mint, and wild asters that grew in the shelter of the three groves Dad had left to protect the house and barn from the wind, and to preserve a little of the original beauty of the prairie for the future. A few butterflies also lingered, but the number had dwindled until where once there had been clouds there were now only a dozen or two. Even the blackbirds were not as numerous as they once had been, and no ducks at all floated on the sloughs. Wild geese still flew high overhead, and always they called down to us, sounding glad to see us in the spring, and sorry to be leaving us in the fall.

The new house seemed like a stranger at first, and no wonder. The lumber in it came from far away, and knew nothing of the surrounding prairie. It had not, like the logs in the old house, grown in a nearby grove. We soon became accustomed to it, however, and enjoyed the extra space, the new chairs and table, and the wide sideboard. I especially liked the big new range in the kitchen, the hanging lamp with the painted shade in the living-dining-room, and the big mirror in Mother's dressing-table. For the first time in my life I could see my head and feet at the same time.

Dad was also proud of the new house, but he said the walls looked bare. He sent some pictures we had saved for years away to be framed, but even they did not quite satisfy him. 'What we ought to have is a piano,' he said at last. 'Then the lasses can learn to play.'

Pianos were rare on the prairie in those days. A few people had organs, but they were considered a great luxury. The catalogues did not even list pianos. Dad, however, looked around, and when he heard that a couple from the States were going home he went to see them. They had brought a piano with them, and they agreed to sell it rather than take it back.

How proud Dad was when he brought that piano home! It was a walnut upright, sweet-toned, and well cared for. We set it carefully against the empty wall, dusted it tenderly, touched it admiringly, and tried to bring a familiar tune out of the black and white keys.

'How do you like it, Sarah?' Dad asked, his thin face and his ocean-coloured eyes glowing. 'You'd never have had a house like this, and such a piano, if you'd stayed in England and married Edmond Bastow.'

'I wouldn't have had so much grey in my hair, either,' Mother said, but she smiled and touched the piano gently.

'You'd be all doubled up with rheumatics, and choked with soot,' Dad said cheerfully.

'The soot never bothered me, but the winters…' Mother shivered a little. She had not been well the previous winter, and the colder the weather the worse she seemed to feel.

'Another good crop or two, and when Jack's old enough to manage we'll go to Victoria in the winter,' Dad promised. 'They says it's warm there, just like England.'

'Three good crops in a row!' Mother said. 'Canada will never be that generous.'

'We'll have good crops every year,' Dad said, 'now that we know how to summer fallow, and conserve moisture. Canada is a fair country. Our bairns and theirs will have it easier than we did, but we were in on the beginning, Sally, we helped lay the groundwork. That's something to remember.'

'Perhaps,' Mother said. 'But if I'd known how it would be when I left England wild horses wouldn't have dragged me here. I'd have listened to Sam, and let you come by yourself.'

'You know right well you can't get on without me,' Dad said, his eyes sparkling. 'If you could you'd have gone back when you had the chance after that first winter.'

'I stayed because of the bairns,' Mother said, and tossed her small head. 'They are yours, and it's up to you to look after them.'

'Well, they're near grown now,' Dad teased.

'Marguerite isn't.' Mother looked at the baby just beginning to walk. 'It will be years before she's grown up.' She sounded pleased.

And some forty years later, when early one morning Dad left us all, Mother still insisted she wouldn't be lonely without him. But though she was in fair health for a woman of almost eighty, she waited only five weeks, then she went to him, and her grave is now beside his in the Royal Oak Cemetery at Victoria. When Dad met her on the other side I'm sure he was smiling, and saying: 'What did I tell you, you'd follow me anywhere?' And Mother, I'm sure, tossed her little head and told him with a smile it was her bairn she wanted to see.